D1519033

Playing the Race Card

Playing the Race Card

Studies in the
Postmodern Theory of Education

Joe L. Kincheloe and Shirley R. Steinberg
General Editors

Vol. 244

PETER LANG
New York • Washington, D.C./Baltimore • Bern
Frankfurt am Main • Berlin • Brussels • Vienna • Oxford

George J. Sefa Dei,
Leeno Luke Karumanchery,
Nisha Karumanchery-Luik

Playing the Race Card

Exposing White Power
and Privilege

PETER LANG
New York • Washington, D.C./Baltimore • Bern
Frankfurt am Main • Berlin • Brussels • Vienna • Oxford

Library of Congress Cataloging-in-Publication Data

Dei, George Jerry Sefa.
Playing the race card: exposing white power and privilege /
George J. Sefa Dei, Leeno Luke Karumanchery, Nisha Karumanchery-Luik.
p. cm. — (Counterpoints, studies in the postmodern theory of education; v. 244)
Includes bibliographical references and index.
1. Whites—Race identity—United States. 2. Power (Social sciences)—United
States. 3. Race discrimination—United States. 4. Social status—United States.
5. Social classes—United States. 6. United States—Race relations.
I. Karumanchery, Leeno Luke. II. Karumanchery-Luik, Nisha.
III. Title. IV. Counterpoints (New York, N.Y.)
E184.A1 D293   305.8'00973—dc21   2002156038
ISBN 978-0-8204-6752-8
ISSN 1058-1634

Bibliographic information published by **Die Deutsche Bibliothek**.
Die Deutsche Bibliothek lists this publication in the "Deutsche
Nationalbibliografie"; detailed bibliographic data is available
on the Internet at http://dnb.ddb.de/.

Cover design by Lisa Barfield

The paper in this book meets the guidelines for permanence and durability
of the Committee on Production Guidelines for Book Longevity
of the Council of Library Resources.

Printed in the United States of America

We dedicate this book to all those engaged in the fight against oppression. While we may be differently positioned in the struggle, we must be collectively engaged. We work alongside you, together—in solidarity and resistance.

TABLE OF CONTENTS

FROM THE AUTHORS

As someone teaching graduate courses in anti-colonial thought, indigenous knowledges and anti-racism in a Western academy, I have often found myself at a crossroads regarding the possibility and hope of change because we work within the very institutions that we critique. It has been a struggle to resist closure in the academy and to shift away from stable and comforting knowledge in terms of our thoughts and practice. For us, as minoritized bodies speaking about race, we are confronted by huge risks. There are personal academic, political, social, emotional and spiritual consequences for the work we each undertake when we write about oppression in a climate that seduces bodies into denial. Personally, I have come to see these ventures not simply as places for academic engagement, but also as opportunities to implicate ourselves in the struggle for social change. We take up these personal and collective responsibilities because we believe we have something to say. We enter into these discussions well aware of the incompleteness of discourse and the search for epistemological diversity and equity, so we engage multiple approaches to anti-racist work in the hopes that integrative strategies might better interrogate the realities of race, knowledge and power as axes for resistance.

George J. Sefa Dei, PhD

As researchers and academics, we often tread a thin line between working for, with and in spite of the *other*. Often, rather than writing with the oppressed, we end up writing about 'them' and for 'them'. In my desire to see this work support, develop and engage the critical education of the oppressed, I am dedicated to the belief that *they*, as participants in the struggle, must also play a significant part in the framing and re-framing of the anti-racist project. Recognizing, like Freire, that knowledge emerges in one continuous rhythm, inquiry—invention—inquiry—re-invention, I am firmly grounded in the belief that truly transformational projects are framed within cooperative paradigms. That being said, I am both encouraged and excited at the prospect of engaging in this collaborative effort. Often, lost in the academic arena of doctoral research and publication, such opportunities serve to remind us that community, cooperation and solidarity are key to a resistant politics for transformative social change. It is our greatest wish that this work finds its way into the hands of the oppressed who are on the journey toward a greater critical consciousness. We hope this work informs your praxis, such that one day your work might inform ours.

Leeno Luke Karumanchery, PhD

As anti-racist educators, we know that this work is not always easy or painless, yet we continue in our struggles because we share a vision of hope. I entered into this collaboration from a very pointed positionality in that my work has always been informed by my lived experiences as a South Asian woman growing up in Canada. Interestingly, I began graduate work wanting to learn more about race and racism and ended up discovering feminism. As a Professor of Women's Studies I engaged this project reflective of the feminist praxis which has so deeply impacted my engagements with race and I sought to bring those knowledges and that framework to this collaborative project. However, just as the evolution of anti-racism work has been marked by continuous shifts that have helped to develop and advance our knowledge in the field, so too have my engagements with feminism been impacted and informed by the anti-racist lens employed through the writing of this work. We are all partners in 'the project' and it is my greatest hope that you will find the experience of reading this work as critically challenging as I did in helping to write it.

Nisha Karumanchery-Luik, PhD

PREFACE

In all struggles against oppression it is important to understand our oppressor and to understand the logic/rhetoric he uses to justify and/or overlook our oppression. The writing of this book arose from our desire to do anti-racist work that could resist the whims and caprices of 'privilege.' As our point of departure from other works that exist, we have set out to use this book as a platform from which to critically address and resist the foundations and machinery for racism. Crucial to this framework is an understanding of what racism means to the oppressed and how/why it continues to be maintained/supported by those with skin color privilege. That is to say, we wanted to address how the subtleties of racism go unseen, unacknowledged and denied in the eyes and ears of privilege. Critical teaching must equip all learners to develop the ability to see how privilege is enacted daily in the academy and in the social sphere. We felt it necessary to combine our interrogations of the structural/material relations of power[1] with an investigation of how racialized subjects are constituted and regulated through the ideology and discourse of racism.

That being said, there is growing resistance to critical knowledge today. So how does an anti-colonial lens by its focus on questions of resistance help us address the open denial and renunciation of race and difference? To address this question we must acknowledge the futility (or should we say fatality) of unmatched theory and practice. As argued elsewhere, the worth of a social theory should not simply be measured by its philosophical grounding, but also by its ability to offer a social and political corrective. In fact, our belief in this political task moves us to affirm that we frame 'praxis' in terms of agency and relative to a constant confrontation of the varied forms of domination and subjugation that are implicated in our lives. Importantly, in this political call, we are wary that the seduction of intellectualism often parallels a certain degree of arrogance. There is usually little expression of humility in such 'knowledges' and, as a result, the power to 'know' often mutes the recognition that there is also a power in not knowing. In our mutual awareness that there is no one model for engaging anti-oppression work, we offer an open investigation of racism that our readers will hopefully read, write and re-write on route to a more nuanced critical consciousness and anti-racist politics.

In this work, we do not separate the politics of difference from the politics of race because this practice helps dominant bodies to deny and refuse to interrogate White privilege and power. We must be acutely aware of how "anti-essentialist" discourses can serve to bring White hegemonic power and privilege to the centre of supposedly critical political pursuits. In other words the emphasis on the individual and dispersed identities can be paralyzing to the extent that it can and does deny the ways centralized dominant systems of power work to establish and sustain particular advantages. The articulation of White hegemonic power can also deny and silence the experiential realities of bodies of color. In the creation of this discursive space (a space through which we might interrogate the processes of oppression and decolonization), we speak about multiple knowledges and how such *ways of knowing* engage and implicate each of our various embodied connections to knowledge.

In engaging these embodied knowledges, we uphold the idea and understanding that equity, in its holistic character, is not forced but rather flows through actions and thoughts—it is marked by genuineness and sincerity. Unfortunately, while years of research and dialogue have pointed us toward engaging a pedagogical and administrative praxis that speaks to social justice within a holistic framework, we continue to find the routes toward such ends to be blocked by those with power and privilege. While social change calls for us all to make enormous personal and collective sacrifices, we must recognize that such a commitment to insurgent change is rarely embraced by those who enjoy the advantages produced, supported, reproduced and sustained in/through the hegemonic relations of the status quo. Now, while we are cognizant of the uphill battle that we fight, we engage a philosophy of hope in the writing of this work. It is a philosophy that we share with a great many others who also believe in the potential of ideas to bring about social change. We believe that in the critical interrogation of race knowledge, multiple voices should be listened to without interruption; thus we engage this work in an effort to speak both to and with *other* voices.

Importantly, making this assertion does not mean we ignore the fact that gender, ethnicity and indeed class inform Whiteness and that it is problematic to generalize when we speak of White privilege. But our approach to understanding the relations of power and difference requires that we speak of the saliency of race even as we recognize the intersections of race with other forms of difference. Recognizing that there are relative saliencies for different identities as well as contextual variations in intensities of oppression, our theory and praxis reflects an acknowledgment of the severity of these intersections and interlocks for certain bodies. In situating decolonization in the anti-racist project through the cultivation of identity and collective consciousness, we engage a politics that moves beyond reactive responses in the moment, toward an agenda that is framed in/through the power of self-definition. We pursue the insurgence of a resistant praxis that might contest the oppressive future that is, even now, being designed for minoritized peoples. Moreover, we urge a mobilization of anti-oppression work that might proactively interrogate and oppose the colonial relations that are being produced and reproduced in the everyday.

To these ends, we look to the sights from which we are oppressed in an effort to examine racism, as it exists within the mind and experience of White privilege and, in turn, for the racially oppressed. Our aim is to not only identify the everyday arguments that seek to trivialize, devalue and mute the impact and experience of racism, but also to establish, for racialized people, a point of departure from conventional anti-racist strategies. We contend that this book, in its *organic* approach to social change, serves an important function within the anti-racist struggle. In the writing of this work, we hope to create a bridge between academia and the pragmatic world. Each chapter of this book engages in a theoretical interrogation and critique of privileged perceptions of racism. It is our hope that in advancing the development of critical consciousness among the oppressed, we will help them to re-examine their own subject positions and generate new, insurgent strategies for survival and social change.

ACKNOWLEDGMENTS

I would like to thank the many students in my graduate courses who have enriched my ideas and thinking on issues of anti-racism studies and anti-colonial thought. Also, my community work and practice have been personally rewarding in pointing to the necessity and importance of academics allowing our discourse to speak to lived reality and community practice. While the work we do is challenging and often disheartening, I am encouraged by our collective and collaborative struggles and truly hopeful in their potential to rupture the status quo. Our collective engagements have helped to frame my understanding of the importance of practice-informed theory and I have endeavored to speak through that voice in the pages of this work. — George

I have been fortunate in the last decade to meet people who have not only helped me to grow as an academic but as a human being. I am deeply indebted to those friends and colleagues who have encouraged and inspired me to look beyond myself and to the greater cause of social justice and liberty. I would like to extend heartfelt gratitude to my co-author, Dr. George Dei, who teaches me through his politics and pedagogy, what type of educator I aspire to be. I would also like to offer a special thanks to my parents, Omana and Peter, for their gift of unconditional love. — Leeno

I would like to express my gratitude to several people who have impacted my contribution to this book. I would like to thank my brother Leeno for his support and for our ongoing discussions around issues of race, racism and liberatory praxis. I would also like to thank my parents, Omana and Peter and my mother and father-in-law, Laine and Heino, for all of their help with childcare—I couldn't have done this without you. My deepest gratitude goes to my husband Peter for his unwavering support and for providing me with an environment where I have the freedom and opportunity to think, write and engage this important work. — Nisha

---

We would all like to extend particular thanks to Joe Kincheloe for his commitment to the cause of social justice and the fight against oppression. Educators like you make it possible for 'us' to meet our collective responsibilities in the opening of spaces in/ through which minoritized voices might be heard and acted upon.

INTRODUCTION
Anti-Racist Tapestries: Threads of Theory and Practice

The starting-point of critical elaboration is the consciousness of what one really is and is 'knowing thyself' as a product of the historical process to date, which has deposited in you an infinity of traces, without leaving an inventory...therefore it is imperative at the outset to compile such an inventory.

—Antonio Gramsci, *The Prison Notebooks*[1]

The strange God settles himself humbly on the altar beside the God of the country. Little by little he establishes himself firmly. Then one fine morning he gives his neighbour a shove with his elbow—crash!—the idol lies upon the ground.

—Diderot's Metaphor[2]

Why are you reading this book? We realize that this is an unconventional way in which to begin an academic text, but the question is necessary. You see, in doing academic work, it is essential that we[3] constantly check ourselves, the reasons that we write and who it is that we write for. This is particularly important for anti-racist pedagogues and activists in that we face so many pressures to do work that will be accepted by the 'privileged' few— those who have the ability to make or break our careers. In fact, ours is a constant struggle for legitimacy—legitimacy in the eyes of our peers, our partners in 'the anti-racist project' and legitimacy for ourselves. As Sawicki notes, we face constant pressure to write without regard for audience or purpose.[4] That is to say, that we are not encouraged to do work that will transform the world. We are not motivated to affect social change with an eye toward equity and social justice. Rather, we are pressured to publish, to gain authority—to become eminent. Placing those pressures to the sidelines, we wrote this work with a very specific eye toward audience and purpose. That is why we ask the pointed question: Why are you reading this book? We hope that those who read this work share in our vision and philosophy. Moreover, we truly hope that this work finds its way into the hands of those oppressed who are at the beginning of their journey toward a greater critical consciousness.

This work is political and we make no pretense to the contrary.[5] We are all socially/politically located, situated and positioned and we bring these various subjectivities to any and all, of the work that we do. In fact, we would challenge social researchers and theorists who assign claims of neutrality to their work. By denying the politics, beliefs and experiences that contextualize academic research, claims to neutrality are used to secure the authority and validity assigned to "traditional empirical/Western thought and research."[6] We strongly assert that while generally unspoken and unacknowledged, academic explorations into the social world are always governed by political intent and ideological ontology.[7] Understanding our positionings is fundamentally important to the work that we do.

So in that light, how do we position ourselves relative to this work? In engaging this project within an anti-racist spirit and framework of collaboration and mutual respect, we felt that it was important to speak with one voice. That being said, the experiences that we drew upon, the narratives that we engaged and the research that we did were all reflections of our stories, experiences and pain in the face of racism. So clearly, as observers, researchers and academics who experience racial oppression, we were/are anything but objective or neutral here. We could not divorce ourselves from the implications of why, when, where and with whom we chose to do this work. Recognizing that and mindful of the various social positions and identities that we each brought to this work, we needed to engage the complex issue of how to speak from intersecting vantage points. We each brought intersections of race, class, gender, sexuality, age and power to this collaboration. We could continue…we also saw the interplay of academic experience, familial ties (as two of the authors are related), academic interest and politics, etc. Like the skin of an onion, the positions could be peeled off almost endlessly. So where did we draw the line?

> At every turn, I add layers and layers of complexity…. These intuitive awarenesses of positioning—one of solidity, of concreteness of definitive understanding of who we are and where we are placed; the *other* of increasing complexity, of fragmentation, of change, of being something more or less than—work together as I struggle to define who it is I am.[8]

Like Arber, we found ourselves drawing the line at those positions that seemed to be timeless or essential parts of our collective identities as we wrote this work. So in this reading of "positioning" as strategic and pointed, we focused on our marginalized positions as people of color in what is a racially oppressive society. Through our individual constitutions relative to the dynamics of race and racial oppression, we focus our gaze through the lens of race. Importantly, that is not to say that we are placing some hierarchical importance to racial oppression, nor do we wish to obscure or dichotomize other subjectivities of identity that function internally, externally or interspersed throughout that category. We firmly recognize the theoretical and practical value of interrogating the interlocks and intersections of race, class, gender and sexuality. It is important that we identify and engage how various systems of oppression work to strengthen and support formulations and constructions of the *other*.[9] So respective of these issues, we chose to do *this* work, in *this* way, because racism stands as a marker of pain, fear, anger, isolation and constant anxiety for us—it frames our lives.

In this very pointed respect, we are focused in our political decision to frame this text within an unabashedly anti-racist framework and with a very specified, localized engagement with race and racism. In agreement with Dei (1996) and Karumanchery (2003), we argue against frameworks that seek to privilege *race* over other forms of oppression. However, that being said, we would add that we must be wary of strategic positions that engender a "political paralysis" of sorts. In an article that makes a case for the strategic essentialism of anti-racist practice, Dei (1999) discussed several disturbing developments in recent political trends related to equity, justice and the denial of difference. He writes:

> My concerns cover a broad spectrum: the denial of the significance of race in academic discourse and practices; the open renunciation of racial differences in social practices and action; the trend towards the use of strictly class-based criteria in formulating social policy for equity and justice; the call for a transracial coalition praxis devoid of any symptoms of politics of identity; and the majority's embrace of the argument that race-specific practices should receive less attention in progressive political agendas and causes.[10]

With these issues in mind, while we cannot allow other oppressions to share the focus of this work, we do encourage our partners in the anti-oppression project to engage and reflect on these interrogations with an eye toward their experiences, interests and politics.

In this light, we would reiterate again in earnest that this work is not a sterile academic project. Rather, it is rooted in our personal battles with racism and oppression. We must be clear on this point: Our struggle for social change and social justice must be understood as nothing short of a revolution. Ours is a search for emancipation from the invisible and not-so-invisible shackles that bind us. So for that reason, we do not make excuses for our use of radical/revolutionary terminology. That is to say, we are very pointed in our use of *oppression, resistance, liberation* and *freedom* as terms that define our experience and struggle. In fact, as discussed, our lived experience as oppressed is what fueled the framing of this project and we believe that this intimate connection only strengthened the resolve and honesty that we brought to the writing of this book. Through a close interrogation of our individual experiences and collective politics, we agreed that we wanted this work to be revolutionary and that it would hopefully clear ground for future political change. Importantly, we wanted that revolutionary change to develop outside the auspices of power and privilege. But how might such social change arise?

In his analysis of social formations, Gramsci once pointed to the basic difference between what he called *organic* historical movements and *discontinuous* ones. He defined organic movements as those social formations that manage to obtain a deep and lasting impact on society over time. In contrast, he felt that discontinuous movements arose through abrupt social revolution and that, as such, they were often "policed" by those in power and subject to serious backlashes. We would assert that many of the problematics that plague and challenge the anti-racist project are, in fact, grounded in this "discontinuous dilemma." Bearing these notions of social formation in mind, where do we see the anti-racist project? Dei (1996) defined anti-racism as "an action-oriented strategy for institutional, systemic change to address racism and interlocking systems of social oppression."[11] Clearly, this is an ambitious project with a pro-active approach. In fact, this framework stands as the fundamental basis for much of today's anti-racist theory and practice: no longer interested in "mopping up the mess," this strategic framework seeks to prevent future spills altogether. However, in addressing issues of power and equity by focusing on systemic and structural change, the revolutionary "flavor" and transformative strategy of anti-racism often leaves 'the project' open to the 'policing' and social backlashes anticipated by Gramsci. Ironically, in our passion for and dedication to social justice, we often forget the level of opposition that we face.

It is not enough that our theories and strategies make sense to us, they must also be able to function within the parameters set out for us by 'privilege.' Those strategies that do not work within the norms set forth by the status quo always seem to exist on ground that is tenuous at best. For example, over the last few decades, we have seen the marginalized and oppressed fight to implement initiatives geared toward social justice in educational, political and social contexts throughout the world and the progress, while slow, had been encouraging. However, in recent years, we have seen the removal, reduction and/or "re-focusing" of many of those same programs.[12] These backslides serve to demonstrate that we work in spaces that are discreetly but carefully policed. We may win a *victory*[13] for equity here or there, but those victories are always regulated and programs adopted in these moments are always in danger of being removed or "re-tooled." As noted by Hall, "what replaces invisibility is a type of carefully regulated, segregated visibility."[14] So in facing this "reality," we must begin to question whether our strategies need to be re-tooled, re-focused and re-written. How can we function outside the auspices of privilege? How can we engage social change that is emancipatory when systemic power and design endorse and sustain status quo?

While recognizing that power is predominantly a social concept, we cannot forget that individuals do have agency and ability to act within and in spite of the confines and constraints of the larger social power structure. In our struggles with systemic racism, we may sometimes neglect to critically address the everyday experience of racism as it exists in the lives of the oppressed. So, while systemic racism and structural oppression need to be addressed and must stay in the forefront of the project, we need to also remind ourselves that there are always decided limitations to single-minded frameworks. Racism exists as more than a socially constructed practice; it exists as a socially constructed experience as well. Therefore, we need to re-assess the false dichotomies that seek to separate and compartmentalize the materiality and experience of racism into hierarchical frameworks that seek to establish the importance of one configuration over another. Among the Malayalee of Kerala, India, there is a parable that speaks to such problematics of cooperation and conflict as they exist within their own community:

> Upon entry into a Kerala fish market, a traveler notes that there are two baskets full of live crabs, one basket open and the other with a lid. In his puzzlement, the traveler asks the shopkeeper if he is not worried that the crabs in the open basket will climb out. The shopkeeper replies, "I'm not worried at all because the crabs in the open basket are from Kerala. If one of them tries to crawl out of the basket, the others will pull it back in."

This story is included here because it carries an important message about community, cooperation and resistance. In engaging a truly inclusive and cooperative model for our work, anti-racist leaders, activists, pedagogues and students need to carefully scrutinize our own philosophy and practice. We need to interrogate the false dichotomies that plague our work. The main problem that faces us in this task is our submersion within Western paradigms that support individual achievement and foster negative attitudes toward cooperation and community. In many ways, it seems that we find ourselves struggling against not only privilege and power, but also against those *others*, who should, in fact, be our partners in the anti-racist project. Why do we do this to each other? The question is very familiar to anti-racism workers because the threat of appropriation, cooptation and competition continually surround our work. In preaching a cooperative and collaborative pedagogy, we must reflect that same practice within our own work.

The anti-racist project is a tapestry and each strategy is a thread in that tapestry. Some threads run through the heart of the work, while others run along the edges. Many of the threads run in the same direction, while others run divergent courses. However, regardless of the direction or location, each thread adds to the strength of the tapestry and when any one of the threads is pulled, the integrity of the whole necessarily begins to falter. We believe that racism, in its constitution as practice and experience, requires amelioration from all sides of the struggle…through each thread of strategy. To elevate one method over another is problematic because every avenue for resistance must be engaged if we are to affect lasting social change.

Our efforts must reflect and engage the dynamic nature of experience. There is no one "right" method. Sparks reminds us that the evolution of cultural studies is marked by continuous shifts that have helped to develop and advance our knowledge in the field.[15] These shifts are a necessary part and product of the contested space in which we work and they serve to remind us that theory and method rarely arise as complete, well-formed entities. In recognizing these limitations, it becomes possible to critically address the theoretical ground upon which we stand and the methodological tools that we would employ. We work not only with an eye as to whether one strategy is more appropriate than another in a given space and place, but also to determine the various ways in which the strategies we employ might enforce, complement and reinforce each other.

In following a Freirian politics and tradition, we see transformational potential in the writing of this book. We see an opportunity to reshape the social sphere and, more pointedly, we see enormous potential to help transform and re-write *the experience of racism* for the oppressed.[16] But how can we initiate this radical transformation? We are earnest in our position that 'organic' strategies can only help to re-inforce the anti-racist tapestry. Further, it is our contention that strategies designed to increase critical awareness and consciousness among the oppressed are crucial to the development and insurgence of such social reform. The critical gaze is a necessity of libratory praxis; without it, the oppressed remain blind to the reality of their oppression. Therefore, we must ensure that we take nothing for granted in our efforts to develop the critical consciousness of the oppressed. We (the authors), as leaders in the struggle, cannot begin what is to be a mutual journey by assuming that the oppressed know what we know: that they understand what, why and how we resist. This is a problematic that must be taken up. In fact, an examination of these questions is at the heart of why we wrote this book.

So why do we fight? If the question seems somehow unnecessary, we need to remind ourselves that in mainstream discourse, the fight for social justice is neither clearly defined nor openly accepted. We must all remember that the nature of racism, as it exists in Western contexts, is insidious and we are all disciplined to see the world through the eyes of privilege. For those who recognize their oppression and particularly for those who are unaware, in denial of, or blinded to it, living itself can be a struggle. As asserted by Memmi (1967), the colonized mind is transfixed within a duality that both rejects and welcomes the colonizer.[17] In our constitution within a privileged reality, the desire *to be* our oppressor, works to oppress us from within. This personal duality prevents us from perceiving how the "true order" of society works, because in spite of our pain and our hardship, we are still disciplined to see the world through the eyes of privilege.[18] We are conditioned, indoctrinated and educated to be blind to the existence and reality of that privilege, so through this duality we both support and deny our own oppression. The tragedy of not being able to interrogate our duality is that, in not knowing, we take our pain and our oppression into ourselves; we become them, they inform our experience and we suffer for our lack of understanding.

The leaders of the anti-racist project must take this into consideration and work to establish critical education as crucial to the success of their efforts. However, awareness of racism does not necessitate freedom from it. Awareness alone may allow us to look reflexively at ourselves as subjects within the moment, but it does not necessarily help us to move away from the guilt, solitude, insecurity and pain associated with those moments in which we could not understand why. Why we couldn't defend ourselves. Why we were set apart from the others. It is the paradoxical and painful duality that makes both sense and non-sense out of our oppressor's words. This is why a critical education is so important: because the oppressed cannot be expected to resist without understanding what they are resisting and why they are resisting it. Consciousness and awareness of racism helps us to analyze our place within the racist experience. However, consciousness in and of itself is not enough. We must also strategize for resistance because the journey toward *conscientização*[19] can be arduous and painful.

Is racism real? Is oppression real? How is it real? Such questions and challenges to the reality of racism are always fraught with problematics in that they serve to silence and devalue the subjective account. The emphasis that is often placed on recounting and/or quantifying instances of racism suggests that it cannot be understood to exist in politically "real" space until it is both perceptible and understandable. However, we must always remember to ask ourselves: Who requires this proof? To whom must racism be made both perceptible and understandable? As certain privileged interpretations become accepted while others are excluded, we can see the politics of the moment and we know whose reality is meant to be perceived. (We) are assigned the task of providing the evidence and (they) are vested with the authority to either dismiss or validate it. But what condition or circumstance would be sufficient to "prove" the existence and scope of racism to the eyes and ears of those with skin color privilege? What proof would be capable of quieting the circular rhetoric born within such oppressive formations. There is a fable that speaks to this dilemma:

> A wolf came upon a lamb who had wandered too far away from the security of the fold. Instead of simply attacking, the wolf resolved to justify to the lamb why it was that it should be eaten. "Last year, you grossly insulted me," said the wolf. "Impossible" cried the lamb, "I was only born six months ago." Then the wolf said, "You feed in my pasture." "No," replied the lamb, "I have not yet tasted grass." The wolf then said, "You drink of my well." "No," blurted the lamb, "I have not tasted water for as yet my mother's milk is both food and drink to me." The wolf responded to this final declaration by seizing and eating the lamb, saying, "Well, I refuse to go hungry simply because you refute my allegations."

In its assertion that tyrants will always find a pretext for their tyranny, this parable carries a valuable message about power and oppression. It serves to remind us that resistance to racism and oppression is best made on the terms of the oppressed. How can we affect positive social change within frameworks that are designed to support and sustain the status quo? How do we prove the existence and scope of racism and oppression to the privileged if they cannot, or choose not to acknowledge it? This demand for proof is an imperative that always originates in spaces that are specific to privilege: spaces that deny and/or contest the very reality of racism and oppression.[20] We can no longer afford to focus our efforts on proving the existence and scope of racism. Intrinsic to such strategies is an implicit assertion that our work and our pain can only be validated if they are accepted as real by those with privilege. The time has come for a radical departure from the politics of negotiation and toward a new politics of reclamation. That is to say that we cannot continue to struggle within sites that are afforded to us by privilege. We need to establish politics and strategies of our own and we need to implement them in spaces and places of our choosing. We may be forced to "play the game," but the time has come for us to "play by our own rules."

For us (the authors), this is *why we fight*. We fight because we recognize the duality within ourselves, we recognize ourselves as oppressed and we would resist that oppression. We also fight because we see that same duality in our oppressed sisters and brothers and we would have them recognize their oppression and we would have them resist it. This declaration is simple, clear, to the point and we do not leave it open for debate. Ironically, the clarity of this anti-racist philosophy is often used to place us on the hot seat of public scrutiny as our politics are challenged as partisan and our engagements with racism are dismissed as subjective, emotional and self-serving. Realistically, such privileged responses to our efforts should come as no surprise to us in that the nature of our work is oppositional. These roadblocks serve to remind us of the importance of moving beyond the auspices of power and privilege and toward sites and strategies that neither look for approval nor require support from our oppressor.

Having clearly asserted why we fight, it is important to address the complex issue of how we fight. With respect to the processes and practices through which we affect social change, the question of *how* is almost always more complex than the question of *why*. In fact, one simple statement could not adequately summarize how we fight because the battle rages on multiple levels. As Brunner asserts, "Complex problems do not have simple solutions."[21] The enigmatic nature of racism and oppression necessitates that we view them through more than a commonsense lens. They require analysis on multiple levels, from the micro to the macro. We must be able to focus our gaze upon both specific moments of oppression and the larger social components that actively interlock and intersect those moments. This is a serious consideration for those oppressed who are at the beginning of the journey toward *conscientização*. It should be realized that racism and oppression are such an integral part of our history in Western contexts that they have attained an almost accepted/acceptable station in our cultural/political/social milieu. That position is solidified through the commonsense beliefs, rhetoric and practices that seek to mute and downplay the impact and scope of racism and oppression.

The commonsense gaze is not enough. It is an entry point to social analysis that proves deceptively disorienting to those with privilege and decidedly problematic for the oppressed. After all, the *commonsense* world, while built upon personal and shared experiences, is a domain that rarely involves a probing look at the myriad factors that developed, structured and executed those experiences. This text is not intended to provide concrete answers to the problematic of racism and oppression rather, we intend to introduce new perspectives on how the oppressed might view and re-write their constitution as subjects within the oppressive experience. In doing this type of critical thinking, we hope to develop new insurgent possibilities for resistance, agency and social change. However, before the oppressed can interrogate and tackle the issues of, and strategies for, social change, they must first engage their own critical consciousness.

One of the main tasks of critical theory is to delineate the myriad factors that sustain and contribute to racism and oppression in order to offer alternative solutions to that complex. So let us interrogate the structures and practices through which we are oppressed such that we might better understand how we are oppressed and how we are implicated in that oppression. Let us take up the project of "knowing ourselves" as a starting point to personal and social change. That is not to suggest that we place the impetus for social justice and reform as a responsibility of the oppressed alone. Rather, we would develop strategies that might work alongside conventional anti-racist praxis; strategies that in their organic nature might sew seeds of social change that are capable of moving from the self to the collective. We feel this ontological framework to be an exciting and innovative alternative to the stereotypical study of failure and hardship that has marked our project for so long. As previously discussed, anti-racist strategy cannot and should not be subsumed under one methodological school of thought. Our call for "a new set of rules" reflects our desire to see the oppressed re-assess and side step the paradigms of policy and practice that have been traditionally set out for them by their oppressor. It is a call for the oppressed to do work that carries personal significance, work that will make a positive difference in their lives and the lives of other oppressed peoples. It is a call to see the oppressed working together in solidarity and collaboration. In fact, the issue of cooperation is a good point at which to begin an interrogation of the methodology employed in this work.

While we assert the pivotal role played by education in the transformational project, we must also be clear as to the cooperative paradigm that must be engaged in any such endeavor.[22] The anti-racist project must work to support and develop the critical education of the oppressed. It is not sufficient that pedagogues, activists and other leaders in the struggle are alone in understanding the goals and strategies that frame the work. As asserted by Spivak, there is an impulse among academics and other intellectuals, a sort of Messiah complex, that often seeks to save, describe and speak for the oppressed.[23] It is of paramount importance that the oppressed and their leaders work together in the development of strategy, the implementation of practices and the evolution of new ontologies. Without a role as subjects of the revolution and without an awareness of that role, the oppressed are relegated to a sort of proactive limbo. It is a paradoxical space, where they participate in the business of social change without knowing why and how they struggle. We cannot subscribe to such strategies because they treat the oppressed as victims to be saved. [24]

The anti-racist project is a cooperative endeavor and we work toward a collaborative paradigm, not because it is important to the work, but because it is fundamental. We must monitor our pedagogy and practice to ensure that conventional didactic dynamics do not encroach upon the educational models that we would employ. For those of us who were educated in Western contexts, this is a particularly complex pitfall to avoid, in that top-down models of education are intrinsic to our experience and difficult to transcend. While we cannot ignore the reality that leaders are necessary to the success of the project, it is imperative that we eschew traditional teacher-student relationships and power structures. We assert that the mechanical, almost sterile atmosphere that accompanies such frameworks cannot be conducive to real libratory praxis. Such educational practices serve to alienate students from the truly liberating potential of education. Rather than challenging students to grow and critically evaluate their world by engaging their experiences and knowledges, such educational models tend to treat students as containers to be filled by the teacher's knowledge.[25]

Teaching the oppressed is an activity that must develop within a spirit of solidarity, cooperation and mutual respect. It is a process whereby students and teachers might interrogate racism and oppression together in an atmosphere of shared exploration and discovery. Of course, the teacher will work to educate the student with the various skills and information at her disposal, but the relationship is not a one-way process, it must be understood to be reciprocal. The teacher-student relationship should facilitate an exchange of ideas rather than a transfer of information. If open to the concept of education as a shared opportunity for growth, the teacher will leave having learned from the student as much as the student has learned from the teacher.

In our desire to do anti-racist work that might truly be liberating, we would ask that this book not be read as unidirectional. It was never our intent to produce a dogmatic work for students to read, memorize and repeat. In much the same way that we (the authors) engage the work of educators like Paulo Freire and bell hooks in our inquiries, we ask that you (the reader) engage, interrogate and re-visit your own work after reading this book. We firmly believe that knowledge is never born wholly and perfectly in any one given moment, nor in any one mind. No theorist ever came to hone her craft without first engaging with and emerging through the works of those who came before her. We concur with the contention that knowledge emerges in one continuous rhythm: inquiry–invention–inquiry–re-invention.[26] So, we ask that you read this work and re-create it through and within your own experience and knowledge.

Having outlined our dedication to the collaborative and reciprocal nature of critical education, we need to explain its relation to *how we fight*. In framing our methodology we contend that true 'organic' social change has three main intersecting phases: the critical education of the oppressed, social transformation and, ultimately, the liberated world. In our conception of the liberated world, we do not mean to suggest the possibility of a perfect human society. That would be unrealistic. As suggested by Marx, social formations are always imprinted by the preceding stages through which they arose.[27] The reality is that racism and oppression exist today, exactly as they exist, because of a very specific historical context. What we have now is a complex of disabilities that is intrinsically tied to the history and continuing reach of colonialism and imperialism. While future social formations will also undoubtedly struggle with these same historical problematics, we work toward a stage of development at which their influence and reach might be somewhat muted. We envision the third stage of social development as a stage in which the task of social justice has become the concern of all members of society and not only those at the lowest social strata.[28] Rather than fighting for freedom, this stage would encompass a fight to retain freedom, eternal vigilance being our reminder of an oppressive legacy that we hope to leave behind. This vision is admittedly optimistic. However, we must adopt a philosophy of hope if we are to proceed in this work…anything short of that would be self-defeating. We must believe that a state of liberation is possible. Otherwise, why would we even bother to engage in the struggle? Having discussed our philosophy of hope, we still need to address the two stages that occupy the direct interest of this work.

The critical education of the oppressed, as the first phase, should be understood to be a necessary pre-condition for participation in the project. We draw the distinction of pre-condition because, as discussed earlier, our efforts are policed and so critical education must exist in our minds and in our work as untouchable. A grassroots approach would ensure that critical education takes place in spaces that are beyond the reach of privilege. That is to say, in helping to equip the oppressed with the tools to critically evaluate and address their oppression, we incite within them a resource not easily muted by our oppressor. It is for this reason that we chose to do this work in communities, families, through literature and word of mouth...all sites that hold the potential to engender organic social change.

The majority of contemporary strategies designed to engender systemic change necessitate a protracted confrontation with sociopolitical power. A showdown of that nature is not our intent at this time. For the purpose of this work, we leave systemic battles with privilege to our partners in the project. Our strategy here is to make a pointed move toward developing a greater critical consciousness among the oppressed through small-scale, grassroots efforts. This is not to suggest that knowledge is enough or that understanding is sufficient to engender social change. Such a position would fall into commonsense pitfalls that suggest racism and oppression are questions of attitude and individual ignorance. Thought alone cannot change reality, because attitudinal change without systemic/structural transformation would do little to dislodge and undermine the intersecting/interlocking problematics of oppression. However, as asserted by Freire:

> The insistence that the oppressed engage in reflection on their concrete situation is not a call to armchair revolution. On the contrary, reflection—true reflection—leads to action. The conviction of the oppressed that they must fight for their liberation is not a gift bestowed by the revolutionary leadership, but the result of their own *conscientização*.[29]

In truly understanding the "reality" and condition of oppression, we must collectively set the groundwork for the development and implementation of social change. There is a deep political, philosophical and personal significance that develops in and through the process of "coming into consciousness," because our exposition and interrogation of the oppressive world immediately and forever alters our relationship with it. In "doing the work,"[30] we find ourselves to be more than interested participants in change, we find that we are implicated subjects as well. It is that implication that compels us to resist our oppression.

The second stage will see the oppressed take their grassroots efforts into the systemic realm where confrontations with privilege are a certainty. In this stage we will see the oppressed begin to work within the public sphere to affect change on a structural level...an "open warfare" of sorts. The obvious backlashes in policy and practice that will result from open encounters with privilege demonstrate clearly that the success of the second stage is in no small part dependent upon the success of the first. Simply put, it would be far more difficult to discourage and limit a politically aware revolutionary body than a loosely formed collective that is merely following orders. A solidarity and clarity of purpose come with a critical consciousness, so it follows that, if we are to develop strategies for resistance and social transformation, we must first critically understand what it is that we are resisting. Our coming into consciousness and the ensuing change to our perspective and experience as oppressed has significant effect on a micro-level because it changes how we see the world and our interactions within it. In gaining "true" critical consciousness, we emerge from the commonsense sphere into the critical sphere where our world, the world of oppression, is unveiled in structure, politics, ideology, culture, context and interaction. This critical gaze compels us to analyze everything that was once hidden from us: what we hear, think, feel, see, sense—everything that once fed our duality can now be employed to fuel our resistance.

Importantly, in much the same manner that critical education is crucial to the oppressed, the critical consciousness of the oppressor is also of great significance within the continuum of social transformation. We must remember that racism, however perceived and experienced, is deeply ingrained within our system and our lives. The banality of racism constitutes both the marginalized and the oppressor and so like those who unknowingly participate in their own oppression, the oppressor does not perceive his privilege. This fundamental issue is what guides our framework in the writing of this book. If racism and oppression constitute the experience and lived reality of both the oppressed and the oppressor, if both feel its effects, then why do racism and oppression continue to flourish? The answer is simply this: while both oppressor and oppressed are constituted through the experience of oppression, they both feel, live, experience and know that reality differently.

The oppressed that recognize their plight do so exactly because they are marginalized and because they carry the burden of oppression. The privileged, who only benefit as a result of their position in the relations of oppression, have no cause to look beyond that experience. It is a problematic more complex than simple denial. For the privileged to accept the scope and nature of oppression, they would also have to accept their complicity in that condition. As a defense mechanism, it becomes necessary not simply to deny the reality of oppression, but to see that reality from a perspective that is less personally injurious. The resulting rationalizations of social stratification and inequality invariably function to pathologize victims of oppression as the source of their misfortunes. Eventually, these rationalizations and beliefs become culturally cemented as commonsense knowledge and adopted as a virtually universal worldview.[31] As aforementioned, the development of strategies for resistance and social change must be conceived through a critical understanding of what we are resisting. This implies not only a knowledge of system and structure, but a knowledge of our oppressor as well. To these ends, while we focus our efforts in this work within the first phase of the anti-racist journey—the critical education of the oppressed—we do so through a unique approach. As our point of departure from other works that exist, we have set out to use this book itself as a platform from which to critically address the theoretical foundations for racism as it exists in Western society today.

We feel that it is important to combine our interrogations of the material/ structural relations of power with an investigation of how racialized subjects are constituted and regulated through the ideology and discourse of racism. Our purpose in employing this framework is the development of a "critical gaze" through which oppressed peoples might examine and resist their own subject positions. But it is not actually "the gaze" that is crucial here. It is how we connect thought with action—well aware that we will meet with strong resistance along that line of struggle. So our gaze must be sharp and continually focused on the possibilities of interruption. Crucial to that resistance is not only an understanding of what racism means to the oppressed, but also what it means to our oppressor. In the anti-racist struggle and in all struggles against oppression, it is important to understand our oppressor and to understand the logic/rhetoric he uses to justify, overlook and mute our oppression. With that in mind, each chapter in this text is geared toward a theoretical interrogation of myths and rhetoric that consistently obscure and/or support privileged distortions of racism and the racist experience.

In Chapter One we focus on an interrogation of the race concept itself. We engage in a historical analysis of the processes and dynamics of racism, as well as its implications for understanding and interpreting human relations and conflict. The purpose is to establish the historical basis for racism in contemporary Western contexts. We begin this work, in this way, because it is important to interrogate privileged interpretations and understandings of what race and racism are. Of particular importance in this chapter is the interrogation of the historical specificities that engender "the reproduction of races" in socially structured spaces. Our purpose is to establish a firm theoretical account that will, in turn, set the groundwork to better analyze the contemporary ideological, material and social meanings of racism, as well as the practical applications of power and privilege. Only through this type of theoretical analysis might we do away with conventional arguments that seek to place racism as relative to all races and cultures. Racism is about far more than mere attitudes; catchy slogans calling for all people to "Stop Racism!" do little more than accent sugarcoated strategies for tolerance and cultural sensitivity. Race is real and we take this chapter to set the groundwork for an interrogation of that reality.

In Chapter Two we examine ideology as a framework for understanding racism. We address how racism functions relative to individual and collective beliefs systems and we take on the racist ideology that seeks to obfuscate the reality of oppression. The ideological rhetoric is familiar: "Racism is just a remnant from the past and slavery. It's not as bad as it used to be." These are sentiments all too commonly echoed in mainstream discourse. The claims serve multiple purposes. First, they work to mute or silence marginalized voices that speak to the hardships and everyday problematics faced by people of color and secondly, they belie the truth, power and influence of racism as it exists today. This chapter examines how racism gains strength and sustains itself. It examines how hegemony constructs and maintains racism and how hegemonic discourses work to create an environment ripe for racism. The production of meaning is intimately connected to how concepts and beliefs are developed based on the power of the ruling elite. This chapter explores theoretical arguments that address these connections, as well as the ways in which ideological power allows one group to influence another group's beliefs, values and under-standing of reality.

Chapter Three takes on issues of *power* and *difference*, recognizing that the voice of White privilege commonly seeks to speak for the racially oppressed (e.g., "If I were Black, I wouldn't care if all my teachers were White, I would just want the best person for the job." "Don't be so sensitive." "If someone calls me Honky, it doesn't bother me."). Statements like this fail to acknowledge the roles of power and difference in social formations. In this discussion, we take on the issue of power to examine how difference is constructed through racist discourse and how power plays out relative to oppression. This chapter looks closely at how the overarching structures of dominance are interconnected and interdependent on each other (i.e., racism, sexism, classism, heterosexism, etc.). We take this very pointed direction because although skin color cannot be overlooked in discussions of racism and oppression, organizational categories such as race become oppressive in and through their relation to power and the language of difference. As a socially constructed phenomenon, racism serves to position individuals and groups into different social locations—locations that are based on access to privilege and power.

By deconstructing how words and meanings function relative to power, we interrogate the political nature of language and its role in the maintenance of oppression. What are the power relations that make the racist experience intensely painful for some while deniable to others? Is the difference an issue of sensitivity or is it an issue of power? In this chapter we examine the relations of power that exist in Western contexts, how they came to be and how they develop as a result of the systemic and structural nature of oppression. We also examine the concept of difference, particularly in relation to race and ethnicity and how difference is constructed through racist discourse. Also, we will work to deconstruct elements of commonsense racist knowledge in order to make links between the theory of power and difference and racist experiences that people of color have in their/our everyday lives. In addressing these problematics through an anti-racist frame, we contest the normalcy of Whiteness, the construction of non-Whites as *other* and the power structures that function in the development of such discourses.[32]

In Chapter Four we expand beyond notions of an "oppressive/oppressor consciousness" to interrogate why those with skin color privilege commonly resist engaging the existence of racism and the necessity of doing anti-racist work. We use this space to address White power and privilege in a way that interrogates why people with skin color privilege often deny the impact that racism has on the lives of people of color. It examines comments and beliefs that are often used to deny, mute and trivialize experiences of racism. This chapter looks at how White people can afford not to see racism or be offended by it and argues that White complacency is problematic because doing nothing re-inforces the status quo. It examines unacknowledged and unmarked White privilege and invisibility. As Whiteness is always taken for granted, we argue for the production of a discourse on race that closely examines Whiteness. Finally, we argue for a critique of Whiteness that interrogates the silence, denial and fear that surrounds the issues of racism and privilege.

In recent years some scholars and activists have contended that the true institutional task of the Western world's socioeconomic system is the sustaining of oppression and maintenance of the *status quo* (see, Bolaria and Li, 1985; Dei, 1996; Dei and Karumanchery, 1999; Goldberg, 1993; Miles, 1989; West, 1992, Henry et al., 1995). However, while it is essential that we bring these issues to the fore of research and pedagogy, establishing the *material* necessity for discourse and curriculum development within an anti-racist frame continues to be a site for debate and controversy. In Chapter Five we take on one of the major problematics faced in the anti-racist struggle: the imperative to understand how racism is manifested in the lived experience of the oppressed. Too often in Western society, racism is tied intrinsically to overt acts of physical violence and/or organized groups like the KKK. This allows those with skin color privilege to conveniently over-look the banal nature of racism. In order to understand the materiality of racism within democratically framed contexts, we need to interrogate and understand the structural forms of racism that allow it to impact the everyday experience and structure of society. In interrogating these systemic, structural and democratic forms of racism, we employ this chapter as a springboard to discuss how structural/systemic change is fundamentally connected to the realities of ameliorating racial oppression in the long term.

In Chapter Six we walk down some of the less traveled roads in anti-racist theory and practice. Thus far in this text we will have shown that, at best, mainstream discourses work to mute the exploration of the lived experience of racialized peoples and, at worst, pathologize the racially oppressed by implying that their experiences of oppression are somehow self-inflicted. We make a very clear distinction in this chapter with regard to the nature of racial oppression as an experience etched in trauma. As will have been framed in the preceding chapters, the insidious and pervasive nature of race and racism is of paramount importance relative to how racial trauma is to be taken up. Orthodox psychological tenets have assessed exposure to race-related stressors along a continuum that rates discrete/ markedly memorable events, subtle exposures and duration of harms. In contrast, we engage a critical anti-racist perspective that frames those stressors as part of a larger ongoing complex of oppression and trauma that infuses every aspect of racially oppressed people's lives. We make this distinction because regardless of the impact on the individual, family or community, the chronic and pervasive effects of a racialized existence are intrinsically individualized in the intersecting and interlocking moments that circumscribe us as oppressed. We take this chapter to engage new interdisciplinary work on the experience of racism and racial oppression. Within this psychosocial framework, we interrogate the pain, trauma and pathology of racism in new and insurgent ways.

In Chapter Seven we interrogate the political rhetoric that suggests public resources cannot and should not be allocated toward the needs and/or demands of special interest groups. This book has a clear mission to "re-think" commonsense understandings of what we need to combat racism and the resulting implications for strategy and resistance. We endeavor to pose questions and explore possibilities for social change based on the politics and theory of integrative anti-racism as a framework for achieving equity in Western society. While this entails a radical re-visioning of the status quo in our current cultural climate, it is also a project that is realistically attuned to the political and institutional formations that make such a project onerous within our society. Critical anti-racist approaches to social reform have a transformative social agenda. They focus on the asymmetrical power relations between and among social groups within society and seek a redistribution of power to ensure fair representation, not only of the actors themselves but also of the subjects of knowledge production. It seeks to equip individuals with knowledge and skills to confront their own biases and prejudices and to work for social change. In the process, it legitimizes the oppositional and subjugated voices of minoritized peoples.

Critical approaches also cultivate a project of transformative possibility in which all people can challenge and resist structural forces that continually reproduce social oppression and inequality. The theoretical orientation employed in this chapter highlights the saliency of race in order to shift the talk away from tolerance of diversity and to the marked notion of difference and power. Race and racism are central to how we claim, occupy and defend spaces in society. An important task of critical anti-racist research is to delineate the causes and/or factors that contribute to social inequality and to proceed to offer alternative solutions. Our politics of research and study is not simply to generate knowledge but to produce new knowledge and perspectives that will help oppressed peoples to re-think their subjectivity in North American contexts. The purpose of this chapter is twofold. First, we pay particular attention to the public discourse against anti-racist politics, practice and educational reform and secondly, we take a critical look at how anti-racist pedagogy and practice might fit into Western contexts in this age of Diaspora.

And in Chapter Eight we have set out to examine the commonality of our experiences relative to the possibilities of solidarity and resistance. Throughout the preceding chapters, we will have established the various patterned interactions and relations of power that frame our oppression. We have framed this chapter such that the new knowledges and inquiries that arose through these discussions might act as a lynchpin for the reader to engage in movement toward a greater critical consciousness and toward more praxical opportunities for resistance. Much of the anti-racist theory discussed in Chapter Seven points to the notion of solidarity and community as a fundamentally important starting point to our liberation. Through an integrative analysis of relationship between group solidarity and resistance, we use this space to interrogate the fundamentally empowering nature of *universality* and self-reflexivity in the moment. Underlying the theoretical applications put forth here is an implicated understanding that standing alone in the face of racism is often anything but empowering. We contend that the discovery of commonality in group settings teaches us the simple but forceful message that we are not alone and that our experiences of racism and oppression are the experiences of *a people*.

If, as suggested by Gramsci, the starting point of critical elaboration is the coming to consciousness of what one really is, then it is indeed imperative that we compile an inventory of what it is that has constituted us. Our purpose in this text is to help compile this inventory. We seek to remind our readers—the oppressed—our partners in the project, that we are the ones being made and re-made in/through discursive formations: we are socially constructed within discursive practices. The framework employed in this work supports an interpretation of *the subject* as a living, thinking and feeling agent, capable of both reflexive thought and proactive action. Utilizing this conception of subject, we are dedicated to the belief that the reality of racism and oppression is a function of our ability to understand it. As soon as we come to the realization that we are submerged within power relations, then the possibility of resistance is also created. If we are to gain/access agency in these situations, we must come to recognize that we are never trapped by power. That being said, we truly hope that this work might support the advance of an organic social transformation. The nature of which, like the strange God of Diderot's metaphor, places us in a position to slowly establish ourselves more firmly, until one fine morning we might give our neighbour a shove with our elbow and—crash!—the idol lies upon the ground.

CHAPTER ONE
Theorizing Race & Racism: Focusing Our Discursive Lens

The meaning and salience of race are forever being reconstituted in the present... There was a long period—centuries—in which race was seen as a natural condition, an essence. This was only recently succeeded, although not entirely superseded, by a way of thinking about race as subordinate to supposedly more concrete, 'material' relationships; thus we have become used to thinking about race as an illusion, an excrescence. Perhaps now we are approaching the end of this racial epoch too.
> —Omi and Winant, *On the Theoretical Status of the Concept of Race*[1]

White teachers commonly insist that they are 'color-blind': that they see children as children and do not see race...What does it mean to construct an interpretation of race that denies it?
> —Christine E. Sleeter, *How White Teachers Construct Race*[2]

Race is real! As a concept, race is complex and ever-changing...but it is real and it does matter. We begin with this clear assertion because in this age of political correctness, the word *race* is commonly eschewed in favour of less incendiary terms such as *culture* and *ethnicity* (terms which in themselves do not exist in uncontested space). In fact, within mainstream discourse, it has become almost stylish to suggest that 'race doesn't really exist'—that a color-blind policy is the best policy—that there is no salience to skin color. Unfortunately, such negations and dismissals only serve to downplay the significance and reality of 'racial existence' and oppression. As the axiom asserts: denying a problem does not make it disappear.

'We share certain mythologies. A History. We share political and economic systems and a rapidly developing, if suspect ethos'.[3] When playwright August Wilson vocalized his desire that a Black person direct the film version of *Fences*, his Pulitzer Prize-winning play, he took a very specific political stand. His argument, that race would greatly determine the nature of the director's vision and interpretive style, spoke to several key contentions that continue to run through present critical race theory. Is race real, or is it just a tool employed in hegemonic struggles for power? Is race defined by biological essence or in temporal interpretation? Is racial understanding a function and province of experience? The meanings, readings and very notion of race and consequently racism are continually in dispute, contested by both *insiders* and *outsiders* because, ultimately, there is no single core of symbols and interpretations to be definitively examined. So, is race real? Whether or not one agrees with Wilson's assessment that cultural manifestations of race are ideally the province and possession of the "group" that produced them, the argument itself points to the powerful ideological and experiential impact of the race concept.

So why begin here? Why re-hash and re-address critical race theory relative to the social construction of the race concept? Well, simply put, an understanding of "race" is central to this work and, as such, an interrogation of the concept itself is not only prudent but necessary. How race manifests, how it is approached in social analysis, how it regulates/constitutes the social world, how we understand it and how we perform it—these themes are all critically important to this study. In this chapter, we have set out to examine some of the processes and dynamics that inform/constitute the ever-shifting meanings of race and their implications for understanding racial oppression. We hope that this provides a valuable entry point, an overview of sorts that will explore the contemporary landscapes of race, racism and racial oppression. We use this space to interrogate various theoretical engagements with race: what it is and how its "reality" impacts racially oppressed peoples. Or more simply put, the whys, hows, wheres and whens of our oppression.

We began this chapter with two quotations. The first spoke to the changing face and meaning of the race concept, while the second addressed a more pointed concern: the denial of difference and the denial of race and racism. As we interrogate the ground upon which these denials and meanings meet, we hope to review/re-assess and possibly re-imagine these problematics in ways that may prove useful to the analyses of resistance and healing taken up later in this work. As we mentioned earlier, this work intersects a wide range of disciplines and in doing so we hope to do more than merely re-state existing understandings or perceptions of race.[4] Rather, as asserted by Said and again by Awkward, we tackle both *the familiar* and *the new*, hoping that insurgent challenges and examinations may arise in *the space between*. As a starting point to this dialogue, like Omi and Winant, we assert that the main task facing racial theory today is to address the continuing significance and changing meanings of race: the space between contexts.

Biology has not left our social and political perceptions. Today, even while the concept of race is being increasingly employed as a social, political and historically contextual construct,[5] there continue to be deep-seated forces in Western society that argue for biological differences as the fundamental signifiers of racial variation. The difficulties in challenging these contentions arise in our own innate propensity to categorize. Importantly, while tribalism and the exploration of human biological difference may have fostered primeval notions of race in early social formations, the varied nature of today's racial framework is evidence to a very clear, if not pointed, evolution from those ancient origins.[6] So what is race? Where does the concept come from? How do we define it? These questions must be addressed because, while race is a permanent fixture of the human landscape with far-reaching social and political consequences, we can no longer afford to either deny its salience nor imagine it to have a fixed or concrete nature. Rather than assigning constant signifiers to the race concept, we echo Omi and Winant's theoretical assertions that seek to define race as a process: a fluid and unstable complex of meanings that are constantly re-formed through social and political conflict.[7]

The variety of meanings ascribed to the race concept indicate that there is a basic difficulty in establishing any general theory on the subject, and so as a result, we need to read it as fluid. However, relative to that fluidity, we must also take care to acknowledge that, while skin color cannot stand alone as the singular lynchpin by which the race concept is held together, there is a permanence and salience to skin color in relation to the problematics of categorization and social differentiation. Therefore, in interrogating race relations ostensibly as power relations, or as relations of domination and subordination, we unlock important theoretical space that critical anti-racists might use to articulate the salience of skin color racism beyond other forms of racism.[8] So bearing that in mind, how do we define race? How do we operationalize racial oppression? How do we understand and sift through the competing interpretations of race as (a) biologically determined, (b) ideologically constructed and (c) socially constituted?

The enterprise of assigning biological objectivity to the race concept has never been an easy one. As noted by Dei (1996), early theorists and social scientists found the task of defining and operationalizing the race concept to be enormously problematic. It is an uncertainty that continues today because, like those researchers before us, we are still constrained by our use of conceptual and analytical categories that are themselves social constructs. Historically, attempts to define race met with operational problematics on two main fronts. First, there was always some question as to the criteria by which human groups were to be classified, [9] and secondly, the problematics of fitting those human groups into definite racial categories multiplied as European colonization and exploration "uncovered new and as yet, unclassified peoples." After all, where would "they" fit South Asians, Arabs, Native Americans and other "newly discovered" peoples into their neat Caucasoid, Negroid and Mongoloid hierarchy? Moreover and not to belabour the point, but where in these categories would we neatly fit inter-racial children?

Regardless of the obvious problematics and evident inconsistencies, the fixed conceptions of race became reified through the use of theories and "objective" sciences such as Polygeny, Craniometry and IQ testing. Consequently, as these pseudo-sciences gained in credibility, so too did our belief in the intrinsic inferiority of those held up against the standards of European Whiteness.[10] White scientists gathered or, rather, fabricated "hard data" in order to elevate Whites above *other* peoples. Strengthened by such claims to "scientific truth," theories that worked to hierarchically classify races as entirely separate biological species began to emerge and cement themselves in the social consciousness.[11]

In recent years we have seen a re-emergence of similar attempts to reify biological racism in the work of authors such as Charles Murray, Richard Herrnstein and Philip Rushton.[12] Such contemporary socio-scientific racists produce biologically determinist works that continue to insert fallacious racial signs, symbols and "facts" into the social consciousness. Under the guise of "objectivity" and scientific exploration, these pseudo-scientists obfuscate their political agenda and work to foster a continued reading of race as a signifier of innate or natural differentiation in human qualities such as intelligence, morality and potential.[13] Notwithstanding the popularized works of these and other such pseudo-scientists, in reality today the business of linking race and biology remains the province of only a very few who exist on the fringes of the conservative agenda.

In a concerted effort to limit and curtail the continued infiltration of such "scientific truths" into the world consciousness, the United Nations Educational, Scientific and Cultural Organization (UNESCO) declared in 1978 that:

> Any theory which involves the claim that racial and ethnic groups are inherently superior or inferior, thus implying that some would be entitled to dominate or eliminate others, presumed to be inferior, or which bases value judgements on racial differentiation, has no scientific foundation and is contrary to the moral and ethical principals of humanity.[14]

This formal statement issued by UNESCO arose as a sort of counter-discourse to the historically constructed conception of race as concrete.[15] Still, regardless of the purpose and prestige behind such declarations and while the biological determinism of race has been generally disavowed in the latter third of the 20th century, those same "racial/racist truths" still manage to slip into our everyday understandings of the world. So much so that concrete notions of race are still commonly employed in both the mainstream and surprisingly within accepted fields of academic study. Omi and Winant commented briefly on the problematic:

> ...race is treated as an *independent variable* all too frequently. Thus, to select only prominent examples, Daniel Moynihan, William Julius Wilson...and many other mainstream thinkers theorize race in terms that downplay its variability and historically contingent character. Even these thinkers, who explicitly reject biologistic forms of racial theory, fall prey to a kind of creeping objectivism of race.[16]

This is in fact one of the great problematics that we face as anti-racists. Whenever we do this work and tackle "the race-concept," we run the risk of making assumptions and interpreting the world on the basis of the very theories and knowledges that we would contest. While the notion of race extended its reach and grasp through the development and application of racist pseudo-sciences, we would contend that, if there is a concrete aspect to the concept, it is set in our inability to shake the "biological fact" of race from our psyches. After all, here we are at the outset of the 21st century and we continue to be plagued by the legacy of what Dubois termed "the problem of the color-line" 100 years ago.[17] Even now, while the linkages between race and biology are being so clearly contested and denounced, we continue to find ourselves interpreting race through intrinsically biological signs, symbols and meanings. As asserted by Lopez (1995), our fates continue to rest upon our ancestry and appearance as "the characteristics of our hair, complexion and facial features still influence whether we are figuratively free or enslaved."[18]

Simply put, while we live for the most part in a post-biological era, the language of science has been subsumed within the more covert discursive language of racism and cultural markers. Age-old claims to the scientific truth of race are now commonly encoded in and through cultural forms as they work to add currency to the already prevalent image of racial/cultural inferiority. Notions of cultural difference manage to mark inferiority in much the same way as, and in sometimes more insidious fashion than, the basic biological notion of race.[19]

> What does it mean when a White judge takes the cultural contexts of Aboriginal men into account during a rape trial? It can mean and it has, that the rapes are viewed as a kind of cultural practice: these people do these kinds of things. [20]

In this new era of post-biological racism, we may speak of culture, but what we are doing is recognizing and tapping into an already established source of meanings that have been made available to us. These are meanings, signs and symbols that are deeply etched within our biological understandings of what race is. The scientific canons, the genetic markers, the very history of race have all left indelible prints within our cerebral landscape.[21] That is to say, when the media speaks of gang violence, what images do we conjure? When we hear that a liquor store was robbed, what do we imagine the skin color of the culprit(s) to be? If we are walking down an empty dark street and we hear footsteps, who would we rather have behind us? What color would we want their skin be?[22]

That being said, if genetics are no longer an accepted lynchpin for racial thought, then where and how do we continue to construct, legitimate and ground our understandings of race? Because racialized bodies have been historically framed, positioned and pathologized in specifically negative ways, the discourse of biological determinism has been deeply naturalized and legitimized as "truth" and "commonsense." The deeply seeded nature of these commonsense "truths" makes it intensely problematic for theorists to suggest that the scientific bases for racism have been banished by the intervention of social theory.[23] Following Lawrence's (1982) assertions as to the role of commonsense knowledge in the development and continuation of racism throughout history, we would assert that commonsense understandings of race have attained almost universal acceptance as undeniable truths in contemporary Western contexts.[24] As noted by Gramsci:

> Every philosophical current leaves behind a sediment of commonsense; this is the document of its historical effectiveness. Commonsense is not rigid and immobile but is continually transforming itself, enriching itself with scientific ideas and with philosophical opinions which have entered ordinary life. Commonsense creates the folklore of the future, that is as a relatively rigid phase of popular knowledge at a given place and time. [25]

It is the taken-for-granted nature of commonsense ideologies that pose the greatest difficulty for insurgent social formations. The problematic arises in that the struggle is not a balanced battle between philosophical systems vying for supremacy. It is, in fact, a one-sided conflict that forces insurgent theory to pit itself against the fragmented, episodic traces of a tradition long since gone, yet deeply enmeshed in the society's historical, social and mental fabric. Our discrete constitution within what is a racially, culturally and ethnically charged social sphere impels, incites and induces us to resonate with a commonsense racial consciousness, regardless of whether or not we ever openly speak of race.

In Winant's (1994) assertion that race could only be understood as an evolving historical construct without objective/concrete interpretation, he inadvertently paved the ground for social theory to re-address race's connection/relation to ideological formation.[26] That is to say that, if race is not to be viewed as a material/objective issue, then it might seem logical to take the next obvious step and frame it as immaterial or illusory. While we would not presume to suggest that ideology has no place in the construction of the race concept, we would question assertions that place race as an exclusively ideological construct. Furthermore for that matter, we contest interpretations that see race as ideology, existing solely as a form of *false consciousness* whose purpose is to explain and support society's material conditions.

To clarify, with respect to the notion of false consciousness, Marx worked to establish a strong relationship between ideology and the interests of the dominant class. He asserted that within a capitalist framework each successive generation would have a ruling class and that each class's control over the means of material production would undoubtedly lead to its control over the means of mental production as well.[27] It was this belief in the notion of a *dominant ideology* that led Marx to posit that ideology as false consciousness would function to invert reality in favour of the dominant classes. This *dominant ideology thesis* places the apparatus for the trans-mission of ideology (e.g., schools, media, law, state, etc.) at the centre of this analysis and suggests that the ruling class's control over social consciousness arises in its ability to manipulate that apparatus. Further, the imagery that develops is of one class controlling and manipulating another. This is clearly a class-theoretical account of how the dominant ideology functions within capitalist society.[28]

Similarly, theorists such as Fields (1990), Bolaria and Li (1985), in line with Marx's notions of ideology as false consciousness, contend that the race concept arose as a direct ideological consequence of capitalism and that its sole function was/is to justify the oppression and exploitation of peoples of color. In their interpretations of the connection between ideology and materiality, there is a very decided assumption that the concept of race was/is intrinsically rooted in the process of material production. That is to say that (a) racism was able to prosper because of the obvious benefits of colored labour and (b) after overt means were no longer necessary to pacify the oppressed, the dominant group resorted to the covert means of ideological domination.[29] Mirroring Marx's notions on ideology, these accounts suggest that the ability of the ruling class (in this case White Europeans) to manipulate the apparatus of ideological production precludes the necessity of an overtly oppressive system.

This interpretation suggests that in oppressive systems all groups are incorporated within the same intellectual universe, the universe of the dominant group.[30] But are social groups the subjects of established group ideologies? Can specific concepts and ideas belong exclusively to one particular class, one particular socio-political bloc? These are serious points of contention for many critics, who would assert that the "rulingness" of a class does not necessarily guarantee the dominance of its ideas; to do so would mean that particular forms of consciousness can be class/group specific. Such interpretations seem to view ideological production as unidirectional.[31] It is important to recognize that while the discourses that organize this terrain do appear to be most greatly influenced by the privileged few, ideological constructions occur on a contradictory and contested terrain that is dynamic and polyvocal.[32] As asserted by Freire, knowledge and ideology are not simply imposed upon the "unthinking masses" and racial thoughts and understandings of the world are not merely poured into the heads of the oppressed. This general movement away from abstract theories of *ruling class ideologies* directs us toward the analysis of how specific socio-historical situations organize social ideology.[33] As asserted by Tonnies (1957), there are other influences at work adjacent to economic base and political superstructure. He defends this position in recognizing that all capitalist societies are not identical and that all artificially developing human collectivities need not adopt the capitalist mode of production. Such ideological influences and their ability to affect social development are of singular importance to our understanding of why social variations exist from region to region.[34]

According to Fields, the ideology of race is intrinsically tied to these very specific social, political and economic origins. She contends that it is imposed upon the oppressed as an illusion that does the ideological work of our oppressor. In such interpretations, there are no efforts made to interrogate how the race concept has evolved since its outset. Fields neglects to address how race has evolved parallel to the world's shifting socio-cultural conditions and she declares vehemently that the continuation of the race concept exists as a function of society's continued usage and engagement with the term. In fact, she disparages anti-racists and other "opponents of racism" for their part in unwittingly perpetuating racial talk, racial meaning and racial ideology. In her analysis, race has ceased to serve the purpose of justifying racial exploitation and social inequality and so should by virtue of that immateriality, "fade into the ether." Fields contends:

> Nothing handed down from the past could keep race alive if we did not constantly reinvent and re-ritualize it to fit our own terrain. If race lives on today, it can do so only because we continue to need a social vocabulary that will allow us to make sense, not of what our ancestors did then, but of what we choose to do now.[35]

There is in her work, a very clear assumption that race is in some way ethereal; that its presence today would and could be "jettisoned" from the social consciousness if we would just stop working with it. Needless to say, this contention is at best naive and at worst dangerous. Such theoretical work paves the ground for the equality versus equity debates and other similarly problematic notions such as *color-blindness*. As noted by Omi and Winant (1993), these interpretations neglect to recognize the fundamental character of race as a social construct that has developed over a millennium or more of diffusion in and throughout every fiber of the social world. Whatever race was in its origins, it is now an intrinsic part and fundamental principal of social organization and identity formation and, as such, it cannot and must not be trivialized as a mere illusion that could be dispensed with if we "chose" to disencumber ourselves of it.[36]

In moving beyond the questionable reliance on the phenotypical markers of race and in rejecting simplistic notions that call for the jettisoning of race as illusory, we are compelled to re-imagine our constitution as racialized beings within a framework that is marred by a biologically determinist past. Rather than interrogating the constructions of early racial discourses and moving through an analysis of the economics and history of race, we will focus on the ideological, political and material meanings to race as they relate to our oppression today. In this respect, we feel it important to move beyond questions surrounding the validity of racial categories and the "reality" of the race concept, to discuss the materiality of race as a social, ideological and political category.

As a socially constructed category, race is often framed as lacking any real quantifiable validity or objective condition. However, in that the race concept's influence stretches throughout the experiences of both privileged and oppressed alike, it must be recognized that race has/is power in our society. While mainstream rhetoric and discourse will assert fervently that the very nature of a free and democratic society precludes the possibility of oppression, the continued growing utility of race in the distribution of unequal power and privilege reveals that the race concept is gaining in social currency. It is an ever-widening sphere of influence that works to keep us oppressed symbolically, emotionally, spiritually and experientially, despite all claims to the contrary. As asserted by Freire (1970), the oppressor's perception is that those with more have earned their status and privilege by virtue of hard work and that, conversely, if others have less it is exactly because they are incompetent, lazy and unwilling to take risks. Once such situations of violence and oppression have been established, it engenders an entire way of life for both oppressed and oppressor alike—a way of life that constructs and constitutes both of their lived realities.[37] In this sense, by employing methods that seem perfectly natural and proper, race has become an effective tool with which our oppressor rewards, penalizes and punishes. As Lopez asserts:

> [R]ace dominates our personal lives. It manifests itself in our speech, dance, neighbours and friends—our very ways of talking, walking, eating and dreaming are ineluctably shaped by notions of race...race determines our economic prospects... race permeates our politics... In short, race mediates every aspect of our lives.[38]

Despite this pervasive influence, the commonplace acceptance of racial categories as real but irrelevant speaks to the underlying reality that few seem to know or understand what race is and what it is not. So it should be clarified that we work with the concept of race because in/through that interrogation, we make sense of and work to rupture the racially constructed power relations of the status quo—the power relations of oppression. Again, we would assert that it is of paramount importance that we do not seek to simply abandon the term. To do so would be to deny its social, ideological and political materiality. We cannot afford to ignore it; we cannot afford to proceed with problematic claims to *color-blindness*. We cannot allow ourselves to fall into commonsense interpretations that see race as an ideological construct to be simply jettisoned from our thinking: a thing to be abolished by simple act of will. Rather, we must continue to engage it through dialogue and political practice.

As suggested by Miles (1989), in the contemporary sense, rather than abandoning the race concept altogether, it seems appropriate that we speak to the process of racialization. That is, the myriad contexts and moments in/through which we are defined, constructed and constituted relative to the signs and symbols of human biological and cultural characteristics.[39] We mention cultural characteristics because the process of racialization cannot be understood to exist and function solely within the biological contexts of skin color alone. While the salience of skin color cannot be overlooked, it is important to acknowledge the centrality of other historically specific meanings entwined in the race concept and so we interrogate race relative to the multiplicity of racial practice, experience and constructions.[40] As Dei (1996) argues, this framework calls for a non-reductionist, historically specific analysis of racism that touches on the internal character of the race concept itself.[41] As with similar shifts in contemporary critical studies, this expansion, beyond theories that assume race to be natural and static, allows us to take important steps toward the interrogation of new conceptions and expressions of race and racism.[42] Moreover, it allows us to rupture the false dichotomies that seek to place racism and the race concept as features of a shameful past and irrelevant in the present. It allows us to interrogate the threads that bind *the then* and *the now*.

Many of us came to theory because we wanted to understand why we were hurting and where that pain came from. In seeking to understand this pain, the issue of silence that we touched upon earlier is again relevant. The internalization of pain, the repression of suffering, the suppression of the unspeakable—these are all natural and normal human responses to violation, oppression and trauma. As Herman (1992) would remind us, "The ordinary response to atrocities is to banish them from consciousness."[43] Much of the pain that drove us (the authors) to do anti-racist work, struck us at times in our lives when we couldn't name or understand the "truth" of our situations because we had dislodged it from our memory. Our pain is magnified by our silence in the face of it and it intensifies in our inability to identify what it is. So again, we come to theory because we want to understand why we are hurting and where that pain comes from.

We see theory as a location for healing, a fundamental step in our journey toward a closer, more nuanced understanding of our oppression. With that assertion in mind, we don't mean to suggest that theory should be looked to in terms of universal knowledge. Rather, in recognizing that there is a partiality to knowledge, we work within anti-racist frameworks that reject notions of an essentialized reality. Dei (1996) notes that anti-racist theory has expanded its epistemology to include a critical inquiry of the practices and dynamics that organize and constitute the lives of marginalized people. However, in order to do so, we look to practices that focus on the complexities of the lived experience rather than rely on traditional quantitative methods that risk developing oversimplified definitions of social phenomena.[44] It is a paradigm shift away from traditions of meta-narration and universal theory that have sought to speak for and dictate to, the oppressed. As asserted by Freire:

> We must not negate practice for the sake of theory. To do so would reduce theory to a pure verbalism or intellectualism. By the same token, to negate theory for the sake of practice, as in the use of dialogue as conversation, is to run the risk of losing oneself in the disconnectedness of practice. It is for this reason that I never advocate either a theoretic elitism or a practice ungrounded in theory, but the unity between theory and practice. In order to achieve this unity, one must have an epistemological curiosity—a curiosity that is often missing in dialogue as conversation.[45]

It is considerably difficult to work toward practical, pragmatic change without also having an understanding of the theoretical ground upon which that change is to take place. The dilemma arises in our inability to differentiate between what we see, know and understand as reality and the complexities of how that reality has been constructed and constituted. In relation to our discussions, this problematic translates into our continued need to view race as either fixed or illusory. Interestingly, as discussed earlier relative to the work of theorists like Fields, such interpretations leave little room for intermediary possibilities. Omi and Winant employed the concept of *racial formation* to proceed beyond both objective assertions of race's fixed, biological nature and the metaphysical/illusory notions that race would be non-existent in an ideal social sphere. In their place, they posit that race is best understood as a de-centered and unstable complex of social meanings constantly being transformed through political struggle.[46]

In following this conception of race as socially constructed and historically-contextually specific, we contest the theoretical conflation of biology and reality. It is problematic to argue against the reality and utility of the race concept, based solely on the fact that pseudo-sciences backing *biological functionality* have no scientific grounding. To do so negates the practical applications and circumstances of race's social, political, economic and material impact on societies in general and on racialized bodies specifically.[47] Winant (1994) reminds us that the realities of race and racism are evident in the ability of both the oppressed and oppressor to identify them.[48] Our awareness has become so finely tuned and ingrained in our everyday lived understanding of the world as racial that it is now second nature to us. We see it. We recognize it. Moreover, in our development of this ability—this racial gaze—we have come to naturalize race and, in turn, solidify its place in reality. In other words, if race has become so identifiable, tangible and clear, then for all intents and purposes it has become real.[49]

In their contention that the realities of the race concept lie in its social formation and consequences, Omi and Winant define race as being an autonomous field of social struggle, political organization and cultural/ ideological meaning. To be more specific, they place an emphasis on the historical and socio-political contexts which mediate the construction of racial identities.[50] Because human influence is always directly implicated in the processes that codify and mark our bodies, our racial identities are invariably linked to the knowledges and often dogmatic meanings that develop throughout time and place. Omi and Winant's perspective on the development of the race concept answers the problematic of determinism with a concept of social formation as encompassing practices and levels that function outside the direct sphere of *base* and *superstructure*. Similar to Althusser's notion of social formation, "racial formations" comprise different levels of human practice—economic, political, ideological, scientific, etc.— that each maintains their own specific characteristics, articulations and dynamics relative to society. These formations are constituted through multiple, distinct sites and they encompass their own accumulating contra- dictions through which...at the right time and place, radical transformations might develop.[51]

According to Althusser (1971), the *relations of production* were repro- duced through the various State apparatus' transmission of repressive ideologies. In this perspective, each ideological State apparatus maintains and contributes to the relations of exploitation by transmitting dominant, oppressive ideologies through language and into society.[52] In his notion of interpellation, Althusser embraced a more linguistic reading of ideologies, how they become internalized, how we speak them and how we are spoken by external forces.[53]

> The political apparatus by subjecting individuals to the political State ideology, the 'indirect' (parliamentary) or 'direct' (plebiscitary or Fascist) 'democratic' ideology. The communications apparatus by cramming every 'citizen' with daily doses of nationalism, chauvinism, liberalism, moralism, etc., by means of the press, the radio and television. The same goes for the cultural apparatus...The religious apparatus... The family apparatus...[54]

Omi and Winant made many of these same linkages relative to how racial formation and racial identities are normalized and given currency. In line with Althusser's assertions, they contend that the most productive site through which racial formation occurs is in the everyday experience…the moments when we employ racially coded characteristics to frame our world. There are in these moments and formations a *specificity of the political.* In an effort to move away from notions of ideological formation as either repressive or unidirectional, theorists such as Laclau and Hall go further in asserting that language, as a medium of thought, is multi-accentual and that ideologies always develop with and within these intersecting accents. Hall highlights Laclau's assertions in his own conception of ideology as "those images, concepts and premises which provide the frameworks through which we represent, interpret, understand and 'make sense' of some aspect of social existence."[55] In such interpretations, it is recognized that ideologies need not be related specifically to one bloc or another, but that the character of an ideological concept develops in its articulation within a specific bloc discourse and not through its content.[56]

Similarly, Omi and Winant directly implicate the state and state apparatus as primary sites through which race and racial identities are constructed and maintained.[57] Again, like Althusser, they contend that these constructions occur not only in and through the administrative levels of the state that function mainly through coercion and force, but through the ideological apparatus (e.g., cultural forms and institutions such as churches, schools,[58] families and literature, among others).[59] Lopez (1995) reminds us that many of the racial categories that we employ and consider to be natural or immutable, are in fact the product of human design. Case in point, the transformation of Mexican from a nationality into a race:

> Race is neither an essence nor an illusion but, rather an ongoing contradiction, self-reinforcing, plastic process subjected to the macro forces of social and political struggle and the micro effects of daily decisions.[60]

So, as contended by Lopez, human agency, working through these various levels of practice are in constant interaction with each other, a struggle for dominance in which social constructions such as race develop in relational terms.[61] Today, race is so deeply woven into the social fabric that our existence is fundamentally constituted and charged through it, such that next to gender, race is the first thing we notice about people.[62] In this respect, it organizes and constitutes our understandings and expectations. Race regulates interpretations of who we trust, who we identify with and who we intrinsically see as intelligent, athletic, weak, lazy, etc.[63] Our social-psychological commitment to race, as a category that is basic to our everyday lived experience, regulates and manages our ability to function as anything but racialized subjects. However, as Lopez asserts, this is not to suggest that these meanings are unalterable and fixed. Rather, it is important to recognize that they too will continue to be formed and reconstituted relative to time and context. Gandy (1998), also working with notions of race as place and time specific, asserted that classifications, both material (in the form of legislation or overt coercive action) and ideological (in the form of language, sign and symbol), play central roles in the distribution and allocation of privileges and access. He maintains that racial ideology, as pivotal in the social construction of race, functions as a system of beliefs that are so deeply interwoven within historico-socio-political discourses that they work to reinforce and reproduce the very beliefs and assumptions upon which they themselves rely.[64]

Gandy further asserts that, along with the legislative powers of the state, the mass media functions as one of the most influential sites through which such racial configurations are produced and disseminated. Moreover, because racial meanings arise out of human agency, rather than independently, they gain in both currency and legitimacy through these historical contexts. The millennia that we have spent inscribing the biology of race into our collective psyches. Importantly, while this historical time has been contextualized through conquest and subjugation, it is critical that we recognize the role played by experience, narrative, sign, symbol, language and discourse in those inscriptions. At the beginning of this chapter, we quoted from Omi and Winant. Their question as to whether or not we were reaching the end of a racial epoch is, for me, not as important as the questions it engenders. If we are in fact reaching the end of a time where race is seen as either immaterial or deterministic, then what is the next stage in this racial formation and, perhaps more importantly, how do we influence the next stage to reflect an anti-racist framework?

By interrogating race as a socially constructed phenomenon, we adopt a theoretical framework that places a great deal of emphasis on the historical specificities of social movements. As an approach to race theory, it is more amenable to the complex social phenomena of the modern world because identities are fluid and continually being refined and re-defined through social practice.[65] Paralleling Gramsci's contributions to theories of social formation, Omi and Winant's notion of race as socially constructed is an interpretation of the shifting balance of relations between social forces in society. In its non-reductionist perspective, it allows for critical engagements with the notions of hegemony, commonsense and the relations of force. It is an interpretation of the complex, conjunctural, intersecting nature of social construction that makes a very clear statement about the problematics of reductionism. Their work can be employed against theoretical conceptions that propose to interrogate social relations through a premeditated teleology or law-like epistemology.

> ...societies are necessarily complexly structured totalities, with different levels of articulation (the economic, the political, the ideological instances) in different combinations; each combination giving rise to a different configuration of social forces and hence to a different type of social development.[66]

As noted by Hall (1996), Gramsci's intent when establishing his conception of the relationship between *base* and *superstructure* was to necessarily remove himself from reductionist or economistic analyses that neglected the *relationships of over-determination* interacting between social practices. It is with this conception of social formation in mind that Gramsci developed a three-pronged methodology whereby social situations might be examined.[67] His approach could be viewed as a strategic guideline for research and activism: a body of pragmatic rules that supports a deeper analysis of society's complex nature. It is an approach that we feel works relative to an awareness of the social construction of race.

The first of his rules asserts that an understanding of the basic structure of society is of paramount importance in that those "objective relations" set the fundamental limits and conditions for social development. The degree to which the productive forces have developed will delineate the ground upon which these historical forces move and the possibilities for social change.[68] This perspective clarifies a process through which new social movements might survive periods of early uncertainty and still manage to affect change. There is an importance to historical interpretation and context which must not be overlooked when dealing with issues of social development because new ideological systems cannot be produced ready-made as a type of intellectual construction designed by the leaders of a political movement. Rather, we would agree that such a social change must develop over time, gradually building and evolving through the course of political and economic struggles and that the character of such a society would depend on the relations of force that existed while it was developing.[69] It is in the capacity to assess the feasibility of a given movement in relation to the moment in a society's "objective relations" that reforms might develop within the confines of the existing system.

The second analytic guideline was put forth to distinguish between Gramsci's notions of organic and discontinuous historical movements. As briefly discussed in the previous chapter, he felt that those social formations that managed to obtain a deep and lasting impact on the society were best understood in relation to their organic ability to evolve toward change. To clarify this concept, and not to be over-simplistic, the rise of capitalism can be understood as an organic social movement. Tigar and Levy (1977) contend that capitalism first took form in the material and ideological participation of subjects and then, over successive generations, openly confronted the system and finally overthrew the legal ideology of feudalism.[70] In this moment, the coercive power of the feudal hierarchy was not powerful enough to sustain itself against the advent of capitalism. Tigar and Levy assert that once the ideological movement away from feudalism had been effectively entrenched, the organic social movement of capitalism evolved into a juggernaut with a life of its own.[71] In following a Gramscian frame, we place ideological evolution as crucial to the success of social formations and re-formations and we would further contend that the advance to new social forms could be generated through a moral and intellectual reform.[72] We agree that social changes, in their most enduring formations, tend to arise through ideological evolutions rather than through abrupt social revolution. The nature of this shift develops through a slow process of transformation in/through which some of the elements of the past system are combined and re-arranged to produce a new ideological principle that preserves popular elements of the old system while abandoning others.[73]

The third of Gramsci's rules speaks to the complexity of the organic movement in relation to historical specificity. He contends that a social formation will develop along historically specific lines and that they will move between periods of relative stability and abrupt shift. The historically specific nature of these intervals can act as a lens through which we might re-construct the relationships between base, superstructure and the movement itself.[74] We find this analytic framework to be useful for our discussion of the social construction of race because it helps us to interrogate how the movement of historical forces can work to constitute the terrain of political and social struggle. Employing this understanding of social formation, we would assert that the process of social change is not a contest where the "winner-takes-all." While the relations of force may be unfavorable toward certain tendencies in specific historical moments, those trends do not neces-sarily disappear. Rather, they may remain beneath the surface of the social consciousness until their potentiality can be activated.

In the socio-historically framed nature of these relations, the conditions that position different social forces as static or dynamic, will often do so relative and parallel to a *political moment* of *class unity*.[75] That being said, it is important to note that in this conception of "the political moment," class unity must never be taken as "a given" because any such communal consciousness is always a contingent effect of a great deal of intellectual labor. To elaborate on this point, we work within the pluralist contention that cross-cutting cleavages create competition between various elites and their specific ideological ontologies. However, while the concept of a singular class/group consciousness is likely theoretical at best, it is reasonable to assert that the dominant socio-economic powers, in their parallel privileges, would possess a high degree of cohesion and therefore, would work toward common purposes that supersede their individual differences.[76]

Gramsci elaborated on this concept of class unity in his discussion of the stages in and through which class/group consciousness, organization and unity might develop (i.e., economic corporate, class corporate, hegemonic). In this discussion he details hegemony as the lynchpin in his analysis of civil society and why he privileges superstructure over the economic base. In so doing, he defined hegemony as "the extent to which [a class] transcends its corporate phase and succeeds in combining the interests of other classes and social forces with its own interests in becoming the universal representative of the main social forces which make up the nation."[77] Gramsci later expanded on this conception to define hegemony as "a general term that is applied to the strategies of all classes; applied analytically to the formation of all historical blocs, not to the strategy of the proletariat alone." Through this adjustment, the notion of hegemony moves to encompass the interests of subordinate groups in an effort to develop intellectual, moral and economic notions of political unity. Within this framework, organizations of *collective will* are seen as developing from the hegemonic balance of a leading social group over a number of subordinate groups. In this configuration, hegemony should not be understood to be coercively imposed. Rather, it develops as a type of "manufactured consent" that encompasses the critical domains of culture, moral, ethical and intellectual leadership.[78]

Hall (1986) examined various aspects of these hegemonic formations. He paid particular attention to the temporal/temporary character of the hegemonic moment. By this he meant to suggest that hegemony, as a rare point of conjuncture for a number of social forces, was unlikely to persist indefinitely. He felt that the complexity, dynamics and subtlety of power relations involved clearly demonstrated that hegemony was not always "absolute" and that local resistances, whether invisible and/or unorganized, would always be present and active in social relations despite the influence of global, national and local economic/political forces to the contrary. Thus, we must be careful not to represent power in diffused and meta-physical terms because we then run the risk of failing to isolate how the enactment of differential/oppositional power can be meaningful and productive for oppressed peoples. It is important to uncover how small acts of resistance are understood by local subjects and how such oppositional knowledges might be implicated in bringing about social change. Local resistances reflect the potentiality of individual/collective agency and so it is important that we question how localized resistances might work to subvert the macro/micro practices of "disciplinary power" that forestall equitable social change. These concerns for resistant strategies become all the more poignant when taken relative to Hall's assertion that hegemony could not persist unless continuously produced and constituted. Again, this reading opens up space in which to discuss how our strategies might be directed to best interrupt and rupture the continuity of the hegemonic process.

Like Hall, we eschew determinist applications that frame hegemony as a pervasively static formation in all societies. Rather, by adopting a more fluid interpretation of "hegemonic order" as shifting, provisional and multi-accentual, we can then envision resistant and reformative possibilities for social change. By this we mean to say that while hegemonic systems may be constructed and sustained on a number of fronts (thereby endowing them with a great deal of cohesion and support as they extend across social boundaries and relations), each of those fronts may be explored as a site for resistance.[79] Again, this is not a zero sum game and there are multiple sites through which our oppression is manufactured and multiple sites in/through which we are implicated as actors/subjects in those moments. Not to sound flippant, but some would view the problematic as similar to the 'chicken and the egg' conundrum. Do we work to change the system and thereby affect our positionality, or do we work to change our positionality in the hopes of changing the system? As we have discussed earlier, we prefer to view the whole of anti-racist work as a tapestry in which each strategy is important and vital. So, we firmly assert that in order for us to critically understand, evaluate and resist our oppression, it is vitally important to first deal with the productivity of our experience. We feel this "productivity" to be intrinsically tied to how we are "made" to view and experience the world through discursive and ideological systems of knowledge production.

Gramsci interpreted ideology as being "any philosophy which becomes a cultural movement, a religion, a faith, that has produced a form of practical activity or 'will' in which a philosophy is contained as an implicit theoretical premise."[80] We see this interpretation running parallel to Foucault's notion of how discourses operate to frame what is thinkable. In reflecting on these perspectives, we feel that Gramsci forms a link between philosophical conceptions of the world and the relations that draw those conceptions into practical application as forms of group consciousness; forms that shape the very nature of social movements. In engaging this critical difference between mere philosophy and organic ideological forms, we want to be careful to note that ideologies have a material existence; they not only touch individual consciousness, but they also organize human masses and constitute the territory upon which political, cultural and other social struggles occur. It is important to recognize that if new ideological conceptions of race, racism and resistance are to become historically effective and shape the general commonsense frameworks and perceptions of society, they must first contest and transform the already existing racist terrain.[81] So we would reiterate the importance of social construction theory for the study of race. As an analytical tool it works to contest the manifest nature of race and racism by interrogating the historic, geographical and socio-political forces through which they are mediated, constituted and constructed.

Relative to this research's pointed interest in the possibilities of resistance, we feel it important to move forward from these discussions, to the questions that surround how race as a social formation works to constitute the oppressed. So in an effort to tie together some of these theoretical threads, a theory of resistance raises other fundamental questions. How are racialized knowledges and meanings transmitted and constructed? How are racial/racialized identities constituted? How are those identities performed? And how can we frame our struggles within relations of force that are not favourable toward anti-racism and still work toward social change? If we are to develop anti-racism praxis as part of an organic social movement, it is vital that we begin to shift our interests from recognizing the signs, symbols and markers of our oppression to a pointed concern with the processes through which we ourselves are implicated in that oppression. By this we mean to say that, in some ways, our preoccupation with the physical manifestations of racism and oppression serves to normalize the very state of oppression through which we suffer. Only by engaging in self-reflexive analyses can we hope to understand the role we play in our own subjugation. Only then will we be able to understand our own duality and ambivalence in the face of racism.

CHAPTER TWO
De-Ideologizing Race: Ideologies, Identities and Illusions

The *problem* of ideology is to give an account, within a materialist theory, of how social ideas arise. We need to understand what their role is in a particular social formation, so as to inform the struggle to change society and open the road towards a socialist transformation of society...The problem of ideology, therefore, concerns the ways in which ideas of different kinds grip the minds of masses and thereby become a 'material force'.

—Stuart Hall, *The Problem of Ideology*[1]

To divide the oppressed, an ideology of oppression is indispensable. In contrast, achieving their unity requires a form of cultural action through which they come to know the why and how of their adhesion to reality—it requires de-ideologizing.

—Paulo Freire, *Pedagogy of the Oppressed*[2]

How might we interrogate ideology as a framework through which to better understand the manifestations and constructions of race and racism? In this chapter, we address the belief, systems and dialogic relations that serve to obfuscate and maintain the reality of oppression as it exists today in Western contexts. As clarified in the introduction, the ideological rhetoric is familiar: "Racism is just a remnant from the past and slavery. It's not as bad as it used to be." This ideological polemic infuses mainstream discourses with perspectives that effectively silence racially oppressed accounts of pain and trauma by belying the "truth" of racism. This chapter will examine how racism gains strength and sustains itself through unidirectional monologues that construct and maintain racism and hegemonic discourses.

The problematics associated with understanding the race concept remind us that we must pay close attention to the methods through which meanings are constituted; otherwise, we run the risk of perpetuating commonsense readings and interpretations of the world. Several questions are of specific interest to us here: How, in what contexts and through what processes are racial/racialized meanings acquired? How do such meanings change? How is it that some notions of race emerge as "intrinsically truthful," while others fade? What do these processes tell us about how we are constituted as *other*? What do these processes tell us about how, when and where we are oppressed? In working toward a closer scrutiny of *meaning* relative to the social construction of race and racial/racialized identities, we think it is important to acknowledge the ever-changing and unstable contexts through which meanings arise, because they are not only constructed, but resisted as well. While we have touched on the significance of historical context in the previous sections, we must again examine the various links that exist between colonial expansion, the racial *other* and the construction of meaning in relation to Western discursive fields (e.g., science, art, literature, etc.). We undertook a cursory theoretical examination of these issues in the previous chapter because such analyses help to establish critical spaces in/through which we might better understand our constitution as colonizer/oppressor and colonized/oppressed. With this in mind, we take this chapter to build on those concepts as we work to interrogate the dominant narratives, knowledges and "regimes of truth" that constitute White and non-White bodies.

Discursive fields constitute knowledge and meaning by working with and through social and subjective power relations. In this respect, discourses should be recognized as more than simplistic ways of thinking and producing meaning. Rather, they seek to "establish the very nature of the body, mind and emotional life of the subjects they work to influence."[3] However, in constituting the lived experience of subjects, it should be noted that discourses are always relational in nature and dependent on a variety of interconnected power relations that sustain each other: the stronger their mutual connection, the more stable their foundation. Following from our discussions in Chapter One, we engage this exploration of "discursive fields" relative to Gramsci's concept of the relations of force in order to bridge the gap between ideological systems and materiality while at the same time addressing the durability and persistence of hegemonic systems. An example of this bridge can be seen in works that look at representations of race throughout colonial expansion and relative to the construction of the Western self versus the colonized other. For example, Goldberg (1993) asserts that the movement toward modernity marked the emergence of discursive fields through which "race" was disseminated to the world. This shift to organized racial thought originated within the historical frame of colonial expansion and relative to the ever-shifting balance in the relations of force. In effect, racialized discourse emerged to re-assess, re-tool and re-invent the common-sense world.[4] There was in this moment an overriding ideological construction of *otherness* that developed into fields of knowledge through which racialized peoples could be known, understood, regulated and subjugated.

The notion of racism tends not to be associated with that of discourse and to be more recognizably related with overt manifestations such as discrimination, slavery and Apartheid. However, while discourses are often seen as existing within linguistic spheres and therefore "immaterial," the sign, symbol, text and talk of discursive fields are crucial to the production and re-production of racism in contemporary contexts. The manufacturing and molding of the markers and meanings that underlie verbal and social practices of racism largely function through systems of text, talk and communication. So, particularly in contemporary information societies, discourses exist at the very heart of racism. As asserted by van Dijk (1993), this is particularly true in relation to "elite" forms of racism (e.g., political, bureaucratic, corporate, educational and media). In their access to and influence over the most crucial elements of information production and exchange, the impact of such elites on the social world are quite wide-ranging.[5] For example, racial knowledges and "realities" have developed relative to discursive fields and their rational/objective hold over the "intrinsic" inferiority of non-White peoples. Held up against the standards of European Whiteness, science and social theory became the primary discursive fields through which race was reified, catalogued and disciplined. In demonstrating the invasive nature of such racial discourse, Said (1979) quotes from A. J. Balfour's 1910 House of Commons speech on 'the problems with which we have to deal in Egypt':

> I take up no attitude of superiority. But I ask [Robertson and anyone else]…who has even the most superficial knowledge of history, if they will look in the face of the facts with which a British statesman has to deal when he is put in a position of supremacy over great races like the inhabitants of Egypt and countries in the East. We know the civilization of Egypt better than we know the civilization of any other country. We know it further back; we know it more intimately; we know more about it. It goes far beyond the petty span of the history of our race, which is lost in the prehistoric period a time when the Egyptian civilization had already passed its prime. Look at all the oriental countries. Do not talk about superiority or inferiority.[6]

In his analysis, Said illustrates how the *other* was constructed, the ways in which domination was/is validated and given meaning and how the West became the subject of the political discourse of "savior" roughly from the 18th century onward. *Power* and *knowledge* arose as the two pivotal themes through which Balfour cleverly validated the need for a British occupation of Egypt. The discourse of Orientalism acted as a sort of "corporate institution" for managing the Orient. It was the lynchpin in the machinery of Colonial domination and it was through this discourse that the West gained the ability to settle, describe, marginalize, rule and denigrate all things *other*—in effect, all things non-White/non-European.[7]

We feel it is important to recognize and examine this discursive machinery if we are to critically interrogate the systematic order through which the Western world managed to construct and discipline the *other*. In fact, the "Colonial Machine" took such a stance of authority over all things non-European that the literature, politics, science and imagination of the time reflected that command. As asserted by Said, "no one writing, thinking, or acting on the Orient could do so without taking account of the limitations on thought and action imposed by Orientalism."[8] Through the strength of its support structure, particularly the legal and institutional means by which the *other* was managed, these racist discourses gained in authority and became solidified within "regimes of truth." The various discursive domains constantly overlapped, influenced and competed with each other such that those with a common ground found themselves not only affiliated with one another, but looking to each other for strength, legitimacy and validation. The more influential and far-reaching the discourse, the closer that "regime" came to being accepted as truthful, objective knowledge, beyond dispute and above the need for validation.

Said's work helps to drive home the degree to which European culture had/has managed to control and constitute every social aspect and meaning attributed to the concept of this new racialized *other*. Through both implicit and explicit contrast, the dichotomy between the West and the East was drawn and meanings were established. In this respect, we can infer that all racialized concepts of Whiteness are to be understood in their relation to another repressed or negated notion. This is a powerful realization; it teaches us that any and all analyses of "meaning" must necessarily involve a critical inquiry of the dichotomies that are operating therein, an examination of the oppositions and negations at work and an investigation of how these meanings operate in specific contexts.[9] These racialized meanings are understood in their relation to an established difference and not due to any innate property. As binary oppositions, the primary terms are defined and ascribed meaning in direct relation to that which they repress.[10]

So within the scientifically, politically and culturally validated atmosphere of positivism that arose relative to the race concept, the bodies of the *other* became charged and embedded with meaning. Every interconnected support structure for the race concept developed new and useful methods through which racialized peoples could be seen, understood and represented. Moreover, each new discourse developed new "truths" about the *other*. It was within this context of empire building that the race concept truly began to take form and shape. European discursive fields not only created these bodies, but, as can be seen in the earlier quotation from Balfour, they effectively formulated a manageable and violable classification of people: a stylized subspecies both inherently inferior and intrinsically in need of administration. These *others*, in all their biological inferiority, moral depravity and mental deficiency, became the perfect foil for the Western archetype and as they became further objectified, so too did their existence become manufactured as a product of classification and stereotype.

As asserted by Bhabha (1994), the ideological construction of the *other*, as fixed and knowable, is a major feature of colonial discourse.[11] We would extend that assertion to contemporary racial/racist discourse in general in that today's manifestations of race and racism still rely on that same fixity.

> Fixity, as the sign of cultural/historical/racial difference in the discourse of colonialism, is a paradoxical mode of representation: it connotes rigidity and an unchanging order as well as disorder, degeneracy and daemonic repetition. Likewise the stereotype, which is its major discursive strategy, is a form of knowledge and identification that vacillates between what is always 'in place', already known and something that must be anxiously repeated.[12]

Bhabha makes an important division here in the seemingly oppositional structure of racist discourse. At the same time that the *other* remains intrinsically knowable within the social consciousness, the stereotype, as the main mechanism of racist discourse, needs repeating, needs constant re-generation and re-integration into the public consciousness. It is as though this "truth" about the *other*, which needs no proof, must still be constantly re-invented and re-stated to retain its currency.[13] It is exactly this nature that allows racist discourses to engage and function within changing social contexts and shifting historical specificities and conjunctures. This "ambivalence" marks the various strategies through which the *other* is constructed as an effect of discourse.

This discursive construction of racialized peoples requires, by definition, an articulation of difference. As we addressed earlier, the colonial subject became the perfect image to offset the European model of civility and normalcy. By the same token, as racist discourses intersect and change to suit contemporary hierarchical dichotomies, we see shifts that allow for the changing face of race knowledge. Where colonial images of the *other* were steeped in an intrinsic inferiority and an overt racism that could not and would not be contested in the mainstream, contemporary discourse, relative to the hegemony of today's political and social climate, makes allowances that always work to ambivalently support/condemn racism. The construction of the oppressed in contemporary discourse is an exercise in balancing these same fixed notions with flexible allowances for variation and anomaly. Contemporary racial/racist discourse vacillates along a continuum where the *other* exists within a sphere of predictability and probable "truth": "Of course Black people are lazy, unintelligent and violent, but some of them are OK— some of them aren't that way." Even when faced with daily personal examples of the fallacious nature of the stereotype, racist discourse's reliance on the "truth" of racial inferiority and degeneracy allows for exceptions to the rule—"When I say they are that way, I don't mean you. You're different. You're not like them. You're normal." The language and action of the oppressor suggests a determination to objectify the *other* and locate them within the realm of the knowable.

These rhetorical tools serve to walk us in circles—that is their function. By leading us in a never-ending struggle to distinguish between real pain and what we only think is pain, between real acts of racism and what we only interpret as racism, they function to prevent us from "thinking about things that we shouldn't think about." But whose explanations of the moment are constructed as narratives of "the real"? Who gets to tell us what is and what is not violence, what is and what is not painful, what is and what is not racism? The discourse is pervasive in its transmission of hegemonic effects. This complex of articulations assert, teach, insist, constitute an understanding that while racism comes in many forms, the only forms that can truly be "known" are those perceptible through the eyes and ears of "privilege"— lynchings, beatings, Neo-Nazi rallies—those types of "in your face" occurrences. But since we have never been taught about the commonplace intrusions that occur in our everyday lives, our inability to understand how the moment is framed adds to the internal problematic of duality that functions as psychic anathema for oppressed peoples—it is a subject effect. Respective of the shifting positionalities of its subjects, racial/racist discourses function as an apparatus of power through which various spheres of activity are governed and directed in order to mark out what Bhabha calls a *subject nation*.

> It is an apparatus that turns on the recognition and disavowal of racial/cultural/ historical differences. Its predominantly strategic function is the creation of space for a 'subject peoples' through the production of knowledges in terms of which

surveillance is exercised and a complex form of pleasure/unpleasure is incited. It seeks authorization for its strategies by the production of knowledges of colonizer and colonized which are stereotypical but antithetically evaluated. The objective of colonial discourse is to construe the colonized as a population of degenerate types on the basis of racial origin, in order to justify conquest and to establish systems of administration and instruction. [14]

So, working from Bhabha, contemporary racial/racist discourses function to produce a social reality for both the colonizer/oppressor and colonized/oppressed such that the world is at the same time knowable and known. Not to be repetitive, but these discourses produce both the oppressed and the oppressor relative to their shifting subject positions; thus the resulting cultural/knowledge production engenders both material and nonmaterial effects for both. Said engages these effects and makes particular distinctions between the *latent* qualities of Orientalism (the subconscious knowledge/truth of the *other*) and the *manifest* ones (the stated views and written doctrine).[15] We employ these distinctions, not as polarized divisions, but as points of tension that exist on the continuum of discursive functionality.

Colonial discourses, much like our contemporary modalities of racism, are on the one hand, an avenue through which the *other* is discovered, unveiled, known and practiced while, at the same time, imagined and mythologized (see, Memmi, 1969). It is, as Said puts it, a form of "radical realism" through which anyone employing this discourse could then designate, fix, name and ratify the object/point of their attention with nothing more than the use of positivistic language. "The tense they employ is the timeless eternal; they convey an impression of repetition and strength... For all these functions it is frequently enough to use the simple copula *is*."[16] Moving from Said's point to reflect on the rhetorical use of stereotypical language, part of the connective tissue that runs between representation and "representation as regime of truth" is the totalizing language of *the now*, and *the certain*. As the primary point of subjectification in racial/racist discourse, stereotypical language inscribes administrative control over the *other*.

In addressing racism as existing and operating within discursive fields, we are not suggesting that all aspects of racism can be understood in discursive terms. Rather, we are addressing those moments of everyday racism that violate and intrude upon the lives of people of color. In many ways, these moments can be understood as a question of interpretation and subjectivity. As such, they need not be seen as inevitable features of our lives—moments that we must learn to live with. We need to do more than address our place within the language of the moment. We need to interrogate our place in the pre-existing script in/through which we participate. There are numerous methods through which we may define these moments. One prevailing intersection refers to the almost constant stream of images produced about the experience of racism: portrayals that perpetuate and sustain common-sense ideologies, beliefs and inconsistencies that exist in relation to race. These representations are framed as assumptions and contradictions that serve to dichotomize subjects of discourse.[17] Another intersection can be interpreted in relation to the context and structure of discourse as it is produced in each moment.

It is important to understand the manner in which oppressive "truths" are produced in order to examine how they become hegemonic through practices, techniques and technologies of power that run through racial discourse. Foucault (1987) forwards the notion of bio-politics as the calculated management of life: the methods in which truth discourses are employed to manage the bodies of subjects.[18] These discourses operate to constitute who can know the "truth," who can speak of the "truth" and what can be said about that "truth." These discourses frame the oppressor and oppressed subject in ways that both encourage and suppress the "will to truth." The dynamics of these moments are framed such that oppressed peoples are made cognizant of what can and cannot be said in any given moment: we have been "educated" to know that certain "racial rules" must be abided by in certain social contexts. These are internalized controls through which we are taught to "discipline" ourselves and these self-enforced restrictions frame our experience in as many ways as the actions of our oppressor. However, as we alluded to previously, these moments are conjunctural and our polite, non-combative responses to/in the moment function to reassert the oppressor's hold on power, space and place. The discourse structures our subjectivities and lets our oppressor know that s/he has the power to violate us…that we are paralyzed and unable to defend ourselves.[19] So if we are to refuse the categories and positions that constitute us as violable, it is essential that we first learn to subvert and alter the discursive positions in which we find ourselves. It is imperative that we are able to interrogate the discourses and dialogues that discipline us to frame ourselves within positions made available to us from sites of power and privilege. That being said, how might we engage in such radical re-imaginings of self and society? Moreover, are such "internalized" or self-contained sites of agency even possible?

In 1637, René Descartes put forth *Cogito Ergo Sum* as his attempt to resolve the epistemological problematic of "truth." This privileging of the "cognitive self," as the terrain in which authenticity arises, situates the individual as existing independent of social context and within static discourses of history, self and memory. This Cartesian notion of "psychological agency" is often linked to the problematic assertion that experience can be somehow built and controlled through direct cognitive analysis and internal monologue irrespective of social context. We find this position to be dangerous in that such applications suggest an "internalized" perspective of individual functionality and development that places cognitive processes as a priori to affective and/or behavioural aspects of *the self*. In addressing individuality, *the self* and identity, we problematize applications that seek to elevate cognitive interpretations of the individual while muting or excluding the role of behaviour and emotion in identity development.[20]

Proponents of "psychological agency" attempt to discern *the self* in terms of two distinct parts: *the self* as a set of contents and as a set of processes. As suggested by Rychlak (1997), in this formulation, "contents" refer to an "ingredient that is produced, conveyed or otherwise employed by process" and "processes" refers to "a discernible, repeated course of action on the basis of which some items under description are believed to be sequentially patterned."[21] The not-so-implicit assertion here is that individuals "think and therefore are." Reflecting a similar conception of "self-formulations," Heelas (1981), in his notion of the "indigenous self," put forth the idea that cultural distinctions are a reflection of *the self* and therefore arise out of the organized content of that individuality, serving to anchor the individual while s/he is submerged in the social world.[22] Within these formulations, the individual is framed as a "universally contained" being that experiences the world and recognizes itself as unique.

The natural progression of such notions of self, as they apply to human agency within social contexts, can be found cemented in the nature of "meanings." In their defense of agency as "dialectic mental process," theorists such as Jenkins (2001) and Edelson (1971) are particularly pointed about the individual's ability to develop and attach alternative connections to meanings that are already firmly established within social contexts. Jenkins asserts that a "defining feature of dialectical thought is the human capacity to imagine alternatives even in the presence of a clearly defined stimulus situation."[23] This assertion, or rather, assumption that the individual has an innate capacity to organize her/his experience into a cohesive concept and then apply it to given situations is problematic at best. Jenkins' work places the locus of social change almost solely in the "mind" of the oppressed.[24] That is to say that, while such humanistic theories almost always concede that culture and social context have powerful mediating influences over the individual, there is always an implicit assertion that the individual, as "psychological agent," has the final say and is always responsible for his/her fate. See, for instance, some of Jenkins' profoundly disturbing contentions about social oppression:

> Granted that a culture establishes powerful guidelines, it is ultimately up to the individual to decide that in order to 'get along' with one's group s/he will 'go along' with what is expected. In principle, the person, *able to appreciate the opposite*, could do otherwise—though, granted, at possibly great cost to the self...socially oppressed people often must make use of dialectical thinking capacity. For example, for people of color in America, personal and group survival has required that they sustain the recognition that the Euro-American world view that relegated people of color to an inferior status represents *just* one (self-serving) construction of events. Of course, the oppressive nature of the social relations imposed on these people has powerful effects on their lives and is real in that sense. But it is very important to understand that liberation has been effected to an important degree by the capacity of people of color first to rise above the present social givens imaginatively and then to work to bring such alternative conceptions into more concrete reality.[25]

Ultimately, these analyses fall short of praxical applicability because, if for no other reason, they fail to consider the agent as a "socially constructed individual." In his assertion that the oppressed make the *conscious/cognitive decision* to "go along to get along," Jenkins ignores the relationship between *the self* and the discursive complex of statements, terms, categories, beliefs and meanings as constituted in/through and relative to historical, social and institutional specificities.[26] Moreover, he overlooks the various ways in which knowledges are constituted relative to social, subjective and power relations as well as through them. Interrogations of the lived experience must address how meanings are inscribed and, in fact, how those inscriptions function to establish the very nature of the body, mind and emotional life of the subjects.[27]

Our interrogations into identity and *the self* must consider the realities of "psycho-social imprints" as a part of the everyday lived experience of people in general and oppressed peoples specifically. The imprints of oppression are very much a part of life for the oppressed. It is a part of life for the racialized child who is etched with the intrapsychic image of outsider and is a part of life for the parent of color who has to console their children after a racist attack. Or perhaps, as Jenkins suggests, they should be able to "recognize that racism is just a self serving construction of events and rise above the present social experience of oppression." In harsh terms, such frameworks almost always imply a "get over it" rhetorical sense without acknowledging the agent's submersion within social, psychological, political and historical contexts. In such humanistic frameworks, there is little space to recognize and engage the oppressed as constructed, constituted and constricted. Moreover, there is certainly even less room to discuss the ambiguities of a democratically oppressive society. These tensions remind us of Bhabha's incisive comments in his interrogation of identity:

> The analysis of colonial depersonalization not only alienates the Enlightened idea of 'Man', but challenges the transparency of social reality, as a pre-given image of human knowledge. If the order of Western historicism is disturbed in the colonial state of emergency, even more deeply disturbed is the social and psychic representation of the human subject. For the very nature of humanity becomes estranged in the colonial condition and from that 'naked declivity' it emerges, not as an assertion of will nor as an evocation of freedom, but as an enigmatic questioning.[28]

So how would we answer such an enigmatic question? Bhabha's (1994) questioning goes beyond problematizing the idea of the "enlightened man" and comments on the very notion of "how we know what it is that we know." Whether we are discussing Western historicism, the human subject or the generalities of knowledge, we think Bhabha's point is well taken: the practice of locating "knowledge" as innately within the individual has undergone a tremendous shakedown in the last two decades and is presently under a considerable amount of fire. The notion of the "rational subject" as a figure of enlightened thought and outside the relational spheres of history, culture and context must give way to a politicized view of a "socially constituted self."

Social psychologist Stefan Hormuth (1991) asserts that *the self* can be interpreted as "a moderator between person and society" in that our understandings of self are acquired and cultivated through social experiences.[29] However, like Cushman and others who have allied themselves to a more postmodern philosophy and theory, we engage *the self* as more than a mere moderator in these interactions and more than just in the social sphere, but rather as "part of social interactions" and "of the social sphere."

> Culture infuses individuals through the social practices of the everyday world...[C]ulture is not indigenous 'clothing' that covers the universal human; rather it is an integral part of each individual's psychological flesh and bones...[T]he material objects we create, the ideas we hold and the actions we take are shaped in a fundamental way by the social framework in which we have been raised.[30]

While we won't spend a great deal of time in this discussion, we don't want to be interpreted as seeking to establish some type of dichotomy between a "social constructionist" view of the individual and a more orthodox psychoanalytic perspective of agency as "mental origin." We feel that the explanatory locus of human agency must be shifted from interrogations of a "rational-cognitive self" to frameworks that are more reflective of the processes and structures of social interaction in historical/cultural context. Like Scott (1992), we assert that it is not individuals that have experience but, rather, subjects who are constituted through experience.[31] That is not to say that we would agree with Gergen's (1997) assertions that the "chief locus of understanding" is to be found in social relationships *rather* than the psyche. Nor would we agree with his implication that "all that psychology traces to mental origins" should be traced to "micro-social processes." [32] Bearing those corollaries in mind, we employ "subject" in contrast to the notion of the individual as "enlightened" and engage an interpretation of the "subject" as a living, thinking and feeling agent, capable of both reflexive thought and proactive action. We place the subject as socially constructed within discursive fields, her cognitive, behavioural and affective productions developing relative to the socio-historical contexts in which she lives.

Praxical theories need to explain these interdependencies without reducing the one to the other. Therefore, in tempering Gergen's assertions, we would prefer to engage these processes of thought and agency as ongoing "social reconstructions of the individual."[33] In other words, a process in which we find a *balance* between *the self* and society: *the self*, being all of those intrapsychic and affective qualities that arise in and uniquely to the individual and society being the world in context. Individual aptitudes, whether creative, intuitive, introspective, analytic or otherwise cannot and must not be relegated to a social reductionism where physiological specificities and the internal mechanisms of the individual are lost in a "social shuffle" for meaning and origin. Rather, we would like to bridge the gap by approaching the individual as an organized and particularized locus for various cultural influences and socially shared mental representations.[34]

So in other words, the individual exists as part of the society and the society exists as part of the individual. It is a dialectic where *the self* and society "mutually presuppose each other and subjects manage their actions within contexts as a function of their personal as well as shared interpre-tations or representations of their social environment."[35] This notion of a "dialogical self," as co-constructed, guided, relational and mediated, is a relatively new articulation of identity and has been taken up by numerous theorists in the last two decades.[36] Bakhtin (1986) asserts that *the self* is polyvocal in social contexts, which is to say that negotiations of identity take place through multiple mediations and within the various social, political, cultural and historical contexts. Therefore, when individuals come into contact, they communicate within an ongoing social conversation that is multi-voiced.[37] The presumptions, knowledges, ideologies, perceptions and other mediators that impact that moment are reflective of each individual's specific vocalities as they respond from and speak to any number of positions and/or sites of identity.

In discussing the ongoing re-formations and productions of identity, Bakhtin (1981) employs "heteroglossia" to reference the multiple voices, languages, knowledges and discourses that develop within *the self*. Importantly, these knowledges and discourses neither settle nor rise in uncontested positions. Rather, they are often contradictory, always shifting and they are deeply influenced by the moments in which they arose in *the self* as well as the socio-historical contextualities in/through which they relate to the world. Hermans et al. (1992) referred to this as a movement between a multiplicity of *I positions*.[38]

> Only when there is an Other can you know who you are…and there is no identity…without the dialogic relationship to the Other. The Other is not outside, but also inside the Self, the Identity. So Identity is a process…an ambivalent point. Identity is also the relationship of the Other to oneself.[39]

Similarly, Hall (1991) engages the previously discussed notion of the "socially reconstructing individual" in relation to the polyvocality of self. As an "ongoing social product," identities form both in and through the various interactions of *the self* within society. As Bakhtin asserts, this "dialogical self" is a congress of different times and different knowledges that are constantly being re-inscribed and re-assessed within and into identities that are heterogeneous, multi-voiced and contradictory.[40]

Kristeva (1974), in her notion of "transpositionality," brings several murky problems into specific relief. In particular, one of the major contentions to the notion of a "socially constructed self" has been whether specific voices gain ascendancy within an individual as part of a selective polyvocality and if so, how? The problematic being that if a selective process of positionality in fact arises in the individual, does that then infer a fall back to a Cartesian notion of the unified cognitive self. Kristeva addresses the issue by theorizing the notion of positionality within *the self*. That is to say that, the multiple positions taken by subjects is dependent on the specifics of the moment: who, where, why and when we are speaking. Simply put, these multiple identities are formed within and through diverse discourses and so emerge, submerge and float as the moment dictates.[41] It is in relation to these distinctions that we must engage the notion of the "dialogical" self.

> The polyphonic novel, with its multitude of characters, each with his or her own voice and ideological positions that are independent but yet linked to the voices of the other, through internal or external dialogue, plays a crucial role in the formulation of the dialogical self.[42]

To illustrate, the phrases "I feel safe" and "I feel safe" are connected by a relationship of identity and so from a purely logical point of view, they mean exactly the same thing. However, Hermans et al. (1992) would suggest that when taken from a dialogical perspective and described as a sequence in a conversation that involves two people agreeing with each other, the phrases become different utterances in a speech act; thus one becomes a statement and the other a confirmation.[43] But even further, we would point out that other options are still available to us in this interpretation dependent on context. If the conversation involved two combatants conversing about their position in a match, both arise as statements. Moreover, if one individual utters the same words at different times, the phrase takes on different meanings as to whether we feel safe: in a crowd, in our homes, with our friends, when we are alone, etc. Therefore, dependent on the constraints of culture, history and context, our multiple identities always carry the potential to intersect and interlock with other positions such that various positions will regularly be found in agreement, disagreement, opposition and contrast with each other. The fluctuation and intersectionality that runs between even opposed positions ensures that dialogues will exist within *the self*. Therefore, "the dialogical self is conceived as a social—not in the sense that a self-contained individual enters into social interactions with other outside people, but in the sense that other people occupy positions in the multivoiced self."[44]

This brief formulation recognizes multiple *identities* as both relatively autonomous and fluid in their relation to real and imagined others, such that they shift dependent on time, space and situation. In some sense, *the self* acts as a contested space where competing discourses jockey for leverage if not supremacy. So why is this important to our discussions of identity, racism and oppression? Simply put, it is important that we recognize that identities—whether personal, cultural, national or otherwise—are not fixed to some universal or essential property. In her interrogations of personal identity, Spivak suggested that:

> 'India', for people like me, is not really a place with which they can form a national identity because it has always been an artificial construct. 'India' is a bit like saying

'Europe'. When one is talking about European identity, for example, one is obviously reacting against the United States...Indian-ness is not a thing that exists. Reading Sanskrit scriptures, for example—I can't call that Indian, because after all, India is not just Hindu. That 'Indic' stuff is not Indian...it isn't a place that we Indians can think of as anything, unless we are trying to present a reactive front, against another kind of argument. And that has its own contradictions. For example, when I'm constructing myself as an Indian in reaction to racism, I am very strongly taking a distance from myself. If an Indian asks me what I am, I'm Bengali, which is very different.[45]

The interviewer replies to Spivak: "It seems that India is often positioned as the "other" of the West." An accurate point, but more importantly to us in this discussion is that for Spivak, India, contextually speaking, is positioned against a great many things. In the multiplicity of Spivak's positionalities, India means different things, in different times, spaces and places. However in her statement that India is an artificial construct employed in reaction to racism, she is very clearly interrogating its positioning as an internal *other*: one of the dialogical negotiations that one undertakes in the face of dislocation in the Diaspora. National and cultural identities are not concrete, rather, they are formed and constructed within historical contexts that by definition arise and are negotiated in relation to other identities that are inherently unequal. Bammer (1998) posits that these fundamental inequalities arise in the relationship between colony and empire.[46]

Within colonial frameworks, the identities of both the colonizer and the colonized alike have been formed and constructed relative to both difference and *otherness* (see Memmi, 1969). So in these oppositional dialectics, our notions of self and our communal, cultural and national identities are all played off and against one another in a shifting terrain of meanings and re-negotiations that mark and manage our Diasporic selves.[47] This "Diasporic identity" is mediated through various practices and dynamics that are linked to and shaped by the internal polyphony that marks our differences and our *otherness*: voices of race, culture, history, nation, oppression and power. As discussed previously, these voices do not exist in uncontested space, so in dialogical terms, the identity is constituted through an eternal movement between and within voices that speak of "belonging" and "longing."

Racialized peoples in Western contexts are in many ways locked in a process through which they must come to terms with who and what they are...where and if they belong. Bearing this in mind, we assert that studies of racial oppression might do well to reflect how the ideological and dialogical contexts of race are constituted within the asymmetrical power relations of culture as constructed within a Diasporic identity. That is to say that negotiating our Diasporic identities must necessarily involve interrogations of the "political and historical practices that are linked to and shaped by *voices* of race, culture, colonial/postcolonial history and power."[48]

In asserting that our multiple identities can be both enduring and transitory, Hermans (1996) suggests that the multiplicity and dynamically shifting nature of these positions will depend on the stability and regulation of the social contexts in which they arise and exist. So in other words, some voices will be backed by socio-cultural systems and structures, while others will be silenced and/or condemned. Those positions that find backing in the social world and particularly through the "apparatus of power," will become solidified within *the self*. Importantly, as positions will fluctuate between positive and negative dimensions, some being enjoyable and affirming, while others are threatening and oppressive, the impact of social and historical context is paramount.[49]

Respective of the shifting positionalities of the dialogical self, racialized identities develop and function through various spheres of social activity to solidify oppositional voices of Diasporic alienation, frustration, tension, disharmony and dislocation within the racially oppressed self. The intricacies of engaging such a multiplicity of varied and incompatible identities often send us into a state of existential crisis, where the daily task of living means confronting a constant juxtaposition of selves. This constant shifting between positions reflects our existence in the borderlands of power, culture and community and speaks to the inability to feel anything but "isolation," to be anything but an "outsider." The resulting crisis often places us at a crossroads of identity where we cannot feel truly at home anywhere. In these moments, the dialogical contentions that run between our *I positions* reflect, not as polarized divisions, but as points of tension that exist on the continuum of our identities. Our sense of self becomes the most "contested" aspect of our identity in that we equate the world as unfair and then situate ourselves in that unfair world as an *other* in our own skin. We struggle with an intrinsically Diasporic sense of homelessness and a marginalized view of what home can never be. Importantly, these displaced, discarded and *othered* voices are not innate, but rather unveiled and assigned to us through the practices and challenges of culture, discourse and language that arise in both external and internal political locations.

Relative to contemporary academic engagements with the dialogical self, we would draw attention to the use of dominant *I positions* as a point through which to critically interrogate the connections between racial oppression and identity. In many ways, examinations of race invariably lead to studies of identity, identifications and their relation to the other. As Martin (1995) contends: identity derives its meaning from what it is not…or, from the other.[50] Moreover, to paraphrase Hall (1991), who saw identity in its dialectic and dialogic relation between *the self* and the other as a structured representation that only achieves its positive through the establishment of the negative.[51] So what is all this other/*other* business and how are our multiple voices managed through the dominant *I positions* of the other? First, in addressing the other/*other* dialectic, Grossberg (1993) formulated the distance between the two concepts in relation to difference and exclusion:

> In commonsense terms, difference makes the identity of one term depend totally on its relation to, its differences from, another term, while otherness recognizes that the other exists in its own place, independently of any specific relation of difference.[52]

We would extrapolate from these formulations to add a third coordinate to identity triangle: self-*other*-other. In engaging Grossberg's formulation, we add that *otherness* carries more than an exclusionary tone, it is also an inscribed articulation of hierarchy. It is within these asymmetrical relationships of position and voice that identities develop and shift: *the self* in relation to difference and in relation to domination. So difference is not only constituted dialectically relative to the other, but also within *the self*.

In that our identities are not formed in isolation, our multiple voices and their positionings are contextualized and mediated through socio-political contexts. So, by necessity, the dialectic between voices will both consciously and unconsciously inscribe the content of "the conversation" to each individual's multiple identities—to be formulated internally as applicable.[53] So, in other words, the dominant identities can and will seek to engage and overpower the voices and *I positions* of the *other*. As discussed earlier, dependent on the social power positioned within the dialectic, these asymmetrical constraints and relations will influence us to privilege one voice over another, the result being that some of our *I positions* will find themselves struggling within the psyche's intermittently oppressive milieu.[54] In our dialogical engagements with the other, we (the oppressed) enter into the moment as an interlocutor in an ongoing conversation through which streams of intersecting/interlocking discourses and voices seek to position/ manage us, our voices and our various positionalities. Sampson (1993) spoke to this particular intersection of power and culture in dialogic formations when he cautioned that dominant groups would seek to maintain their power and privilege by "masquerading their monologues as dialogues."[55]

Similar to our previous discussions of how repressive ideologies are transmitted through various socio-historical apparatus, we contend that social power in general and those with privilege in particular play important roles in the transmission of the ideologies, discourses and voices that in turn function to constitute the oppressed. In this reflection of the Althusserian notion of how we speak and are spoken by forces that exist outside our bodies, Hermans (1996) posits that the nature of our "relative dialectic autonomy" leaves certain less developed voices open to domination and mastery from other sites. In these theoretical connections to the formation of racial identities and the normalization of racially coded knowledges in the everyday, we see these ideological codes and translations as forms of interpellation as asserted by Althusser. We come to know our own voices, language and selves as they are perceived in the voice, language and self of the other; therefore, we come to know ourselves as *other*. This is the lived experience, where we can never just be Canadian, American or British, but must always also be from somewhere else, in the minds of both the other and *the self*. As suggested by Bhatia (2002), these are the contradictions and tensions of a hyphenated reality...a reality to which we adhere in spite of ourselves.[56]

CHAPTER THREE
Theorizing Power: Rupturing Dichotomies

Power must be understood in the first instance as the multiplicity of force relations immanent in the sphere in which they operate and which constitute their own organization; as the process which, through ceaseless struggles and confrontations, transforms, strengthens or reverses them; as the support which these force relations find in one another, thus forming a chain or a system, or on the contrary, the disjunctions and contradictions which isolate them from one another; and lastly, as the strategies in which they take effect

—Michel Foucault, *The History of Sexuality*[1]

It seemed that everyday of my Grade 7 and 8 career, Dominic tormented me. 'Paki', he'd say, 'Smelly Paki', 'Fucking Paki', 'Go home'. Grade 7 and 8 were very difficult. Mr. Marshall was my grade 7 English teacher. He was young and hip and we all looked up to him. One day, he sat on his chair and we gathered around him on the carpet. He said that he was told that he *had* to discuss racism with the class. He rolled his eyes. As I was the only student of color in the class (I think the others were in ESL) he turned to me and said, 'We should probably ask someone who might know about this. Nisha, have you experienced racism?' All eyes were on me. I was horrified. I had tried so hard not to be seen as different and now I was discovered. A few feet away Dominic grinned and squirmed uncomfortably. I was afraid and ashamed and embarrassed. 'No', I replied in my most believable voice, 'I haven't experienced racism'.

—Nisha Karumanchery-Luik, *Personal Experience*

How was the rolling of her teacher's eyes silently positioning and violating? Did the teacher's obvious political stance carry the same meaning, intent and influence on the White children in the class as it did for her? Was the difference an issue of sensitivity or was it an issue of power? Why didn't she just speak the truth? As discussed earlier, these moments are conjunctural and our polite, non-combative responses in the moment work to re-assert and re-establish our oppressor's "hold" on power, place and privilege. In the above narrative, the author's subjectivity was implicitly structured in ways that clearly established her inability to defend herself. But is that state of helplessness static and unchanging, is her powerlessness intrinsic to her oppressed self? In addressing issues of power and difference, we interrogate the methods and avenues through which privileged voices are "able" to speak for the oppressed. As discussed in the introduction, we need to interrogate how White privilege is bolstered through the application of power in relation to racial difference. We began this chapter with these two very pointed quotations because we felt that they served as the perfect entry point to our discussions of power, its influence and how that interplay is manifested in the everyday. However, if we are to begin with this general line of inquiry, it necessitates that we first engage the basic question of power's seemingly clear facility within a dichotomous racial continuum. In other words, why does it seem that Whiteness has a hold on power and privilege?

Traditional juridico-discursive readings of power tend to articulate three basic assumptions: (a) that power is a possession, (b) that power flows downward from a centralized point and (c) that power's primary function is repressive. For example, along these lines, Bishop (1994) in her more orthodox applications of "power," argued that there is a complex of systems that are "designed" to keep people in unequal and unjust positions in our societies. She further asserts that these systems are held in place by several interrelated expressions of "power-over": political, economic, physical and ideological power over. These formulations seem to suggest power as being located *beyond* discourse, which is to say that as discourses gain "authority" through their locations relative to the State and other institutions, power is *bestowed* upon them, while being *denied* to others. However, we (the authors) recognize that these institutional sites are themselves contested spaces and that the dominant discourses that govern them are therefore under constant challenge as well. While discourses will extend specific selected forms of subjectivity, the internal conflicts that are constituted within their organization allude to the possibility of other subject positions and the possibility of reversals. As tactile elements operating within "relations of force," power must not be interpreted to exist within simple bipolar relations of power or powerlessness.[2]

All that being said, the exercise of power, more so than its nature, is what occupies our interest in the writing of this chapter. What we hope to address in these pages are the specific arrangements between productive activities, resources of interaction and power relations as they relate to racial difference and racism. By focusing our attentions on power relations in this respect, we are effectively engaging the issue of power relative to the production of racialized subjectivities and the material practice of oppression.[3]

Importantly, while criticisms of essentialism can sometimes be misguided or misinformed, our intent here is to discuss the possibilities of anti-racist theoretical frameworks that would not suffer from positivistic political or ideological essentialisms.[4] We didn't want to handcuff ourselves by relying entirely on any one theoretical analysis of power because we firmly subscribe to Hall's contention that "one-sided accounts or interpretations are always a distortion of reality."[5] So instead, we draw from multiple sites of theory in the hopes of engaging an inclusive and open perspective on power and the resulting relations of oppression that circumscribe our lives as racially oppressed.

The image and belief that power somehow exists/functions beyond our reach continues to be one of the major dilemmas with which we must contend. Again, through commonsense articulations, the answer might seem obvious: power is associated solidly with Whiteness and White privilege in a top-down hierarchy of access requiring the oppressed to struggle "against" it. But is that the case? Can/should we engage power as flowing exclusively between sites of privilege and oppression? As asserted by Hall (1986), it is not surprising that Marx and other orthodox theorists might interpret the systems in which they are enmeshed with respect to the everyday factors that constantly engage them and are easily "knowable." This is the basic problem for macro-interrogations of power: they are too willing to take the "market" and "base" for granted without questioning what it is that helps/helped to make such social systems viable in the first place. In such essentialist views of centralized power, little importance is placed on the issue of transmission because, within these frameworks, ideologies, power and social change are seen to be functions of the "relations of production." If orthodox theory were to move forward from this point, it would necessitate that we consider the relevance of other forces working beyond class and market boundaries.

Realizing that orthodox theorists never firmly established a connection between ideology, the material world, power and social change, we think there is a connective circuit that must be interrogated. As indicated thus far, we depart from meta-theoretical applications of power as framed primarily relative to the maintenance of hierarchies and an oppressive status quo. Rather, with our reading of the adversarial and complex nature of power, we engage understandings of how we, as subjects, discipline ourselves and internalize the surveillances, discourses and other "immaterial" forces that relate to our constitution as subjects of discourse.[6] We feel this approach to be a necessity if we are to develop insurgent readings of power that might re-inscribe possibilities for resistance. In preceding discussions we have addressed two main points of inquiry: what race/racism is and how society's belief systems and dialogic relations maintain and constrain our "will to truth" in spite of our experience of oppression. So following this theoretical development, we recognize the importance of moving our discussions toward a more pointed interrogation of how we are implicated in that oppression. To these ends, we have placed this examination of power and difference here because we feel that it is a natural and necessary continuation to the discussions taken up thus far.

As taken up in the previous chapters, our adhesion to this racist reality is fundamentally articulated through our muted and restrained engagements with and within various technologies of power. Importantly, we engage these discussions with the recognition that "power" exists in contested space and that differing theories of power rely on various epistemologies, ontologies and assumptions. Recognizing these tensions, our treatment of power in this text will, by necessity, reflect a theoretical and political application that is ultimately appropriate for the anti-racist project. In other words, we need a praxical theory of power. To this end, we feel the work of Michel Foucault to be particularly relevant to these discussions and worth re-visiting—as a starting point, if nothing else.

In his attempt to elude the repressive, bipolar definitions of power put forth by Marx and other historical materialists, Foucault developed a conception of "the relations of power" that we find to be quite useful. As evidenced in this chapter's opening quotation, it was in his rejection of traditional top-down models of power that Foucault theorized power as extending beyond notions of State, law and class. Through this unorthodox framework, we (the oppressed) find ourselves free to locate power in forms, spaces and places that are generally obscured to us. Importantly and contrary to much orthodox theory, he asserts that power neither existed solely on a macro-level nor within a centralized body. Rather, he contended that the various forms of power occurring on the micro-level were, in fact, the very relations of power that made coercive discursive models of power even possible. In other words, for Foucault it was through the complex of micro-powers that we discipline and through which we are disciplined.[7]

In developing this bottom-up model, Foucault made several assumptions that separated his work from more conventional conceptualizations of power. His first assumption—that power is relational—asserts power to be a complex that functions between discourses and subjects: a complex that resides within differences. He developed this relational concept in an attempt to draw attention away from questions of ownership that necessarily frame power as an object to be possessed. Secondly, he suggested that power relations at the micro-level could have global repercussions for oppressions such as racism or class. Furthermore, he was pointed in his contention that locating power in class and other centralized sources could only serve to obscure the endless networks of power relations that invest our bodies, knowledges, relationships, sexualities, etc. In following his second contention, he further asserted that the function of power was primarily productive. He made this presupposition because he could not determine why power would continue to hold such a grip on so large a number if it were purely coercive and repressive.[8] In many ways, the exercise of power continues to be a circular dilemma for the oppressed. The problems arise in that power often functions by positioning individuals and groups into "different" social locations. However, we must remain cognizant that these locations develop relative to the historical contexts of those same relations.

Respective of this dilemma, we have found that deconstructing how language and meanings function relative to "power" allows for the possibility of examining the political nature of the resulting dialogues and monologues. We draw from these main theoretical tenets to ask how power relations make the racist experience intensely painful for some while deniable to others. Moreover, we interrogate the relational dynamics functioning within categories and notions of difference, that guide, indoctrinate and discipline both the oppressed and the oppressor into their specific positions. In doing so, we would examine the normalcy of Whiteness, the construction of non-Whites as *other* and the ways in which power structures develop through these discourses of difference to oppress us in ways both subtle and obvious.[9]

Most often, the ways in which power structures work in our daily experiences of racism and oppression are hidden and/or not easily recognizable. Sometimes we make the connection between racist events and "difference": "They harassed me at the store because I looked different." However, "difference," or to be more specific, "being different from our oppressor" in and of itself, is not a sufficient condition to oppress. As a starting point, what we really need to examine is how "difference" is taken up and how it is socially constructed in context to generate an oppressive milieu—to generate power and the relations therein. Importantly, we must first address the power relations intrinsic to the construction and application of "difference" before we can interrogate how those meanings are implicated and constitutive in the moment.

- I'm color-blind. When I walk into a room full of people I don't see color. To me everyone is equal.
- If you call me a name I don't care. If I call you a name and it bothers you, it's your problem because you're too sensitive.
- Where are you from? You're American? But where are you *really* from?
- There is no racism in my workplace.

What do these comments have in common? Statements like these fail to acknowledge the roles played by power and difference in social formations. Because organizational categories such as race become oppressive in and through their relation to power and the "language of difference," such monologues function to inscribe racist knowledge into the commonsense/ commonplace rhetoric that we hear with regularity in the everyday. So when we examine these monologues through a critical anti-racist lens, we uncover the reality that these seemingly innocuous statements and questions are charged with meaning and always arise as manifestations of power function-ing through the application of difference. To further elucidate our position, let us interrogate some of the underlying meanings that frame these seemingly harmless monologues.

Where are you from? This question is a perfect example of how seem-ingly inoffensive questions can prove to be problematic and intrinsically oppressive to racialized peoples. Living in North America, all of us (the racially oppressed) have either been asked this question or will be asked this question at some point or another. What we must recognize is that the words need not be verbalized for the meanings behind them to inscribe and disci-pline us. The question itself is sewn into the fabric of Western society—the fabric of our lives. We all "know" that the question speaks to "belonging" and the dichotomization between the "us" and the "them," even if we are not able to cognitively deconstruct the moment as oppressive. After all, "they" can never really come from here, can "they"? "They" must come from somewhere else. Within this context of nationalism, we are positioned as *other* and our Diasporic identities are clearly marked as exotic, foreign and alien: It speaks to membership and community. Furthermore, if we answer the question with, "I'm from here" or "I'm Canadian," or "I'm American," the response is often re-directed back to us, "But where are you *really* from?" These re-directions function to further rupture our identities by disregarding our sense of belonging and seeking to define us as "alien" based on skin color and other racial markers. Their directive reaction communicates disbelief, it suggests that "they" could not possibly be from here because "they" do not look like us—like people who are "really" from here. The very implicit assumption that underlies the monologue is that "real" Canadians or Americans are White. It speaks to the question of whose image reflects the "Western paradigm" and who is positioned as "belonging." The implication is that being a person of color makes you less-than. It also speaks to the dynamics of racialized "visibility" and the privileges of "invisibility" as enjoyed by members of the dominant group.

So why is it that this question arises so commonly in the everyday lives as racialized peoples? Moreover, why is it that the question is rarely put to those with skin color privilege unless ethnic or linguistic "differences" arise as relevant in the exchange? Is it because racially privileged and oppressed peoples alike are both constituted to normalize Whiteness as the *main* marker of belonging in Western contexts? The words themselves are innocuous, but they act as a delivery system for the potentially violating meanings hidden within. The question itself will convey different meanings, assumptions and expectations into the moment entirely dependent on the context of the dialogue or monologue, as the case may be. The various meanings behind the questions will always depend on the dynamics of the interaction: who speaks, who hears and most importantly the historical contextuality of the moment. To further this discussion of context let us reflect on the second quotation that opened this chapter.

Paramount in this discussion is an interrogation of how the relations of power manage to effectively disguise racially oppressive monologues as dialogues between equals. In examining this narrative, we would highlight the importance that the oppressed come to recognize and acknowledge the multiplicity of power dynamics running through everyday racist interactions such as this one. Her (the author's) silence in the moment was framed by much more than the mere presence of her attacker. Power operated within the context of her racialized body: "different" and *other* in a classroom full of White students who either join in the harassment or, as most students do, collaborate in the moment through their silence. Power operated through the silent but symbolic actions of the White teacher who, in the rolling of his eyes, openly denounced and belittled her pain in front of the class. Even in her child-mind, she knew from experience that he was not an ally and that speaking out would engender a whole new complex of problems—so in that recognition, she stayed silent. The power dynamics were also reflected in the White teacher's decision to ask the only student of color, in a classroom full of White students, to speak about her "supposed" experience of racism—to speak about how her classmates "supposedly" violate her—to explain her "supposed" pain. In reality, however, would her acknowledgment of racism have been taken up as anything other than oversensitivity on her part? Furthermore, it is important that we do not disregard the intrapsychic turmoil that often develops in/through the "decision" to opt for silence. Such feelings of "self-betrayal" can commonly function to bolster and frame future problematics of self-loathing and self-alienation.

We have learned that rules of conduct and interpretation are all contextually framed and so there are rules we must follow in each given space, place and time. We have internalized these controls such that we are constituted to "discipline" ourselves. These self-enforced controls influence and define our experience of racism in as many ways as the overtly coercive systems of our oppressor. These internalized controls and our "disciplined" responses to racism strengthen our oppressor's hold on the power relations that effectively structure our subjectivity as oppressed. As Marcus (1992) suggests in relation to the discursive dynamics of sexual assault, the language speaks through us, it freezes our strength and lets the oppressor know that we lack the resources to protect ourselves.[10] In similar fashion, internalized racism functions to mark and mold our intrapsychic schema with self-hating and other problematic beliefs that are deeply influenced and framed by privileged definitions of "difference." We internalize the value systems of our oppressor and in this way we are produced and reproduced as "racialized" subjects. As suggested by Collins (1990), resistant and oppositional engagements where we find ourselves trapped in the cycle of explanation, validation and accommodation, rarely function to increase our intrapsychic and psychological stability. In his discussions of emotional dynamics, Collins (1990) distinguished between two forms of emotion:

> (1) transient emotions such as joy, embarrassment, fear, and anger that are dramatic and disruptive of the flow of everyday life; and (2) emotional energy, which is a long-term emotional tone that is durable from situation to situation.[11]

We find this definition of *emotional energy* as "a long-term level of enthusiasm, personal strength, a sense of social connectedness, and/or willingness to initiate interaction" as useful to this work in that it speaks to racism's impact on the daily lived experience of the oppressed. In framing people's motivation to develop as high a level of emotional energy as possible, Collins (1990) also suggests that energy may be drained or transferred in one of two ways: by a) developing it through solidarity experiences based in ritual interaction, or by b) gaining emotional energy from a less powerful person in a hierarchical interaction.[12] In following Collins' assertions, it becomes clear that oppression does not exist/function as a monolithic entity that inscribes all cultures, groups and individuals in exactly the same ways. Rather, our various individual contextualities, whether historical, cultural, environmental, psychological, material or metaphysical, position each of us in unique and incongruent ways.

Summers-Effler (2002) also asserted that the more powerful person involved in these interactions is always more likely to leave the experience with more emotional energy than the less powerful. So how might we extrapolate the significance of these individual moments of "energy transfer" to the overall life experience of the oppressed? This distribution and social transfer of emotional energy appears to be a self-sustaining system in that those with power and privilege are optimally positioned to experience, develop, attain and maintain high levels of emotional energy at the expense of subjugated groups.[13] The cumulative impact of being caught in this cycle of oppression speaks to what we know of our potentiality in the world as well as what we can expect from the world. Importantly, while these "internal conversations" can be made conscious, they will tend to continue without conscious effort as we negotiate our ongoing day-to-day interactions.[14] In these ways, the experience of oppression constructs and constitutes our positionalities to reflect internalized understandings of inferiority, limits, regulation and fear that frame these situations in relation to our undesirable identities.

So again, as we reflect on Karumanchery-Luik's personal experience of racial trauma, it should be recognized that there was most certainly a transfer of emotional energy in that moment. The negative effects on her long-term emotional energy gradually developed over Dominic's successive attacks, until the patterned interactions collectively infused her knowledge of social position, inferiority and acceptance—whether consciously or not. She was disciplined to recognize that defending herself was a fruitless strategy and that silence was the only tool that served to at least lessen the social consequences that came with challenging her oppressor in the moment. She was taught to be submissive via the clear and commonly repeating message that she is alone, helpless, and destined to a lifetime without reprieve. As we are beginning to see in/through these critical interrogations, the psychological and intrapsychic dilemmas arising within racial/racialized/racist experiences are anything but simple. Furthermore, in their complexity, they most commonly leave us reeling in attempts to manage a duality and pain that we can neither understand nor frame.

These types of oppressive dynamics intersect all such moments and so we should begin to recognize that the everyday lived experiences of the racially oppressed are intrinsically marked and defined by such power relations. In examining and acknowledging how power is inextricably linked to these experiences of racism, we can begin to see how exposure to other cultures and how the notion of multiculturalism as an anti-racism strategy would be ineffective. In reality, multicultural policies and programs tend to promote surface level changes to perception and understanding without critically examining the social, economic, political and historical factors that frame, construct, support and bolster racism. Multiculturalism frames racism as a cultural issue to be combated through education about *other* cultures, customs and practices. In fact, such policies do little to address power imbalances or issues of equity. Moreover, let us ask ourselves to whom such policies are geared. Multicultural policies address neither the pervasive nature of oppression, nor the impact of oppression on the lived experience of marginalized peoples. Such strategies are neither able to challenge the status quo nor deconstruct/subvert the power differentials basic to such social relations because they only address one very small piece of the puzzle. Because racism is supported by an entire historical complex of disabilities, our strategies must speak to the various intersections of oppression that run therein.

A number of scholars have investigated how race, class, sexuality and gender function as intersecting systems of stratification based on socially constructed hierarchies of oppression (see Hill-Collins, 1990; Dua and Robertson, 1999; Calliste and Dei, 2000; Dei, 1999, 2000; Brewer, 1993; Razack, 1998; and many others).[15] As discussed earlier, we also engage an anti-racist politics that acknowledges "distinct" systems of oppression such as racism, sexism and classism as intersecting and interlocking within over-arching structures of domination. This framework recognizes that categories of oppression operate in/through each other and that each system is functionally reliant on the others. Supporting this perspective, Patricia Hill-Collins suggests:

> The significance of seeing race, class and gender as interlocking systems of oppression is that such an approach fosters a paradigmatic shift of thinking inclusively about other oppressions, such as age, sexual orientation, religion and ethnicity.[16]

Throughout our colonial and post-colonial histories, the image of "the mythical White norm" has been defined relative to the intersections of

White, male, middle-class, heterosexual, Christian privilege. Importantly, within Western contexts and to a great extent beyond Western borders, power in both macro and micro forms, has continued to reverberate through these specific loci: the intersections and interlocks of privilege.[17] Today, racism and other systems of oppression continue to work collaboratively in their support of this mythical archetype. It is through these relations of power that the White standard continues to be reified, imagined and re-positioned as the one true gauge against which to measure and define difference, dysfunction and dissidence. In these contexts, the Diasporic *other* is always relegated to the margins because their very existence creates a threat to the order, structure and balance of "the good White society." Again, however, as a corollary to this simple tenet of Western hierarchy and oppression, it is important to note that this unwanted colonial *other* is also a necessary component of the Western social order because s/he acts as the contrasting model against which the White moral and social order is set. In other words, the very existence of those who comprise the margins, functionally defines and establishes the boundaries for the centre: our exclusion/disadvantage marks the acceptance/privilege of our oppressor.

Through the ever-present influence and power of racial discourse, "multi-ethnic" societies have undergone a paradigm shift away from biological rationalizations for race and racism in favour of socio-cultural justifications that support/bolster the continued subjugation of racialized peoples.[18] In Western contexts, that shift has helped to construct the normative nature of how the "White paradigm" frames what we are as a society and what we should aspire to be. It is an archetype that is intrinsically inaccessible to the racially oppressed; so through various articulations of power that solidify and speak to this culture of "difference," we become positioned as *other* in our own lands. In effect, as discussed earlier, we become locked in a process through which we must continually question our claim to space, place and a sense of belonging. Our voices, languages and "selves" are interpellated through the voices, languages and "selves" of our oppressor so we come to know ourselves as *other* through their eyes as well as through our own experience. To re-assert Bhatia's interpretation, these are the dangers of living a hyphenated reality.[19]

These power relations become constructed such that a Diasporic identity of *other* is forced upon us. The power relations that serve to oppress and discipline us into submission do so without our knowledge. In many ways, it may best be understood as a machine that extends all around us, at all times: its sole purpose to silently control us while blinding us to the truth of our oppression—the truth of our ability to resist—the truth of our access to power. Importantly, because we have always lived within these relations and because we have been slowly indoctrinated into its silent codes and rules, we find ourselves struggling within a prison that cannot be seen or touched—a prison for our minds.

An inquiry of how these "invisible constraints" develop within dichotomous and oppositional discursive frameworks is central to these discussions of identity, difference and power. Again, as discussed in Chapter Two, through both implicit and explicit contrasts, the dichotomy between the "White norm" and the racialized *other* is drawn through discursive formations. In result, the insurgent meanings encased within those contrasts become reified as "truthful" or "real." In these ways, we come to understand that racialized concepts of Whiteness are knowable only in direct relation and contrast to the repressed and negated *other*. Therefore, the exercise of power might best be interrogated relative to the dichotomies that are operating therein. Which is to say that an examination of the oppositions and negations at work here might illuminate how these meanings operate in specific contexts.[20] Moreover, racialized meanings, as well as the power that flows through the interpretation of those meanings, might be best understood in relation to how established differences are constructed through discourse and language. Again, as binary oppositions, the primary terms of race and racism are defined and ascribed "meaning" in direct relation to all that they repress and oppress.[21] In our everyday lives, we engage an almost constant stream of information that works to perpetuate and sustain power relations as they exist by establishing races and cultures as firmly different and dichotomous.[22] As discussed previously, the controls internalized within these representations condition us to "discipline" ourselves such that oppressive powers become organized through both our internal schemata and our oppressor's external loci of power.

There are debates within post-structuralism as to how these contested spaces might be interrogated relative to power and power relations. Some have set up camp outside a number of positions in seemingly direct opposition to Saussure's concept of "deep structure" in language and his assertion that the meaning of language could be found in the function of the linguistic system. Some of these theorists argue that words have *no* intrinsic interpretation and that language must be analyzed with respect to specific historical and contextual meanings. Others assert that words attain meaning only when in relation to other words and that the only "truth" available is that language cannot be taken at face value. As can be seen in the oppositional nature of these debates, the problematics associated with meanings and language remind us that we must pay close attention to the methods through which meanings are constituted. Otherwise, we run the risk of perpetuating commonsense understandings of how power functions through our social engagements and constitutions.[23] But what do these processes tell us about how power is constituted and how it operates within linguistic and discursive relations?

Again, like Foucault, we find it useful to engage discourse in its relation to the social construction of meanings. In this respect, we encourage the oppressed to interrogate the role played by language in the construction of our subjectivities. We are all undeniably influenced, regulated and managed through the power relations that develop relative to discursive relations. Theorizing within this framework, we would contend that our ability to engage these organizations of self is directly related to the socio-political sphere in which we struggle. Importantly, our ability to frame meanings and power as fluid, relational, unstable and fully dependent on history, location, moment and event allows us to imagine the possibilities of constructing new meanings from new locations. However, that further begs the question: If "truth" and reality are constructed by discourse rather than being reflected by/in it, how can we ever know anything beyond our own experience?

In reply, we echo theoretical views that assert discursive structures of subjectivity to be integrated within theoretical conceptions of language and social power. It is a reading that offers both an interpretation of experience as contextualized and an analysis of its constitutive and governing relationship with individual subjects.[24] Like Foucault, we also feel that discourse cannot be simply understood in terms of language or text. Instead, we interpret discourse as an organized complex of statements, terms, categories and beliefs that are structured in relation to historical, social and institutional specificities.[25] In short, discursive fields constitute knowledge and modify the hold of power. Within this framework, discourses are more than simplistic ways of thinking and producing meaning. Rather, discourse, language, sign, symbol and meaning work to "establish the very nature of the body, mind and emotional life of the subjects they influence" by exercising power through "structured" rather than "forced" relations.[26] This constitution of subjects is contingent on a variety of interconnected power relations that sustain each other and again, the stronger their mutual connection the more stable their foundation. Employing notions of ideological and discursive development as discussed in Chapter Two, we address this connection in several ways. As language acts as the medium in which everything is represented in thought, it also acts as the medium in which ideologies and discourses are generated, transformed and transmitted through the relations of power. It is through these types of immeasurable moments that ideologies and discourses must be interpreted as more than simply reflexive or as a matter of perception.[27]

The glaring discrepancies between democracy's promise of human liberation and the reality of human subjugation points to the existence of a discursive machine through which power is inscribed and re-inscribed in/through the oppressed—we (the oppressed) sustain the system and support our oppressor through our implicated positions within the system. But how are we implicated within these power relations? In answering this question, we feel it important to first draw a very pointed distinction between the notions of implication and participation as they apply to oppressed people and their/our role in the maintenance of the status quo. We feel that such discussions of participation often tend to assign responsibility to the oppressed a) for escaping or resisting their/our oppression, and b) for remaining or participating in their/our oppression. This is for us a very dangerous slippage in that we strongly contest and problematize theoretical positions/language that place racialized peoples as partners in their oppression. We are ardent on this point because partnership in this sense implies a willingness to cooperate in the "relationship." Such stances do not consider the psychological, physiological, intrapsychic and emotional consequences of racism as arising within such power relations. Nor do they think about the damages and ruptures to "self" that are formed in environments of danger, insecurity, self-doubt and coercive control. Theoretical stances that place us as anything more than implicated in our oppression neglect to address how prolonged and repeated experiences of racism serve to fundamentally frame our notions of basic trust, autonomy and initiative.

In applying the notion of "hegemony" here, we can begin to see how intersections of ideology, discourse and subjectivity function on both a micro level and in the macro-sphere relative to the encumbrances of State coercion, class politics and market forces.[28] Along these lines, Smart (1989) asserts that the major forms of domination (as per Foucault's theory of power) are best interpreted as *hegemonic effects*, transmitted through the complex of micro-power. Within this perspective, the power relations transmitted through cultural hegemony are constituted in the intersections that run between ideology, language and discourse. That being said, we draw a distinction between externally and internally enforced violence as arising through a historical complex designed to further support hierarchy, power and privilege, while pathologizing the victim of racism.

In interrogating racism as functioning within discursive fields, we mean to suggest that moments of everyday racism that violate and intrude upon the lives of people of color are very much a question of interpretation and subjectivity. As such, they need not be seen as inevitable features of our lives—moments that we must learn to live with. Bearing this in mind, we need to address our place within the relations of power in the moment. There are several methods through which we may define these moments of racism as existing within relations of power and functionally inscribed through difference. One prevailing intersection refers to the almost constant stream of images produced about the experience of racism: portrayals that perpetuate and sustain commonsense ideologies as well as the beliefs and inconsistencies that exist in relation to race.

These representations are framed as assumptions and contradictions that serve to dichotomize subjects of discourse.[29] One part is not simply constituted as different from its counterpart, it is framed as inherently opposed to it. Males and females, Whites and Blacks, gays and heterosexuals are not complementary counterparts; rather they are "constructed" as aspects of difference only connected in relation to their definition as opposites. Objectification is central to this process of oppositional difference because within such dichotomous thinking, the marginalized element becomes objectified as *other*—a thing to be manipulated and controlled.[30] As asserted by hooks (1988), domination always involves an attempt to objectify the subordinate group. She specifies:

> As subjects, people have the right to define their own reality, establish their own identities and name their history. As objects, one's reality is defined by others, one's identity created by others and one's history named only in ways that define one's relationship to those who are subject.[31]

The complex of systems that functionally frame the oppressed as objects to be positioned and controlled do so through both micro and macro-power relations. From the micro position, ideological influences, discourses and the power of experiential knowledge combine in ways that influence not only individual and group perceptions of reality, but also their understandings of how to interact with that reality. Through these discourses, the oppressed learn to engage injustice and inequality as part of the everyday—as normal. In other words, our belief that oppression is natural, in turn, prevents us from engaging in revolutionary practice. Even more problematically, our development within "normalizing spheres of influence" silently constitutes us such that we rarely even see/note/recognize the our existence within oppressive contexts. Our silence, inaction and acceptance of the situation helps to maintain the oppressive status quo. In this analysis of social organization, social meanings and power, we emphasize the importance of discursive relations precisely because they function as far more than a neutral conveyer of ideas; rather, they shape ideas and work to constitute our social reality.[32]

Since discourse is so influential in the shaping of the social world, those who have the ability to construct social symbols and their meanings are in a highly privileged position. They have the advantage of being able to order the world to suit their own interests and legitimate their authority and importance. They can construct a language, a body of knowledge and a reality in which they are the central figures, whose belief systems are beyond reproach. In this interpretation, groups that have the power to develop the structure of discourse, language, thought and reality also have the potential to create a world where they are the ruling bloc. In our interrogations of knowledge production, we have to be conscious of the question: "Who has access to the tools that create knowledge?" Importantly, discourse, theory and knowledge are all always implicated in power and power structures. The production of knowledge about race and the practice of oppression are embedded in power relations and our oppressors' ability to objectify us by defining us in relation to their subjectivity.[33] Since dichotomous constructs help to explain some of the ways in which "meanings" are constituted, any investigation into "meaning" must "deconstruct" these oppositions to understand how they work.

In deconstructing racialized "difference," we reverse and displace the binary oppositions that infuse oppressive relations in order to reveal and engage their interconnectedness as well as their historically contextual specificities.[34] Racist meanings become historically produced through processes of contextualization, de-contexualization and re-contextualization, so by de-constructing them, we de-centre the hierarchical oppositions in which they are framed.[35] So how do we go about de-constructing the discursive relations that perpetuate and uphold the hegemony of race and racism? The assumptions, expectations and contradictions that privilege Whiteness in relation to the racialized *other* speak directly to public discourses that define Whiteness by its normalcy: "We" are White while "they" are not. "We" are from here and "they" are from somewhere else. "We" work hard for what we have, while "they" abuse our social services. These beliefs not only serve to perpetuate racism by re-inforcing the cultural production of racist discourse, but they also attack and violate the oppressed in real, emotional and symbolic ways. Our identities are created for us and our relationships with the world are positioned only in ways that define us in relation to our oppressor.

Recognizing that language and discourse work within the relations of power to name, identify and define us through our oppression, how might we then work within these relations to re-inscribe our hold on power in these circumstances? How do we de-colonize our minds? How do we de-construct the everyday power relations that run through our experience of oppression? For example, in the everyday use of racialized words like immigrant, ethnic, Canadian and American, we speak to notions of "belonging." However, in deconstructing these terms, we find that through their pointed categor-izations, these terms function to include some, while excluding others. In effect, they bring to mind very specific images and notions of "peoplehood" and identity. It is important to note that there is no word that defines immigrant and *equally* Canadian or American: Being the one makes you intrinsically less than the other. In de-constructing the dichotomies that seek to establish the "us" and the "them" within such oppressive power relations, we must begin by asking the following questions: Whose words have merit when one speaks of racism? Is it the person who experiences it and suffers through it, or is it the person who says, "You're being too sensitive, you shouldn't read so much into it"? How do these "monologues" excuse and endorse "privileged" distortions of another's lived experience while actively violating the oppressed?

In relation to racism, the emphasis placed on re-counting the moment suggests that action and experience cannot be understood to exist in politically "real" space until they are both perceptible and recognizable to our oppressor.[36] That is to say that the reality of "the moment" becomes a function of one's ability to understand it and name it. The inherent question that underlies such notions is that if racism and the racist moment are not named for what they are, can the violations and pain be *understood* to have occurred—can the act itself be understood to be traumatic? As certain interpretations are privileged to the exclusion of others, we can see the interplay of power within the moment and we know whose reality is meant to be perceived in those spaces and places. We live in the intersections of experience, where the seemingly innocuous bits of daily minutia might carry the potential to affect our experience in the moment. So recognizing the importance of subjectivity, how might we account for our implication in these moments? Or, rather, how might we address our implicated selves in order to alter or subvert our violability in these moments and how might we alter or subvert the power relations working therein?

We would posit that the relations of power inscribed within *racist moments* function in many respects as learned interactions that follow a generally scripted progression. These scripts are racialized in such a way, through the various socially constructed and constituting systems discussed throughout this work, as to make it decidedly difficult for people of color to resist in the moment. As asserted earlier, social interactions with our oppressor have a profound influence on how we integrate our experiences and how we are implicated in those experiences, particularly within moments that are reflective or reminiscent of such previous violations. In relation to the scripted interactions that take place in these moments, racialized people's disciplined responses reflect our inability to read the script; moreover, they speak to our inability to recognize the script as actionable or resistible.

So how do we define actionable? Where do we locate power in relation to social reform and resistance? Who has the power to change the system? In his classic work, *Words that Wound*, Richard Delgado engages these problematics by theorizing the feasibility of promoting legal action against those who utter racial slurs and insults. He states near the end of his work:

> Because most citizens comply with legal rules and this compliance in turn 'reinforce[s] their own sentiments towards conformity', a tort action for racial insults would discourage such harmful activity through the teaching function of the law. The establishment of legal norm 'creates a public conscience and a standard for expected behaviour that check overt signs of prejudice'. Legislation aims first at controlling only the acts that express undesired attitudes. But 'when expression changes, thoughts too in the long run are likely to fall in line'. 'Laws...restrain the middle range of mortals who need them as a mentor in moulding their habits'. Thus, 'If we create institutional arrangements in which exploitative behaviours are no longer reinforced, we will then succeed in changing attitudes [that underlie these behaviours]'. Because racial attitudes of White Americans 'typically follow rather than precede actual institutional [or legal] alteration', a tort for racial slurs is a promising vehicle for the eradication of racism.[37]

In this most telling section of his work, Delgado makes several assertions and related assumptions. We contend that his reliance on the socially constructive and revolutionary nature of legislation is too facile when interrogated relative to the deeper impact and influence of race's socially constructed nature. After all, not to be too simplistic, but what did employment equity legislation do for the critical interrogation of race and racism in the mainstream? Furthermore, for much the same reason, we find his reliance on tort as a vehicle for the eradication of racism to be so much "pie in the sky" theorizing in that it seeks to place race as an attitudinal issue regardless of its social-psychological framework. Of the several theoretical frameworks discussed in Delgado's paper, he makes three specific assertions that speak to the focus of this work. First, that the violating experience of racism, as a "real" fact of racially minoritized people's lives, is something to be challenged, addressed, deterred and repaired within the field of tort law. Second, that racism exists in a top-down model of power where the oppressor has the innate ability to violate the oppressed. And third, in his reliance on the legal terrain as the crucible in which racism is to be burned away, Delgado makes a problematic conflation between the reality of the moment and the "victim's" ability to prove it—so, as usual, the onus of proof falls to the oppressed.

As Delgado's framework unfolds, he seems to run between several thematics that muddy the terrain on which he would posit his legal solutions. To begin, we would clarify most ardently that the violent and "real" nature of racism, as a major focus of this work, is not our point of contention with Delgado's arguments. Rather, we are specifically concerned with his assertion that racism in the form of racial insults has an innate and immutable ability to injure people of color. We contend that such frameworks limit the potential of the oppressed to merely deal with the aftereffects of the racist moment.[38] In Delgado's inference that the "pain" of racism is a starting point to a new politics for legal change, he employs a perspective on the racial experience that views people of color as either already violated or always violable. By doing so, he unwittingly places the power to oppress and the power to reform solely within the auspices of White privilege, thereby relegating people of color to prostrate, suppressed and powerless positionalities.

The second contention we have with Delgado's argument is related to the first but focuses on his top-down perception of power and his neglecting to address the social constitution of the oppressed as relevant to their positionality and implication in the moment. That is to say that in recognizing race and racism as socially constructed, we conclude that the experience of race is not a uni-directional experience. Rather, race is constituted in/through the lived experience of the oppressor as much as it is in the oppressed. The subtle difference being that in many ways, we (the oppressed) act within the moment and our implication within the moment is intrinsically related to the consequences of those actions. While the potentiality of psychological harm will likely always exist as part of the racialized experience, we assert that it is intensely problematic to define people of color by their violability and White people by their ability to oppress. Such a stance completely removes the possibility of agency for the oppressed, particularly in relation to the development of anti-racist strategies for the young or as yet "uninitiated."

Our third contention with Delgado's paper centres on his efforts to establish the legal impetus for addressing the harms of racism. We find his inference that legislation may function as an avenue through which people of color can acquire "power" and/or healing by proving that they have been violated to be problematic on several fronts. As questioned previously, who gets to validate the experience? What happens if the case is thrown out of court? Does that mean that the hurt, injury and trauma of the moment did not occur? Delgado's focus on legal tort suggests that the "reality" of the moment becomes somehow more/most useful if used to sway the minds of the privileged. We agree that re-counting the racist experience can help to bring the moment into politically "real" and useful space. However, we would emphasize that such analyses should be employed to move the oppressed to a greater critical consciousness of the moment and their constitution/implication within it. Moreover, we would attach the corollary that such moves to engender a greater critical knowledge/consciousness/ understanding of the moment must proceed primarily in the form of a critical pedagogy for the oppressed. Such moves must be about validating the experience for the oppressed and not about proving the nature and "effect" of the experience for the privileged.

As discussed earlier, we contend that anti-racist work appropriately proceeds from an understanding that race and racism are "real" and need to be addressed. However, while we do not argue against the "reality" of these social facts, we would draw attention to interpretations that present psychological injury as an inevitable fact of the racialized experience. It is our contention that such assumptions invest the oppressor with a fundamental ability to violate and that the oppressed, in turn, have no option but to deal with the aftereffects of that violence. Work such as Delgado's, while intended to take up the inequity, violence and horror of racist action, also serves to place the power for social change and resistance in the hands of privilege. For various reasons, we find such frameworks to be intensely problematic. Certainly, the possibility of psychological harm does exist. In fact, (as taken up to a greater extent in Chapters Five, Six and Eight), such harms are very much an everyday part of our racialized experience. However, the "taken-for-granted" status that such approaches assign to the racist moment implies that the pain, trauma and injury of racism are "facts of life" to be feared, denounced and/or repaired. Again, in investigating the social construction of the racialized subject through discursive practices, we engage discursive interpretations of the subject as a living, thinking and feeling agent. Importantly, utilizing this conception of "subject" does not detract from our ability to understand the discursive relations that constitute us and our society, nor does it preclude our ability to affect social change.[39]

These racist/racialized encounters follow, for the most part, a predictable and practiced continuity of cues, moments and events. We contend that these moments are structured such that it is exceedingly difficult to refuse the roles, lines and experiences scripted for us—that applies to both us and our oppressor. We access the signs, markers and symbols within the moment to define for ourselves: what counts as race, racial, racist; what is appropriate or inappropriate; how to recognize and navigate racially charged situations (i.e., what we can get away with and what we can't); how to position ourselves in the moment. We adapt these culturally available scripts to our particular interpersonal contexts and modify/internalize them as "intra-psychic" disciplines and relational scripts.[40]

We are disciplined through these scripts and, while such disciplining controls should not be interpreted as intrinsic to oppression, they are certainly conducive to the oppressive relations of power that delineate our experience as racialized and marginalized peoples. In re-iterating this point, we would specify that the interpretation of discipline as a modality for the exercise of power brings us to a very pointed space in the development of this work. In Chapter Two, we took up discussions of power and discipline relative to the ideological and discursive frameworks that function to adhere racialized peoples within oppressive milieus. Following those discussions, in this chapter we addressed the practical applications of power as fluid, relational and de-centralized. But where does that leave us? If we have established the oppressive functionality of racialized power in Western contexts and at the same time forwarded a notion of power as neither universal nor repressive, then how do we explain the oppressive nature of Western society? How do we take up the realities of White privilege and the seemingly universal extensions of White power that frame the colonial and postcolonial experience?

The answers to these questions may be teased out in the distinctions we have made between "dialogic" and "monologic" interactions. We agree that power relations are always open to modifications and that there is, therefore, no fundamental principle of power that serves to dominate. However, we must take care to remember that power, like discourse, language and meaning, is always contextually specific and will function relative to the historical blueprints that have framed its development into the present. Social fields abound with various fluid and non-homogeneous power relations. Importantly, while the system, dependent on socio-historical contexts, will always be open to the development of both oppressive and libratory relations of power, the directional flow of those relations is what frames our inquiry here. In this light, we feel it important to address and interrogate the relationship between power, discipline and the specificities of White privilege. To these ends, in the next chapter we will work to combine our previous discussions into a coherent analysis and examination of power and discipline. We will do so by focusing on the historical contexts and social dynamics that have intersected and combined to produce the conditions of contemporary racial oppression in Western contexts, the seemingly universal locus of White power and the technologies of discipline that frame "realities" of White power and privilege.

CHAPTER FOUR
White Power, White Privilege

...one can speak of the formation of disciplinary society in this movement that stretches from the enclosed disciplines, a sort of social 'quarantine', to an indefinitely generalizable mechanism of 'panopticism'. Not because the disciplinary modality of power has replaced all the others; but because it has infiltrated the others, sometimes undermining them, but serving as an intermediary between them, linking them together and, above all, making it possible to bring the effects of power to the most minute and distant elements.

—Michel Foucault, *Discipline and Punish*[1]

The bigot's responsibility is generally no more than individual. Of far greater significance is the man in control. He may be sophisticated enough to hide his personal racism from the world; he may even not experience any. It does not matter very much whether he does or not. Because he lives in a racist society, social relations have been structured by him so that the black is not present for him. Negritude, black history, black social existence, are made not to matter. The man in control is technically insulated from the racial reality and influenced only by the capital whose fortunes he must superintend...Later, he will salve his racial conscience by contributing to the black college of his choice. He might even scold the White bigots and feel genuinely outraged at them.

—Joel Kovel, *White Racism: A Psychohistory*[2]

It is through the privilege of Whiteness that "difference" continues to be both defined and articulated. Today, while White privilege is continuously asserted in and through sites of privilege as a justification for racist practice, claims to White "innocence" and the resulting denial of systemic oppression serve to leave the mechanisms for racism intact. Whiteness is assumed to be a right rather than a claim to privilege and, importantly, it is this "privilege of Whiteness" that we target in anti-racist praxis. As many others have demonstrated, it is important that our articulation of Whiteness is seen as more than a sum of White privilege, power and identity.[3] We must connect Whiteness with the reality of White racism. We recognize that the creation of an

open and equal opportunity system with effective and positive social outcomes for all groups requires the disrupting and rupturing of the dominance
of Whiteness and White racism...anything short of this goal will only serve
the status quo. But how do we proceed to interrogate and teach about the
issues of power, oppression and social control when the very natures of these
concepts and the related problematics of privilege are abstract concepts? As
Kovel (1988) so astutely puts forth, those in positions of power and
dominance are "privileged" in their ability to disregard, obfuscate and
downplay the realities of oppression that circumscribe the lives of marginalized peoples—those with privilege "know" they have it.[4] Deep down, in
places that they don't want to talk about, they feel that privilege, but
acknowledging these "freedoms" would require that they recognize and take
responsibility for their participation in the continuance of social injustice and
the relational impact that their liberty has on the oppressive existence of
others.

Again, the abstract nature of privilege and the almost metaphysical
character of social control as applied within oppressive relations of power,
carries the potential to "scar without marking," to "push without shoving." In
fact, one of the peculiar endowments of White privilege arises in its ability to
obfuscate its relationship to the mechanisms of power, while at the same
time, employing those mechanisms in language, discourse and every other
aspect of our lived reality. In rhetorical discussions about racial privilege,
oppressive discourses will often manifest in these disguised and yet very
marked ways:

- The attention to ethnic roots: I understand racism because my parents
  have European accents and they've experienced racism
- Muting the salience of skin color: My last name sounds foreign and
  I'm not Christian so I understand racism
- A hierarchy of oppressions: The real problem isn't race, it's class
- The "What If " Excuse: White people would be oppressed if the
  Chinese had been the ones to colonize
- Geographic Relativism: Our society isn't oppressive. Take a look at
  Afghanistan. Now that is an oppressive society

We do not presume to mute the Diasporic experience of European
immigration, the validity of gender, class, sexual orientation, etc., as valid
intersections of oppression and we take specific care to recognize the painful
realities of religious persecutions. However, in the context of this work, we

must still recognize the salience of skin color as our focus. The above arguments serve to disavow the normative and privileged nature of White-ness by claiming some other identity which allows legitimate victim status. The purpose: to diffuse the "taboo" implications that accompany a recognition of complicity in the continuance of racism.[5] "It's just easier. It is easier to blame oppression on historical circumstance and thereby sidestep one's own complicity in the continuing cycle of social injustice. It is easier to look "over there" to societies that are differently oppressive and claim a "comparative liberty." As the axiom asserts: denying a problem does not make it disappear.[6] Critically addressing White privilege requires an in-depth analysis of how oppression is constructed: How power is accessed by some while denied to others; and how the lack of access to power and privilege effectively oppresses racially *othered* peoples. How does the production and application of White power and privilege directly impact the constitution and performance of racial oppression? Recognizing White privilege and understanding its connections within the larger social relations of power is a basic step toward understanding racism and other forms of oppression.

As discussed, the notion of the "mythical norm"[7] is produced through the intersecting and interlocking of oppressions. The discourses of "normalcy" and "cultural paradigm" that arise relative to these dynamics are productive of a raced, classed, gendered and sexually oriented archetype against which all *other* models are measured and judged as somehow "less than." It is important to recognize that oppressor and oppressed alike are impacted by their positionings in these hierarchies. For example, a White middle-class man's societal placement, his experiences and his opportunities are fully understandable only in relation to the social conditions and oppressions of those located outside that locus of privilege.[8] This is the complex of disabilities through which oppression continues to flourish.

As will be taken up in both Chapters Five and Six, the "realities of racial oppression" remain obscured to the commonsense gaze precisely because any interrogations of those "relations of power" presuppose the ability to think relationally and in abstract terms. Because White privilege is infused into the norms of their everyday lives, it becomes a difficult aspect of experience to separate and recognize, let alone implicate. So, for the most part, while the racially privileged may recognize the existence of oppression, they often do so without perceiving the relational tissue that runs between that oppression and their power. Importantly, however, we must also take care to remember that the ability to ignore the implications discussed here arises directly out of that privilege (i.e. the master never felt the physical pain inflicted by his whip).

Whiteness is defined by a privilege that goes unseen: an invisibility that in many ways places our oppressor outside the racial sphere, vested with a power and social advantage which they themselves need not consider— "That's just the way it is." Importantly, libertarian claims to color-blindness arise in these moments precisely because as Whiteness is taken up as normal, our world-view becomes framed through the "racelessness of White skin." In de-constructing these engagements with skin color, it becomes clear how power and privilege function to shape the social sphere with deleterious effects for some and beneficial effects for others. One such beneficial effect comes to light in the ability of White people to proceed without a conscious reading of their own racial positioning—that is, until they place it in relation to another person's race. Until those moments of "racial collision," the privileged have the luxury of interpreting race as something that *other* people have—they do not see it unless they have to. Even though their skin is infused with meanings and markers, the power that speaks to and through their banners of Whiteness ensures that they do not have to think about race or how it positions them in society.[9] Such self-reflection in the everyday is not a necessity of their experience.

Wildman (1996) points out that "the invisibility of privilege strengthens the power it creates and maintains. The invisible cannot be combated and as a result privilege is allowed to perpetuate, re-generate and re-create itself. Privilege is systemic, not an occasional occurrence."[10] If privilege is kept invisible and not considered real, it can't be examined, it can't be diminished or dismantled. Recognizing that denials of White privilege protect and prevent awareness about how racism works and how it is upheld, we must be able to examine the unacknowledged privilege that circumscribes the lives of White people before we can address the resulting oppressions. McIntosh (1992) defines White privilege as an invisible knapsack of unearned assets which White people can count on cashing in each day, but about which they are meant to remain oblivious. "White privilege is like an invisible weightless knapsack of special provisions, assurances, tools, maps, guides, code-books, passports, visas, clothes, compass, emergency gear and blank checks."[11] She identifies numerous daily benefits of this power and privilege that are available to White people based on the color of their skin. Some of these include (a) the normalizing effects associated with having one's race widely and positively represented in the media, (b) the security of knowing that one's race will not hinder or prevent access to resources (e.g., legal, medical and social service) and that (c) skin color privilege means never having to educate and prepare your children to face/resist/recover from the daily physical and mental suffering that is intrinsic to a racialized existence.[12]

While the categories that speak to human differences are socially constructed and thereby open to change over time, the privileging of Whiteness has remained, for all intents and purposes, constant. But how is that possible? As asserted previously, if power is neither universal nor repressive, then how is it that racialized power continues to hold sway in Western contexts. The relations of racial domination were/are constructed in very specific ways and within very specific historical contexts. Therefore, through the functionality of these historically specific "hegemonic effects," the ongoing manifestations of racism reflect and re-inscribe the conjunctures of space and time in/through which contemporary racial oppression arose. While we agree with Goldberg's (1993) assertion that different racisms manifested themselves at different historical moments and contexts,[13] it is important that we refrain from diluting the contemporary issue and problem. Anti-racism asserts that the oppressed should work with a broad definition of racism that is inclusive of skin color, language, culture and religion, as markers for differentiation and unequal treatment. However, it is equally important to acknowledge the power of White racism as the *source* from which other contemporary racist discourses and practices have emerged.[14]

It is the discourse of Whiteness that prescribes what is (ab)normal, (un)acceptable and (in)valid, so those engaging in racism or racist practices draw from a historical complex of knowledge that is fully entrenched in the racial polity of Whiteness. As discussed, many existing works have undertaken a careful analysis of the historical specificities and contingencies that have engendered the "reproduction of races" in socially and racially structured spaces.[15] Our purpose here is to establish a firm theoretical account of White racism that will, in turn, set the groundwork to better analyze the contemporary ideological, material and social meanings of racism as put forth so far in this work. We contest conventional arguments that seek to place racism as relative to all races and cultures. There is a saliency to White racism and we can afford to neither overlook nor downplay.

How often have we heard these questions from our oppressor: I wonder what would have happened if someone other than the Europeans had colonized? But I would experience racism if I went somewhere like China, wouldn't I? The questions themselves are facetious. There are no answers required. At best, such questions reflect a fundamental ignorance and/or denial of the socially constructed nature of race and racism. At worst, they function to mute White responsibility and complicity in the propagation and continuance of racial oppression while constraining new/creative imaginings of our world. As intersecting strategies, they work to frame power and privilege as mere twists of fate—that anyone would be racist given the right historical circumstances. The reality is that racism exists exactly as it exists, no other group colonized and what we have now is a complex of disabilities that are intrinsically tied to the history and continuing reach of colonialism and Whiteness. As suggested by Spivak (1990), the most frightening thing about imperialism is its long-term effect, what secures it, what cements it and how it has implanted the benevolent self-representation of imperialist as savior into our mass psyche.[16] Thus, we focus on the salience of White racism in relation to what secures and cements it as well as how we are disciplined to implicate ourselves in its organizing effects.

History and contexts are important for understanding the analytical and conceptual "...terms that mythologize our differences and similarities."[17] The privilege of Whiteness is a relational phenomenon that has emerged from the interplay of complex social, cultural, political and historical forces and contexts (see also Frankenberg, 1993; Dyer, 1997, Roediger, 1994).[18] Dei (1996) has rightly noted that the notion of race may have been an essential feature of early social formations, especially as individuals searched for social explanations about the nature and consequences of human differences. Still, as Reynolds and Lieberman (1993) assert, the origins of the race concept may be tied to European philosophy, particularly the European colonial and imperial expansion in the 17th century.[19] So how is it that this colonial gaze, formulated so long ago, still holds sway over us today? How do these invisible chains from a long distant era manage to control and discipline us into oppression in the now? In answering that question, we come back again to the notion of discipline. Foucault asserts that the chief function of disciplinary power is training. Through the use of normalizing judgments and hierarchical observations, those exercising power work to bend its subjects into a differentiated and analyzable assembly.[20] Having addressed the normalizing effects of discursive relations in the previous chapters, let us now look at the pointed issue of the mechanisms through which such disciplinary power functions. To these ends, let us look again to Foucault:

> It 'trains' the moving, confused, useless multitudes of bodies and forces into a multiplicity of individual elements—small, separate cells; organic autonomies; genetic identities and continuities; combinatory segments. Discipline 'makes' individuals; it is the specific technique of a power that regards individuals both as objects and as instruments of its exercise.[21]

"Objects to be inspected, instruments to be exercised." The exercise of "disciplinary" power, as put forth by Foucault (1977), pre-supposes a mechanism that coerces by means of observation in such a way as to induce the effects of power and simultaneously demarcate those on whom that power is applied. These "observatories of human multiplicity" arose in the classical age, parallel to various techniques of subjection and other methods of exploitation, to create an entirely knowable people, an intrinsically visible object of surveillance and control.[22]

Historically, these mechanisms arose and manifested themselves through a multitude of perspectives, structures and languages. They were embedded within the structures of power and domination that characterized all social formations—from the earliest human interactions and perhaps even from the time that humans learned to grasp "difference" and assign meanings to those differences. The process of *othering* was born the moment that we began to classify and evaluate the phenomena of "difference" based on our real, imagined or perceived dissimilarities. However, these social controls came to widespread and tactile use with the ideological invention and application of the binary divisions between "God and Satan," "Good and Bad," "Civilized and Savage," "peaceful and violent," "cerebral and physical," etc. Whiteness, White power and White privilege have been and have become embedded in the fabric of human cognition, understanding and communication in relation to these polar opposites.

Through various ideological and discursive forms, this intrinsic truth of Whiteness has become identified with the "positive" concepts of "light," "purity," "beauty" and "goodness"—in a word, "God." Meanwhile, the negative aspects of that dichotomy have been reserved for the savage and exotic *other*. The visibility, or rather, invisibility of Whiteness positions "them" as the repository of civility and knowledge: it is an image that continues to be written, spoken and articulated in a multiplicity of languages.

> There were the minor techniques of multiple and intersecting observations, of eyes that must see without being seen; using techniques of subjection and methods of exploitation, an obscure art of light and the visible was secretly preparing a new knowledge of man.[23]

Through its biological, scientific and ideological language, White power has implemented its supremacy by "logically," "rationally" and "objectively" proving that the White race alone has complete monopoly over the virtues of "beauty, intelligence and strength,"[24] and that the White race is genetically, biologically and psychologically superior to other races.[25] Moreover, by way of "cultural" discourse, White power has been enforcing the notion that the White man's institutions, belief and value systems, worldviews and ideologies are superior to those of *other* peoples.[26] This is the surveyor society and in their creation of an entirely "knowable" people, they set the foundations for the mechanisms of power as they function to watch, control and oppress racialized peoples in the now.

To further examine the origins of this technology of power, we trace the religious manifestations of White racism to Pope Nicolas V's infamous "Decree of Subjugation," issued in 1455, through which the church officially sanctified the enslavement of "infidel" peoples.[27] From this point on, the devoted Christian missionaries and their governments considered it their sacred duty to subjugate African, Aborigine and Indian peoples as a heretical subclass of people. These moves were predicated on the ideological justification that these White saviors were saving these "savage souls" from themselves and securing, for them, a place in "God's Kingdom." However, the economic truth of this decree spoke to the potential wealth and material gains to be had—and, in fact, a wealth and material production which, in turn, would cement the very foundation of Western industry and commerce.[28] By means of these coercive powers and the modes of surveillance that arose parallel to them, disciplinary power became an integrated system in which both internal and external systems were linked through the central foci of "knowledge" and "dichotomy."

Again, in extrapolating from Foucault (1977), with the advent of these hierarchized controls a whole problematic would develop through which the social schema would turn to surveillance as the axis upon which oppression would spin. Importantly, it was not only the architecture of the coercive system that would establish a racialized people to be seen and controlled, but rather the creation of a "visible" population, cognizant of their *otherness* and thereby constituted as "effects of power." It was, for the colonizer, the perfect disciplinary apparatus in that, at a glance, he knew everything there was to know about the colonized and in turn the colonized knew everything about themselves through their oppressor's gaze. We learned to recognize our powerlessness and inferiority; importantly, we also learned to recognize that our oppressor was aware of all these things. The oppressed became aware of a great many things in this social order, not only that s/he was watched and "known," but that being watched, necessitated self-control as a means to avoid external discipline and punishment.

Interestingly, these external disciplines or, rather, this "art of punishing" exposed racialized peoples to a field of comparisons in which "differences" were marked by rules, one set for their White oppressors and another set of rules for themselves.[29] In short, respectful of the knowledge that the oppressor's gaze was/is both ever-present and all-seeing, the oppressed function under the premise that the domain of nonconformity is punishable. These pointed moments of indoctrination to the "rules of engagement" could be seen in (a) the colonial past, as disobedient and not so disobedient slaves were punished, whipped, hung, mutilated and killed, (b) the early-to-mid 20th century as colonized peoples were imprisoned, shot and murdered for "not knowing their place," and (c) in the contemporary manifestations of imprisonment and social stigmatization for peoples of color who speak too loudly and too often. Discipline and punishment work together to establish for the oppressed and oppressor alike what they are capable of, what is expected of them and, perhaps most importantly, the boundaries of what they are allowed to do. In so doing, the mechanisms of power establish for the oppressed, the "constraints of conformity" by which they must achieve and fail accordingly at risk of punishment. As discussed earlier, this mechanism, set firmly within the White gaze, compares, differentiates, homogenizes and excludes racialized peoples relative to a social hierarchy that elevates the White paradigm and effectively normalizes their privilege against the oppressed and outcast state of *othered* peoples.[30]

Now, with respect to the issue of White power and privilege, we have discussed the normalizing of Whiteness, so let us address the pointed notion of observation or, more pointedly, the disciplinary power of surveillance. In Foucault's seminal work on the development of disciplinary systems, we interpret several themes that speak directly to the modern disciplines of racial oppression that enclose and encircle the lives of the racialized peoples. First, let us look briefly at Foucault's examination of Bentham's Panopticon:

> ...at the periphery, an annular building; at the centre, a tower; this tower is pierced with wide windows that open onto the inner side of the ring; the peripheric building is divided into cells, each of which extends the whole width of the building; they have two windows, one on the inside, corresponding to the windows of the tower; the other, on the outside, allows the light to cross the cell from one end to the other. All that is needed, then, is to place a supervisor in a central tower and to shut up in each cell a madman, a patient, a condemned man, a worker or a schoolboy. By the effect of back-lighting, one can observe from the tower, standing out precisely against the light, the small captive shadows in the cells of the periphery. They are like so many cages, so many small theatres, in which each actor is alone, perfectly individualized and constantly visible. The panoptic mechanism arranges spatial unities that make it possible to see constantly and to recognize immediately. In short, it reverses the principle of the dungeon; or rather of its three functions—to

enclose, to deprive of light and to hide—it preserves only the first and eliminates the other two. Full lighting and the eye of a supervisor capture better than darkness, which ultimately protected.[31]

As proclaimed by Foucault, "Visibility is a trap" and truly, our skin marks us as prisoners, easily identifiable and disciplined to perform based on the knowledge of that visibility. We (the oppressed) are confined to a "cell" that has been fashioned from our skin and our culture in contrast to those same properties of our oppressor. And in much the same way that the cells of the Panopticon function to separate the prisoners, we are separated from a great many things. While we are made visible to our oppressor, the discursive formations that guide us within our oppressive milieu infuse us with a duality and a self-hatred that effectively separates us from our fellow oppressed and from a knowledge of our oppression. We are seen as *other* from both external sites of privilege and internalized sites of Diasporic identity. In these ways, we become objects of knowledge, discursive "effects" to be interrogated and understood and as proposed by Foucault, within these walls, we are never subjects in communication. We hear the calls of our oppressor: "They always stick together—they are always trouble when they get in a group—they always talk about Black culture—he played the race card—everything would be OK if they would stop bringing up the issue of race." In reaction, we choose not to resist. We shun our communities, our cultures and heritages in favour of less problematic spaces—sites that are not so well lit—spheres in which we believe our visibility to be veiled from the eyes of our oppressor. "We go along, to get along." This is the "colorblind" prison in which we find ourselves secured—with little chance or avenue of escape.

This visibility, functioning relative to the markers of White privilege, impacts our ability to oppose and to resist our oppression—precisely because we are identifiable and, therefore, easily policed. Again, our agendas are muted under the socially charged labels of "special interest politics" and "reverse racism." This divisive visibility is in many ways a "guarantee of order" in that our oppressor controls the means by which our resistance is validated in the mainstream and our self-implicated duality prevents us from developing a critical gaze into our constitution as oppressed. At every turn, the possibilities of developing communal action are discouraged and those of us who do resist are singled out for all of the communal, social and economic repercussions that accompany the label of "troublemaker."

Therefore, the major effect of our Panoptic prison is to inflict upon the racially oppressed a permanent and constant state of visibility that exists on both a conscious and subconscious level, thereby establishing an automatic and self-reproducing relation of power between us and our oppressor. In this framework, we feel our oppression, even when in ostensible isolation from our oppressor, because the internal gaze does not allow us that freedom. The permanence of this "self-surveillance" renders that exercise of coercive powers from sites of privilege as generally unnecessary because these particular relations of power are performed in such a way as to function independently of privilege. In other words, we have been circumscribed by a relational dynamic through which we have become the bearers of a power that is self-controlling and self-disciplining.

These constraints do not function in our oppressor's power to control us but, rather, in our recognition that we are in fact being observed and that we should therefore act as they would have us act. Like the guards of Bentham's Panopticon, our oppressor's surveillance is known to us and we are aware of his power even if we never directly see it performed. We see his eyes and ears at work at all levels and in all spaces of the social sphere, but we never truly know when we are being "watched," so we always behave as if we are watched. To a great extent, White power functions in its ability to "regulate" without "regulating" and by that same token, much of White privilege rests in that they need not live through the constrictions and disciplines that frame our lives as oppressed. As noted by Foucault, as a mechanism of power, this system of discipline is particularly important in that it "automizes" and "dis-individualizes" power.[32]

> Power has its principle not so much in a person as in a certain concerted distribution of bodies, surfaces, lights, gazes; in an arrangement whose internal mechanisms produce the relation in which individuals are caught up. The ceremonies, the rituals, the marks by which the sovereign's surplus power was manifested are useless. There is a machinery that assures dissymmetry, disequilibrium, difference.[33]

So how do we move from this interpretation of the mechanisms of power to an interrogation of contemporary White racism? We are pointed in taking a counter-hegemonic position that to claim, defend and maintain the privileges of Whiteness would be to engage in White racist practice: it further enmeshes and supports the application of these disciplinary and systemic powers. In a recent work, Dei (2000) notes that many scholars have argued that critical discussions of difference challenge the normality of Whiteness and the pervasive effects of White privilege as the root of racism in Western contexts.[34] Frankenberg (1993) has called for the unmasking of Whiteness as an un-racialized category.[35] Thus in our anti-racist praxis we must centre the interrogation of Whiteness and White racism in a way that does not shift attention away from the plight and concerns of those disadvantaged in society. A rupturing of Whiteness is crucial to any further subversion of Eurocentrism and racial oppression because Whiteness promotes a particular cultural practice of race-based hierarchies that feeds on the prevalence of dominant forms of racism.[36] As discussed, White racism operates from a power base that effectively defines "normalcy" and notions of meritocracy, excellence, ethical neutrality and rugged individualism as all rationalized in relation to the paradigms of Whiteness and racist practice. As a privileged signifier of difference, we feel that an analysis of the discourse on White racial hierarchies is a necessity.[37]

So what does it mean to claim Whiteness in a racialized context and what does White racism entail? The crucial questions surround the issue of difference: What kind of difference is being asserted and by whom? Whiteness must also be examined as an active component in the maintenance of White domination. Whiteness coexists within a system of economic, political, cultural, spiritual, psychological, emotional and social advantages for the privileged—at the expense of racialized *other*. As such, it is a category of and for the dominant. Like Whiteness, White racism is a social marker and practice of power and privilege. But rather than simply posit "who" exactly is White, we must also ask what constitutes a claim to Whiteness. We must also adhere to Giroux's (1997) caution not to conflate a warranted critique and careful interrogation of Whiteness simply with criticisms of White people. Bearing that caution in mind, we re-frame the question of "who." To the more pointed interrogation of "what" Whiteness is and how/why it is produced, maintained and bolstered in the social order.

Like the race concept itself, Whiteness is a social construction with political, cultural and economic "capital." It is produced by and conducive to the social contexts of power that construct "difference," "normality" and "privilege." It is also an ideology in the sense that it evokes images, conceptions and promises which provide the frameworks through which we all represent, interpret, understand and make sense of our social existence.[38] Whiteness is a form of self-identity and a marker of material, political, symbolic and psychological worth. It is against this worth that the oppressed are measured and examined, thereby turning the economy of visibility into an exercise of power. Arising within the privileged loci of power and control relative to these norms of Whiteness, the disciplinary power of the White oppressor is exercised through both his invisibility and the compulsory racialized visibility of its subjects. Importantly, this self-disciplining does more than tell the oppressed what we can and what we cannot do, it tells us who and what we are. These mechanisms of power speak to our internal/intra-psychic schema in ways that mark our identities as inferior and violable.

Roediger (1994) and Dyer (1997) have both written extensively on Whiteness as a marker of identity that is nothing but oppressive and false: "an empty category" that is fragile and fluid and an "identity based on what one isn't and on whom one can hold back."[39] We would move from their assertions to contend that Whiteness has become much more than an empty category—that it has become a point of cultural attachment. For our purposes in this work and even to a greater respect relative to the anti-racist project as a whole, we must begin to interrogate ways of thinking through Whiteness and the inherent complexities housed therein. Importantly, these examinations must critically examine racial injustice and the deep seeded inequities that circumscribe both the system and our lived experience of it. Respective of its cultural and institutionalized nature, progressive politics for change must maintain a gaze on Whiteness as a system of dominance that has progressed from the initial writings and reports about the newly "discovered" savage to the contemporary knowledge about the third world and its Diasporic progeny. The ontological reality is that Whiteness is a powerful conception of identity and difference that cannot be destroyed.[40]

> Thanks to the whole apparatus of writing that accompanied it, the examination opened up two correlative possibilities: first, the constitution of the individual as describable, analyzable object, not in order to reduce him to 'specific' features, as did the naturalists in relation to living beings, but in order to maintain him in his individual features, in his particular evolution, in his own aptitudes or abilities, under the gaze of a permanent corpus of knowledge; and second, the constitution of a comparative system that made possible the measurement of overall phenomena, the description of groups, the characterization of collective facts, the calculation of the gaps between individuals, their distribution in a given 'population'.

What originally grew out of the colonial gaze has become cemented in the construction of the *other* and our firm knowledge of what is and what is not, what we are and what we are not. However, we must recognize that it is still possible to work toward a critical deconstruction of Whiteness. To that end, we must begin by acknowledging the normality of Whiteness as the overriding paradigmatic archetype of the Western world. It follows naturally that we should not only challenge merit/individuality-based systems that mute and disavow the interplay of privilege, but also that should teach that Whiteness reproduces itself regardless of intent, power differences or goodwill.[41] Whiteness as a property excludes and appropriates.

For example, mainstream educational systems demonstrate how hegemony impacts on schooling in the everyday. In both subtle and overt ways, the "hidden curriculum" works to re-produce and re-inforce the inequalities that exist in society.[42] Studies show that streaming practices, teacher expectations and pedagogy, as well as the curriculum itself, all work to disadvantage certain racialized and minoritized youth on the basis of race, gender and class. Privileged children are provided with an unfair advantage in their educational experience because the rules and regulations for what defines good schooling is based in a Eurocentric model. Beyond the issue of schooling, immigration laws are also a frightening example of how mechanisms of power and privilege create rules and codes that systematically exclude and marginalize people of color. From her examination of Canada's moral reform in the early 1900s, Valverde (1991) reported that the racist, classist and sexual fears of Anglo-Saxon populations were merged into a single moral panic surrounding the notion of the "unfit immigrant." Here, the race, culture, class and "sexual morality" of potential immigrants were problematized and used to explain the supposed inferiority of people of color. The social climate during that time period was clearly reflected in those early immigration policies that established "preferred" and "non-preferred" categories of immigrants. Preferred immigrants came from the United Kingdom and other "White nations," while Orientals, Negroes, South Asians and other non-Whites were framed as "non-preferred" and undesirable.[43] Even today, and without delving into the horrendous post-9/11 era of racial profiling in immigration policy and practice, we cannot overlook the glaring inconsistencies in treatment that separate White and non-White immigrants to Western nations. Immigrant status profoundly impacts the lived experience of racialized peoples in numerous ways. One of the more pointed applications of racism in this context can be seen in how Western societies de-value and often disavow the work experience and educational credentials of non-White immigrants. Many non-White immigrants to North America and Britain find that once they immigrate, higher educational diplomas and degrees in their home countries are devalued and their work experiences negated. Often the evaluative criteria for foreign credentials is based on limited information about these *other* institutions' standards and programs and is almost always based in a considerable pre-judgment as to their relative inferiority.[44] How is it that Western nations rationalize the valuing of some degrees over others? These blatantly racist relations of power are commonly justified through the use of rhetorical explanations to effectively deny racism while solidifying White power and privilege.

Importantly, at this point we would like to reassert our recognition that White racism manifests itself differently along the lines of gender, class and ethnicity. Not to deny the power and impact of White racism on the racialized, this is an acknowledgment of the different racisms, moments and places in which these oppressive mechanisms exert their hold. To understand this position we again reflect on how White privilege manifests itself. Chater (1994) noted that privilege and power have been historically mediated along lines of class, caste, nation, race, gender, sexuality and so on. In this sense, our multiple positionalities frame our experiences such that we have a complex and contradictory relationship with power and powerlessness and with privilege and oppression.[45] She further asserted that the experience of White working class, women, the disabled and homosexuals revealed that we must seriously interrogate all generalizations of White privilege.[46] Because people call on privilege from sundry positionalities, it is also critical that we acknowledge the different ways racism is enacted upon various bodies.

We concur with Harris (1993) that the benefits of Whiteness are available to all dominant groups (and specifically Whites) regardless of class, gender and sexual orientation.[47] However, while those who benefit from their skin color privilege may experience disadvantage in society, it will not be because of their race, but in spite of it.[48] Admittedly, Whiteness is not a universal experience of all Whites, nor is enacting White racism a universal practice of all Whites. Therefore, it is important to explore how gender, class and sexuality make the experiences of being White different for different people, because there is no "fictive homogenous community of Whites."[49] It also calls for a re-negotiation of Whiteness as a productive and critical force within the politics of claiming, knowing and naming difference.

To articulate Whiteness as an oppositional category, anti-racism must work with racial identity as a form of agency and resistance. The political, economic and educational advantage of Whiteness must be utilized to create a resistant space that challenges dominance and hegemony.[50] In the same vein, the claim to normalcy must be challenged and resisted before access to societal resources may be realistically re-imagined and re-distributed. This should be our vision of the 21st century, one in which no group has an automatic right to privilege and power.[51] Because the public discourse of color-blindness is as insidious as the practice of racism itself, [52] our specific academic project is to move the dialogue beyond the theorization of the concept of race to an examination of the significance of race in social and political practice. In order to offer more than simple theoretical perspectives on White racism, we work to move beyond the academic lacunae in which "race" has been framed. To these ends, we argue that engaging race and racism in solely theoretical terms runs the risk of muting the materiality of racism and racial oppression. Furthermore, we must be careful to avoid theoretical positions that assert the race concept to be meaningless because it lacks scientific validity and clarity.

In offering a critical analysis of White racism, it is important for certain ideas to be re-iterated. For example, we believe that an important discursive position is to recognize that racially defined experiences are social constructed through the perspectives of the knower (subjective knowledge) and an objective social reality. There are no illusions to White racism. Denying race and substituting race with the de-politicized term "ethnicity" will not make the problem of racism go away. Similarly, articulating multiple racisms does not diminish the powerful effect of White racism. No matter how hard we deny White racism, it continues to be key to the production and re-production of racial oppression, both in Western contexts and on a global scale. There is connection between race and racism in that the term *race* speaks of the power to define, *otherize* and categorize. Racism is the outward manifestation of that power. Furthermore, there are also social, political, cultural and intellectual meanings attributed to White racism; thus, no amount of intellectual gymnastics can deny that Whiteness carries considerable "currency" in our society. Because society is color-coded, the acknowledgment of racial differences per se is not the problem. The real issue rests in the mechanisms of power that construct and re-construct these differences within very specified and regulated interpretations of hierarchy and preference. Rather than deny race because it is not "scientifically valid," we must critique science for its inability to account for race.[53]

In speaking about White racist practices, our focus should not be on individual intent and motivations but, rather, on the social effects of such practices. As White racism manifests in the effects of specific, historical, social and institutional practices, Ungerleider (1996) asserts that we must see racism in both the intentional and unintentional denial of privilege.[54] The use of language, culture and religion as important markers of discrimination and differentiation, as well as the emergence of cultural racism, signifies privileging practices of White racism. As we continue to articulate and act on the intersections of difference (race, gender, class, sexuality, etc.), it is important for us to recognize the saliency of race and the permanence of White racism. As Fine et al. (1997) point out, raced and colonial hierarchies are embedded in institutions, and everyday racism "travels like a virus through institutional structures, policies, practices, relationships, fights and identities."[55] In its more contemporary form, from an economic viewpoint, White supremacy is manifested in the annals of major national and transnational corporations, international monetary systems, and the functioning of global capital. It is also manifested in the cries of millions of starving children, impoverished southern peoples and the plight of the majority of the earth's population. In the first half of the twentieth century, Fanon had observed:

> The West's opulence has been founded on slavery, it has been nourished with the blood of slaves and it comes directly from the soil and the subsoil of that underdeveloped world. The wellbeing and progress of Europe have been built up with the sweat and the dead bodies of Africans, Arabs, Indians and the Yellow races.[56]

Today, in the age of rapid globalization and internationalization, Fanon's description rings true. As a matter of fact, it has become much, much worse. While the triumphant march of the global capital is leaving millions of southern peoples in a state of destitute, starvation and extreme impoverishment, the colorful TV cameras focus on kindhearted Christian missionaries who are out there in Africa and Asia feeding the world's hungry children, tending to the needs of the sick, the elderly and the dying. Whereas the old missionaries had seen it as their sacred duty to Christianize these infidels and to save their souls by all means necessary, these new missionaries are baptizing the African children into Christianity by offering them warm food, clothing, sanitation and "modern" education. At the same time, the multinational media brings to the bedrooms of millions of White people the image of starving children from Sudan, Ethiopia and Eritrea. The dire problematic that will undoubtedly face us in the near future is that these images of "victim" and "savior," "good" and "bad," threaten to creep into the psyche of the world's indigene, as the new colonials fix their gaze upon us.

Through this *language of domination,* the disciplinary machine of White racism expands through a "tightly scripted narrative of differential power," to integrate the entire world into one frame of racialized knowledge—that of the colonial subject fraught with duality and alienation.[57] With the internationalization of a commodity culture and the widespread effects of the world market, these "New Colonials" rapidly encircled their arms in a stranglehold over the world's sense of identity, inserting powerful images of the "New Other" into the universal consciousness. Everyday, reports of the latest cultural incursions speak to the ever-expanding scope of our headlong rush for globalization. However, in this unchecked charge, we watch our identities re-assess, re-form and re-negotiate themselves relative to the "guiding" model of the Western world. See, for example, Fox News' coverage of a study that links a rise in bulimia/anorexia in Fiji to the arrival of TV and the transmission of shows like *Melrose Place* and *Bay Watch*.[58] Or perhaps the disturbing image of Canadian Professional Wrestler Brett Hart being cheered and "worshipped" by South Asian schoolchildren during a promotional trip to India—he said they viewed him, "like a God."[59]

This image of the Colonial master surveying his outlying territories and subjects has been deeply embedded within our silenced and disciplined identities. It is a narrative that forms and shapes our collective histories, while always working to ensure an innate disparity between the other and the self. It is a unidirectional relationship in which dialogue is abandoned in favour of instructive and constructive monologues that seek to ensure a divide between oppressed and oppressor. As taken up in previous discussions, that dialectic also extends, or should we say inverts, into the interplay of self—other—*other*, on the stage of identity.[60] Our oppressor sees himself as the superior savior of the poor, uneducated and starving masses: the benev-olent patriarch whose "coffee money" could save the lives of a number of children in Africa and Asia. These images re-inforce the notion that those starving Africans are perishing due to their own laziness, backwardness and incompetence. The fact that the north owes its prosperity and opulence to the subjugation and colonization of southern peoples does not register in the psyche of our oppressor.

Parallel to this economic "superiority," a psychological and moral domi-nation is also constantly reinforced and perpetuated within the White mentality and as a result in the mind of the oppressed, who see ourselves through their eyes. We are disciplined to believe that the entire world depends on the charity of the White race and that it is they who work to resolve the planet's misery, to feed and clothe "the wretched of the earth." In spite of the White man's claim to principles of equality and equity, the image of Black bodies as the inferior *other* has not changed in his psyche. As Lorimer (1987) pointed out, "Whenever the Victorians considered the posi-tion of Blacks, they could conjure up an image of a patient suffering slave, a comic minstrel, or a cruel lustful savage to fit the particular situation."[61] Now, with the international appeal of the multibillion dollar sporting industry, images of energetic basketball player, boxer and wrestler have been added to the already existing images. White power is alive and present in all aspects of contemporary life, just as it has been throughout much of modern history. We began this chapter with a quotation from Joel Kovel's (1988) work *White Racism: A Psychohistory*. In it he talks about two kinds of White racists: the hate-filled, rock-throwing, name-calling lower-class racial bigot and the silent, sophisticated, powerful patriarch—the man in control. According to Kovel, it is this "unseen" patriarch who has institutionalized racism and overtly/covertly egged-on the hate-filled rock-throwing bigot.[62] We would further assert that both of these racists exercise power and avail themselves of the mechanisms of that power in every aspect of their lives.

For those with White skin, power and privilege are birthrights that must be recognized and declined in order to reject and manage the personal potential for racism. But as we have discussed, for our oppressors, race and racism are disturbing, embarrassing and unsettling issues. Thus, for the most part at least, the issue of racism will remain taboo.[63] Because critical dialogues engaging issues of race and racism hold an "unspeakable" quality and aura, the taboo is translated into discourses that deny difference and mute all things racial. Such strategies, be they deliberate or inadvertent, work to solidify oppressive power and privilege by preventing our ability and desire to question our state of oppression or their state of privilege. Privileged group members have the implicit option to ignore oppression and not speak out against it, an advantage evidenced in their ability to often "forget" about race and racism for a while, whether unconsciously or consciously, through silence or inaction. In these ways, White people who claim to be allies in the project can take a break from the frustration and despair of anti-racism work and face no consequences in doing so. Olsson (1997) states that one of the basic privileges of being White is the freedom to retreat from and forget about issues of racism.[64] People of color do not have that option by virtue of our skin color and the nature of racism.[65] This "White" option to ignore oppression in combination with being part of the societal norm means that the holder of privilege usually does not see his privilege. What better way to solidify one's hold on power than by challenging and refuting the "realities" of that self-same power base?

CHAPTER FIVE
The Materiality of Racism: Democracy and Dissonance

I used to think things such as employment equity (in effect, hiring quotas for non-Whites) was probably a good idea—until I began to think about it. The more I thought about it, the less sense it made. For instance, who is non-White?...Does it make any sense to favour the children of well-heeled Chinese immigrants over those of working-class Portuguese immigrants...? It's a bit dangerous to ask these questions. Old acquaintances shun you. You begin to get congratulatory calls from people who sound alarmingly like late-movie Nazis...So I was interested to find other non-Nazis with similar, albeit private, qualms. Perhaps the most notable is the Caribbean immigrant (she doesn't want her name used) who has risen to a senior position in the employment equity industry and who has concluded that the real fissures in society are based on class rather than race.

> —Thomas Walkom, *Does Race Really Matter at U of T?*[1]

If anti-racism has become a corrective educational practice for some, it is because social relations and practices of domination have for far too long been presented as the 'normal' and 'fair' way of doing things. It is this sense of 'normality' and 'fairness' that anti-racism challenges...To refuse to promote anti-racism is to engage in the politics of negation. Blinded by racist myopia, a few individuals are revisiting the discourses of colonial racism and propagating hate and resentment.

> —George J. Sefa Dei, *Anti-Racism Education: Theory and Practice*[2]

Competing discourses are what's at issue here. Within Western contexts, the dogma of democracy plays host to a variety of interconnected discourses that work to sustain a firm denial of racial oppression within both institutional and mainstream sites in spite of material proofs to the contrary. Democratic ideology and discourse speaks through cultural emblems of freedom, fair-play and merit in ways that rarely deny the existence of racism, but position it as a marginal matter and certainly unworthy of the implementation of ameliorative programs or practices. Moreover, within mainstream discourse, the 'reality' of racism is always positioned in and through sites of privilege, to be a problem of the 'radical right,' and not as an issue to be taken up on a societal scale. Walkom's piece is particularly telling in that his views reflect some of the main problematics that face the anti-racist project. It is interesting that he mentions "late-movie Nazis" in his editorial because "overt racists" are the least of our problems in that we can usually see or hear them coming. In contrast, subtle, more disguised racists prove to be far more problematic because they speak to us from sites of supposed safety and support. Their attacks take us unaware, unprepared and their "supposedly" apolitical worldviews deceptively mark and position us as *other*, as deviant, and as solely responsible for our pain, marginality and frustration.

That being said we employ this excerpt from Walkom's editorial precisely because, as he asserts, he is a non-Nazi. But are his views anti-racist—or more problematically, are they racist? Even the term he uses in self-defense is problematic. Non-racist—what does that imply? Dei (1996) establishes firmly, in concert with much anti-racist praxis, that we, all of us, are either racist or anti-racist. There is no middle ground. Either we actively support, promote and/or condone racism and oppression, or we stand against it. Because anti-racism is an oppositional praxis that functions to contest the oppressive relations of the status quo, opting to do nothing in the face of racism means that one silently collaborates within the oppressive milieu. The continuum consists of two diametrically opposed points and while the shades of gray that lie between speak to dedication, involvement and ideology, all points along the continuum speak to one or the other. Claiming an affiliation with some third group under the heading of non-racist implies that one chooses to do nothing and that inaction in the face of suffering and subjugation speaks volumes as to one's personal politics and ideology. In fact, it is precisely because Walkom's arguments are so banal, so commonsense, and so liberal on the surface that we engage his editorial as particularly poignant and useful in these discussions.

These are obviously not the words of a Nazi, nor are they the words of someone who "consciously" works to oppress or discriminate. Simply put, these are the commonsense notions of a White male speaking from his personal experience in Western contexts and trying to make sense out of the world in/through that experience. But like so many other well-intentioned people with skin color privilege, Walkom neglects to recognize the one simple truth of such discussions—racism is real—and in that reality, there are real material consequences. What does it mean that he so casually negates the importance of race in favour of a class-based analysis of social stratification? Walkom's words introduce us to just a few of the more common mainstream arguments that seek to position people of color as both deviant and ultimately responsible for their own outcast/oppositional state:

- In a democratic society like ours, racism cannot exist
- Everyone experiences discrimination now and then
- If only minority groups would try to fit in and adapt to "our" society, they would experience less differential treatment
- Racism is about attitudes, so multiculturalism helps by teaching tolerance
- If everybody were treated equally, racism wouldn't exist
- Employment Equity Programs are racism in reverse
- Race is not as important as other factors like class

In functioning to explain away and deny racism and its impact, such arguments minimize the offensive and intrusive nature of oppressive experiences by maneuvering us to believe that we are the ones with the problem. While racism and racialized experiences function relative to "difference," these rhetorical arguments mute that relationship by placing "difference" as unrelated to the social dynamics of success and failure. Racism has very real consequences for our physical, conceptual, physiological, emotional, psychological and spiritual engagements with the social world. Recognizing these connective tissues, we think it is crucial to address how our personal and social struggles in the everyday experience of racism are framed in relation to individual deficiency rather than social pathology.

The reality and impact of racism in the lives of people of color is often minimized when observations about the progression of our society and the current lack of racism are made (e.g., "there is no racism at my workplace"). It is true that the nature of racism has changed over the years; however, hearing a comment like this one should make you suspicious. There are many ways that racism can manifest itself in the workplace, some not so obvious at first glance. Perhaps there are no overt signs of racism—name-calling, put-downs, physical violence, but there are other more covert, less obvious ways that racism impacts the workplace. It is often difficult to identify or prove racism in these spaces because oppressive and discriminatory hiring practices, performance evaluations, and promotions tend to be constructed in subtle ways that are not easily named or identified as such. Unless the particular space has been carefully examined with respect to practices, power relations and structural elements, saying "There is no racism at my workplace" is a naive statement based in power, privilege and/or denial. When most *colorblind* spaces are probed with a critical eye, it is common to uncover the reality that systemic racism and discrimination thrive in spaces that do not turn the gaze inward.

Echoing the sentiments of the "anonymous" *Caribbean immigrant* referenced by Walkom in his article, a South Asian woman interviewed by Karumanchery-Luik (1996) had similar thoughts about her "non-experience" of racism while working in a prestigious Toronto accounting firm.[3] Asserting that she had never really experienced racism at work, she went on to suggest that it was a positive atmosphere, untouched by issues of race and difference. However, as the interview continued and she was encouraged to critically interrogate the policies, practices and bodies at work in the firm, she began to recognize many structural and systemic elements of oppression that had previously been hidden to her. Upon closer scrutiny, she noted that all of the "head honchos" in the firm were White men and that the secretaries were predominantly females. She also pointed out that the majority of the cleaning staff and janitors were minorities while only five of the 130 professionals in the company were people of color. Interestingly, by the end of the interview, while she had come to recognize the structural and systemic oppression that was present in her workplace, she continued to maintain that she had not had any direct racist experiences herself. In fact, she made this claim just before explaining that she felt more accepted at her place of employment because she was very "North American":

> If I were very different, if I represented a [different] culture to people, I would not fit in with my firm and I don't think it would be very easy to work [there]…if you looked to them as if representing a different culture. I don't even know if it would be the way you dressed, but maybe the way you acted…not aware of popular culture…I think it works to the disadvantage of a lot of minorities.[4]

While she recognized the disadvantage of being identified as "different" and she spoke about the privilege she attained by "fitting in," she was still unable to make the connection between her experience of "passing" and the realities of racism and oppression at the firm. Would she experience racism at work if she came to work wearing a sari? If so, does that mean that her everyday experience of "passing" reflects a non-racist environment or a policed and regulated experience of belonging? Furthermore, while her light skin color and ability to blend culturally helps to establish a *relative* safe space for her, many people of color do not have the option, the privilege or for some, the desire to pass. Racial or ethnic markers (e.g., non-White/ European skin color, facial features or accents) are not (easily) altered and have all been linked to discriminatory practices in the workplace. Moreover, shouldn't we be able to retain aspects of culture, whether it be clothing style, food or linguistic difference and still expect to be treated equitably. What are the assumptions and value judgments that go along with those kinds of expectations? In asserting that she hasn't experienced racism at work even while detailing the above discriminatory relations of power and privilege, she is implicitly suggesting that her ability/desire/attempt to pass circumvents any overt experience of racism that might be directed toward her. However, what does it say about an organization/society that covertly policies acceptance, access and potential relative to a White/North American frame of normalcy? How can she say that she is not impacted by racism at work when she realizes that her acceptance and privilege are tentative at best and framed relative to her ability to be "as White as possible." Is this not a text example of racism in the workplace?

Again, key to many of these arguments is the core belief that there is no real salience to skin color—that racism is much like other socially structured disabilities that speak to individualized hardships (e.g., racism is the same as other discriminations). However, because other discriminations do not function in and through the same socio-historical contexts that structure racism as oppressive, they cannot and must not be equated as such. The kind of discriminations experienced by White European immigrants are fundamentally different from racism in several significant ways, not the least of which is the obviously unrelated impact of skin color bias. While it is true that White people can be discriminated against based on a whole host of human characteristics and differences other than race, it is important to recognize that race cannot be transcended like ethnicity, culture and language. In a 1996 study, Karumanchery examined the nature of generational decline in relation to racialized peoples and processes of assimilation and acculturation in Western contexts. He found that skin color would continue to position racialized people as *other* long after markers of "ethnicity" such as in-group territory, endogamy, community involvement and religious affiliation had faded along lines of generational decline.[5] Skin color, as a clear visual marker of difference, positions and frames racialized peoples as *foreign, immigrant* and *alien* long before other features can signal their Diasporic roots. In contrast, first generation European immigrants are hardly distinguishable from the dominant group until they speak, and even then, only if they are audibly different.

In moving to a discussion of linguistic discrimination, we recognize the existence of a hierarchy in which European accents are normalized and framed as preferable in contrast to those of the *other*. For example, in the

Western world, British, French and Italian accents are romanticized and idealized while *other* accents, such as those belonging to Asian and other Southern peoples are ridiculed as fodder for mainstream stereotyping and racist jokes. In their association to specific races and ethnicities, accents are positioned on a hierarchical continuum in which those closest to White-European paradigms are established as the most desirable. Such linguistic hierarchies clearly illustrate that race, ethnicity and culture stand as markers of difference and more pointedly, as signifiers for differential treatment. However, this reality does not quite mesh with the democratic ideals dogmatically glorified in Western contexts. As a result, we invariably have our arguments re-directed with counterclaims that seek to mute the relevance of such differential treatments. By offering up examples of "otherized" European accents also satirized in the media and in society at large (e.g., Scottish and Irish accents), these oppressive voices effectively sidestep the realities that circumscribe the differences that frame "otherized" accents. As discussed extensively throughout this work, such rhetorical arguments fail to take context, history and power into consideration when comparing these accents and the differential treatments relative to each.

It is important to re-iterate that such investigations of differential and oppressive hierarchies are dangerous because they strike at the very heart of the democratic sense of individuality, morality, fairness and justice. More-over, the everyday/commonplace denial and muting of racial oppression is further bolstered by the mainstream refusal to acknowledge that race, ethnicity, gender, etc., are in fact guiding factors in the determining of success in our supposedly *merit-based* society. An acceptance of this oppressive reality is specifically problematic for those who claim hard-fought positions in the upper economic stratum of the Western world. While the problematics of racism continue to surface as a powerful reality in North American contexts, that "reality" continues to be challenged and denied in the mainstream. Within such frameworks, the lived reality of racism as asserted by people of color almost always stands in contrast to reality as defined within and through sites of privilege. The result is that racially oppressed peoples continue to live through and identify everyday racism, while those with skin color privilege continue to dismiss that evidence as attitudinally based and generally inconclusive. The normalizing effects of these racial–racist discourses work within and through hegemonic conditions to bind notions of difference and hierarchy into critical domains of culture. In this way, a moral, ethical and intellectual leadership develops via a sort of *manufactured consent*.[6] The insidious nature of these discourses are reflected in their ability to constitute the oppressor as rightfully dominant, while informing and constructing the experience of the oppressed as rightfully dominated. It is an interplay that effectively maneuvers us to be implicated in our own oppression.

In interrogating these normalizing effects, Henry et al. (1995) employ the theoretical framework of *democratic racism* in order to problematize and investigate the binary value sets that support everyday rationalizations of racism relative to the general tenets of liberal democracy. Following their work, we too assert that democratically racist discourses propose that racism should be dealt with, if and only if, the present social and political structures are not changed. So within these discursive and ideological confines, initiatives geared toward equity and social justice are commonly found to lack public support because they tend to require changes to policy and practice via State intervention. The contention arises in that such interruptions of the status quo work in direct opposition to dominant interests and are therefore positioned as conflicting with the basic ideals of liberal democracy. Ironically, such changes to policy and practice are positioned in the mainstream as arising in *special interest politics*—a maneuver that manages to effectively sidestep the systematic/systemic subjugation and oppression of entire under-classes of racialized and marginalized peoples.[7]

We take the political stance that contrary to much commonsense thought, democratic values as they are presently engaged in Western contexts do not necessarily function in opposition to oppressive structures framed in notions of authority and control. After all, we must ask ourselves why we are increasingly finding that the intersecting and often allied rhetoric of bureaucratic efficiency, "bottom-line" money management and "democratic values" continue to shift social and political agendas away from equity concerns and toward the normalized interests of power, privilege and the status quo. Interestingly, relationships that arise in such democratic spheres are framed as, and positioned to be, *apolitical bi-products* of an *apolitical system*. However, we assert that such democratic dogma has played host to a variety of interconnected and often contesting discourses that effectively mute the oppressive reality in which we live. But before entering into a more protracted discussion of how "democratic racism" functions to reflect the interests of an increasingly globalized socio-economic sphere, it is both important and legitimate to first examine how and why the notion of "democracy" exists in such contested theoretical and practical space.

In attempting to clarify the apparent incongruities that run between these conflicting value sets, we feel it is useful to distinguish between *democracy as governmental form* and *democracy as a way of life.* In making this distinction, we also think it is important to explain that when we (the authors) discuss democracy in these contexts, we are considering how it arose in the North American cultural landscape—and more specifically in the socio-political landscape of the United States. North American models of democracy and democratic values have always been set within two competing conceptions of democracy: the private and the public. Portelli (2001) clarified the nature of this division:

> Theorists have distinguished between participatory, public and critical democracy, on one hand, and representative, privatized and managed/market democracy on the other hand. It has been argued that while the former notion of democracy is associated with equity, community, creativity and taking difference seriously, the latter is protectionist and marginalist and leads to an extreme form of individualism and spectator citizenship.[8]

These two competing ideologies continue to play a major role in the formation and re-formation of Western social politics, policy and practice. The relations of democratic racism suggest that dominant strains of Western political thought and institutional practice are so couched in the "mythos" of liberal democracy that notions of equity, community and social justice are becoming increasingly minimized and muted. It is a carefully managed system through which *the present* and *the promise* of democracy are both cautiously policed. To make this point, we turn again to Portelli's work on democracy in education:

> Although Philosophers of education with different educational and political beliefs have argued for the importance of investigating the relationship between democracy and education, the differences in their ideologies have obviously resulted in differences in how the relationship is conceived. While, for example, some have focused on 'education *for* democracy', others have argued for 'democracy *in* education.'[9]

So extrapolating from Portelli's argument to our discussion of democratic racism, the following questions help us to interrogate the functionality of democratic values in today's ever-globalizing socio-political sphere:

- What kind of social policy is appropriate for a democracy?
- Is there room in our society to develop the character usually associated with the democratic way of life?
- What kind of values ought to influence policy and practice in a democracy?
- What kind of work is required to allow democracy to flourish?

These questions serve to highlight some of the intrinsic problematics associated with privatized notions of democracy. Again, working from Portelli's
focus on the difference between democracy *in* and *for*, we recognize that
working toward democratic ends does not necessarily make sense without
first infusing your work with democratic values. By this we mean to say that
while working for democracy does not necessarily exclude democratic
practices, there is generally too much emphasis placed on how socio-political
means might be employed to obtain/maintain a democracy. And once again,
we are left with the burning question: How do we define democracy in this
context, how is it practiced and performing?[10]

As put forth by Sehr (1997) contemporary engagements with democracy
and democratic values in Western contexts tend to reflect a privatized
interpretation of democracy as "our ability to compete freely for a job, and
then use our income to secure life's necessities, along with whatever luxuries
we can afford."[11] This conception of democracy in its near disregard for
social and political content has been carefully managed and filtered into
mainstream calls for more highly reliable, centralized and monitored organizations. Therefor, socio-political policy and practice that pursue individual
rights and self-interest speak to the underlying Utilitarian philosophy that
society is best served by addressing the interests of individuals. Regardless
of the intentions behind this ideology, the result is a philosophy that engages the
social world through the lens and language of market economy. A critical
interrogation of this *privatized democratic mentality* reveals a complex discursive interplay that functionally portrays the market as both necessary and
natural while painting emancipatory and social justice reforms as self-serving,
inefficient and ultimately, the concern of special-interest groups. Within this
framework, success and failure are delineated strictly on the basis of merit,
but as we clarified earlier, equality and equity are not the same thing. In this
and other similar ways, market-driven relations of power in Western contexts
serve the interests of the most powerful in society while equity considerations are sidelined as neither paramount nor central to the *main business of
a democratic society*. As suggested by Benhabib (1993), a democratic state
must be wary of elevating economic rights and capital concerns to the point
that they curtail the rights of other competing interests.[12]

We assert that the application of this *privatized democracy* functions to
maintain an ideology that alienates and deters certain bodies from successful
engagements in the socio-political sphere. Within these discursive and
ideological confines, policies and initiatives intended to promote equity and

social justice are commonly met with distaste from the public because they tend to question the role of individual and private economic activity. Furthermore, reforms that look to interrupt the status quo function in direct opposition to privileged interests and as a result they tend to be framed as subversive and contrary to these *dominant* conceptions of democracy. As clarified earlier, today most North Americans experience democracy in almost entirely economic terms. This experience of democracy in relation to market-based notions of freedom has arisen through hegemonic relations to stand as irreproachable and almost beyond the ability to criticize. And through hegemonic relations of force, the disparities, injustices and inequities of the system have been naturalized and normalized into the everyday. Because Western society is dedicated to the philosophical proposition that individuals are rewarded solely on the basis of merit and that no individual or group is ever singled out for discriminatory treatment, the truth of oppression is functionally sidestepped while appearing consistent with the discourse of liberal democracy. Again, in these democratically racist contexts, those who experience oppression and suffer its material–non-material consequences are positioned as somehow responsible for their state of being.

Building on Dahl's (1998) assertions, we contend that the likelihood of developing a socially just and democratic society drastically improves if *all citizens* subscribe to, support, contribute to *and benefit* from the ideals, values and practices of that democracy—anything short of such an inclusive and equitable reading of democracy would prove to be problematic at best.[13] However, the discourse of White privilege in concert with the discourse of meritocracy works to disregard and mute arguments that place race and difference as fundamental factors in the development of what has become an oppressive democratic sphere. The problematic and unfortunate bi-product of these oppressive relations of powers is that the role of race and difference in social stratification is rarely interrogated with respect to questions of (a) access to resources (b) the socio-cultural push to succeed or (c) the ability to rise above the glass ceiling. Rather, democratically framed discourses attribute racial stratification to cultural problems, the refusal of minorities to fit into Western society and other conventional explanations that seek to pathologize the oppressed.[14] The ideology of democratic racism, in its insidious nature, allows people to maintain conflicting value sets by minimizing the conflicts that arise within these contested spaces. Through these formulations, democratic racism permits people to maintain racist beliefs and behaviours while appearing to hold a positive notion of democratic values.[15]

A number of racially oppressive forms/practices have developed under the umbrella of democratic racism. Relative to the ever-changing realities of our Diasporic age, racism as ideology, discourse and practice has needed to evolve into more practically applicable relations of power, force and domination. In Western contexts specifically, our multi-racial and multi-ethnic societies have seen the rise of *racisms* that distance themselves from biological arguments for domination in favour of belief systems that support and bolster social and cultural rationalizations for discrimination.[16] When critically investigated, we can see these new modes of racist theory and practice played out differently in varying contexts. Essed (1991) argues that these new oppressive forms signal a *culturalization of racism* through which skin color is being replaced by less incendiary markers of difference such as culture and ethnicity. Importantly, these shifts arise because there continues to be a reluctance to identify race as the basic determinant of White power and privilege in relation to the disem-powerment of racialized peoples.[17]

To follow from Essed's assertion, the strategic use of language allows racist discourse to convey the same oppressive meanings through the use of cultural rather than racial markers. Rather than focusing on skin color variations this specific notion of a *new racism* expresses itself through the negative evaluation of non-White cultures. For example, the custom of arranging marriages is vilified and positioned as "deviant" and inferior in Western discourse, while the tradition of dating leading to marriage is placed as intrinsically "correct." Along these lines, racist discourses that conceptual-ize Black violence and criminality may do so now under the "liberal" and "politically correct" guise of discussing cultural dilemmas—"Of course the fact that they are violent and usually criminals has nothing to do with their race, it is because they come from *broken* families and their culture is very relaxed when it comes to the notion of hard work."[18] By pathologizing "deviant" cultural patterns as the primary cause of racial tensions, "new racisms" avoid the necessity to interrogate privileged culpability in the rise and maintenance of oppressive social formations. Moreover, normalizing discourses are employed in these contexts to place criminal behaviour, low academic achievement, poverty, discrimination in the workplace and other social problems as culturally based and therefore only addressable by the oppressed and their communities.

Similarly, Gaertner and Dovidio (1981) propose the notion of an *aversive racism* that manifests in those with skin color privilege who are "well intentioned."[19] Within this framework, aversive racists appear to have a genuine belief in egalitarianism—a set of beliefs that are reflected in their open affirmations that racism's "real" deleterious social effects need to be addressed. As alluded to in Walkom's (2000) editorial, these "non-racists" openly oppose intentionally destructive, violent or discriminatory behaviours and can rarely be confused with "late-movie Nazis." However, theirs would also likely be the mainstream voices decrying the implementation of government initiatives that might ameliorate the material consequences of racism. These aversive racists enjoy their skin color privileges but truly think themselves to be prejudice free. Problematically, while they take on this non-racist stance, their actions/inactions disguise a firm set of problematic beliefs that subscribe to fundamentally racist notions which are anything but apolitical.[20] Furthermore, when aversive racists take positive steps toward equity and social change, those actions tend to arise from a desire to promote a "non-racist" self-image rather than from a desire to either advance egalitarian values or to combat racism.[21]

Henry et al. also address a third aspect of democratic racism that functions through the use of explicitly color-blind rhetorical rationalizations for the maintenance of the status quo. This notion of a *symbolic racism* speaks to the practices and value systems of those privileged who assert a belief in equal rights and opportunities for people of color while also criticizing those same minorities for actively pursuing these rights. Through the use of abstract ideas and symbols, racialized peoples become associated with certain types of intrinsic behaviours and proclivities that in turn speak to our marginality as deserved.[22] By operating through symbols as opposed to outward and obvious acts of personal discrimination, these symbolic racists may practice everyday racism in ways that are never construed as overtly racist. This symbolic racism may manifest as open opposition to welfare, affirmative action and employment equity programs on grounds that are rooted in racist ideology but justified through political and economic rhetoric.[23] The material "reality" of racism as arising through these discriminatory and oppressive forms invariably impacts on our lived experience in the everyday. But to be very specific, these subversive and covert forms of racism work to regulate our life chances, our social and political opportunities and our access to resources. In and through these far more "invisible" forms of democratic racism, we see the lynchpin that holds systemic racism together in contemporary Western contexts. No longer relying on the fallacy of biological determinism these new racisms employ a more functional and intellectualized brand of oppression that infiltrates our workplaces, governments, educational, legal and healthcare systems by constructing a systemically charged and socially operationalized oppression.

These theoretical formulations force us to question the equitable nature of systems that have always stood for fairness and justice. Do they truly function within the democratically defined frameworks as set out by the mainstream, or are they innately discriminatory and racially oppressive? Case in point, while employment equity programs function to engender workplace equity by directly re-dressing the effects of structural and systemic discrimination, many people continue to oppose these initiatives as so much "reverse discrimination." Such policies, in their proactive anti-oppressive character, are positioned by privilege as being undemocratic, unfair and ultimately a threat to individual freedom.[24] Thus policies like employment equity as strategies for social change are rarely framed positively in the mainstream. Rather democratically racist rhetoric always positions such strategies as "reverse racism" that seeks to punish White people for the crimes of their ancestors. These perspective fail to acknowledge either the long history of racism that infuses our societies or the impact of those relations on the life chances and opportunities of racialized peoples in the present. In order to answer these problematics, we feel it important to first address the pointed issue of framing oppression as intrinsically and defin-itively distinct from other forms of disadvantage or adversity.

Frye (1983) cautions that we must be careful not to stretch the word "oppression" into meaninglessness forms that include any and all human experiences of limitation, suffering or harm because we can be disadvan-taged without being oppressed.[25] Thus, in order to understand whether a particular suffering or limitation is a manifestation of oppressive relations, we have to look at the various situational and contextual specificities relevant in each given situation. Frye explains:

> ...one has to see if (the particular harm or limitation) is part of an enclosing structure of forces and barriers which tends to the immobilization and reduction of a group or category of people. One has to look at how the barrier or force fits with others and to whose benefit or detriment it works. As soon as one looks at examples, it becomes obvious that not everything which frustrates or limits a person is oppressive and not every harm or damage is due to or contributes to oppression.[26]

We often hear this from those with skin color privilege: "It's not just people of color that experience discrimination, White European immigrants have experienced it as well. In fact, everyone experiences discrimination now and then." This statement makes the assumption that everyone can be equally victimized while ignoring the differences that run between racism which is based on systemically and socially constructed barriers of force and other discriminations which are regulated via less material factors. For example, as discussed earlier, our educational systems, school officials, curricula and pedagogy are framed as both fair and unbiased; thus, educational success is said to be reflective of individual ability and merit. Much of this thinking becomes solidified through the unique authority and legitimacy of education as an official governmentally sanctioned and supported institution. However, a critical examination of educational practices reveals their implication in the systemic production and re-production of racial oppression. As an institution that functionally re-produces the social relations of economic and social power, schools at present, work to legitimate systemic inequity by allocating resources to some, while covertly curtailing them for others. Such hegemonic practices work to ensure that educational practices and environments reflect the racist, sexist and homophobic ideology found in the dominant culture.

The oppressive nature of racism in our educational systems impacts on racially minoritized students in a number of ways: among these are (a) the administration's lack of response to racist incidents in schools; (b) the racist or racialized attitudes, expectations and practices of teachers; (c) Eurocentric curricula; (d) the streaming of minority students into non-academic, non-matriculation programs; and (e) the lack of representation of minority teachers as role models.[27] Unlike the moments of overt racial harassment, which do stand as fundamentally painful and detrimental features of school life for both minoritized students and teachers, these less in-your-face racisms carry the potential to implicitly *racialize, otherize* and *oppress.*[28] As suggested by Karumanchery-Luik (1992) among others, teachers' expectations of student ability have powerful mediating influences on self-concept, hope for the future and personal/academic success.[29]

Research shows that processes of student stereotyping and labeling are prominent among even those teachers who profess attitudes of colorblindness—suggesting that such attitudes need to be critically examined. It is entirely problematic that these supposedly colorblind educators refuse to recognize the fundamental impact that differences in race and ethnicity have on the learning processes of racially marginalized youth.[30] Conceding that racially minoritized youth are significantly affected by these power dynamics, it becomes important to acknowledge that pretenses to colorblindness serve only to further bolster the oppressive effects that functionally otherize, marginalize and traumatize us. Ironically, while professing a colorblind approach to education, processes of stereotyping and labeling have become covertly formalized in/through the common practice of "streaming." Here students are assessed relative to supposedly "neutral" criteria and then correspondingly placed into "appropriate" academic levels. Problematically, studies have clearly shown that these processes are fraught with racial and cultural biases that work to the detriment of minority students.[31] As immigrant, racially minoritized, working-class and female students are streamed into lower level as well as non-matriculation programs, these "neutral" placements function to significantly limit educational choices and opportunities for marginalized youth.

In further discussing the implication of these subversive forms of racism as they relate to educational issues, research clearly suggests that we need to engage in a more pointed examination of the "hidden curriculum" that silently disciplines marginalized students. These unseen classroom relations function to sustain capitalist logic and rationality by incorporating processes of socialization that engender stratified skills, attitudes and values to students of different classes, races and genders.[32] By constantly re-inforcing and re-inscribing oppressive patterns into the everyday experience of schooling, these systemic racisms silently and covertly discipline and position students to maintain and perpetuate the existing hierarchy and authority of the status quo. In these ways, schools re-produce relationships of dominance and sub-ordination in both the economic sphere and society in general.[33]

When examining the role of education in the positioning of racialized subjects, it becomes clear that the effects of the streaming process extend well beyond school borders. For example, since jobs with higher levels of income and status most commonly require higher levels of education, students who are streamed into non-matriculation courses will find their opportunities for economic advancement slowed if not stunted. In this way, systems that employ such inobtrusive methods of color-coded streaming function to limit the abilities and potentials of minoritized youth to transcend their racially stigmatized and socio-economic backgrounds.[34] The resulting reproduction of stratification and inequity in the marketplace suggests that important connections must be made between education levels, labour force participation rates and income. In our effort to make these connections, we take the next few pages to conduct a cursory examination of some comparative Canadian statistics as they relate to issues of race and socio-economic stratification.[35] Importantly, we employ Canadian, American and British statistics almost interchangeably in this work because we recognize that relations of force and power tend to mirror/overlap each other across Western contexts. We contend that these various findings can be generally extrapolated to speak across Canadian, American and British national boundaries and into other similar Western socio-economic spheres.

In 1990, according to Statistics Canada, the average yearly income for full-time work in the province of Ontario was $36,031. However, when controlled for race, that figure dropped substantially as racialized groups were found to earn approximately $6,300 less per year than their White counterparts. Moreover, if we take race and gender into consideration when examining this wage gap, we find that women of color earned only 61% of what White males earned. These disparities appear to be racialized as well as gendered in ways that have real material effects for the oppressed. Interestingly, when we look at these effects in concert with other problematic socio-economic disparities such as labor force participation, the picture becomes even more intensely troubling.

Using the same data sets to examine workforce participation trends, we found that the average rate of 69.6% stood in slight contrast to the racial minority rate of 72.1% for that same year. However, we find it noteworthy to mention that Filipinos, Blacks and South Asians displayed some of the highest rates in these racialized groupings at averages of 81.5%, 75.2% and 74.5%, respectively. Now if we expand this brief analysis to consider the intersections of race and gender, the disparities become even starker and more troubling. When race and gender were controlled for, the average total participation rate of 62.1% was markedly different from those of Filipino (81.7%), Black (71.3%) and South Asian women (66.4%). Traditionally, labour force participation rates have been interpreted as being directly reflective of employment opportunities. However, as suggested by Woo (1985) disparities in participation rates might just as easily be explained by job market inequalities and/or the economic necessity to compensate for relatively low wages.[36] We would contend that when race and gender are factored into the equation, it becomes increasingly problematic to interpret high participation rates as indicative of "better" employment opportunities. When placed relative to the realities of income disparity and the oppressive relations of power as examined thus far, these arguments become spurious at best. In analyzing these disparities in the division of labour, Glenn (1992) argues that the U.S. labour market works to ensure that minoritized workers are relegated to low-status, low-wage, dead-end, marginalized jobs. After all, while these racialized groups display higher participation rates than the total population, they also continue to earn less than their White counterparts. Like Glenn, we would argue that Western labour markets are generally stratified along raced and gendered lines and as alluded to in the above analysis, systemic barriers function to prevent the upward mobility of certain marginalized peoples.[37]

Building on this discussion, we must begin to trouble the rhetoric of today's liberal democracies in their efforts to support existing images of Western labour markets as fair, equitable and based in merit. Functioning within these hegemonic systems, the discourse of democratic racism molds the marginalized into a compliant and complacent pool of "workers" fully circumscribed within/by the myths of individualism and meritocracy. Importantly, these problematics extend far beyond market lines and into every other facet of the social schema. Case in point, critical examinations of Canadian, American and British healthcare systems have revealed problematics of discrimination and inequity to be systemically supported and reproduced. Moreover, these oppressive problematics invariably work to regulate and establish how "care" is administered and, in turn, who has access to resources. In this light, the connective lines that run between oppression, illness and the distribution of health services in Western contexts cannot be overstated. Similar to Sherwin (1992), we contend that social power, privilege and oppression are central mediating factors in (a) how marginalized peoples perceive healthcare (b) whether we can access it and perhaps, most importantly, (c) who needs to access it.[38]

We place a particular emphasis on illness and assessment because the intersecting and interlocking of oppressions serves to position certain bodies at risk of experiencing disproportionate shares of mental and physical illness. After all, how can we continue to disregard the fact that in North America racialized people in general and women of color in particular are at a much higher risk of having life-threatening conditions than those with skin color privilege? For instance:

- African American women are four times more likely to die in childbirth and are twice as likely to die of hypertensive cardio-vascular disease than their White counterparts.
- African American women have three times the rate of high blood pressure and lupus than White women.
- Women of color in the United States, are more likely to die from breast cancer, even though they have lower rates of incidence than their White counterparts.[39]

Importantly, these types of disparate health statistics reveal vast inequities between the "center" and the "margins," even when socio-economic status is taken into consideration. To be clear on this point, even when income levels are the same for both Blacks and Whites, African Americans still experience higher rates of illness.[40] Also, these disparities extend far beyond treatment of illness and to the more banal experiences of oppressed people as they struggle to access a space and place in the healthcare system. Todd (1992) contended that skin color and socio-economic status were also indicative of poorer care and more hostile, less respectful clinician-patient relations.[41] It is important to recognize that healthcare professionals interpret medical practices through their own class, race and gender biases. Which is to say that social expectations and stereotypes invariably impact on the quality of care minority members receive. For instance, psychiatric and other health-care clinicians tend to pathologize cultural differences while labeling ethno-racial minorities with the more severe psychiatric disorders such as schizophrenia.[42] A prime example of this tendency to pathologize can be found in the everyday treatment of natives and First Nations communities in the health care system.

When White healthcare workers discuss the problem of alcoholism in First Nations communities and suggest abstinence as a solution, they fail to recognize how racist stereotypes are integrated into their worldview.[43] Images of *drunken Indians* who lack the discipline to curtail their alcoholism and other such commonsense interpretations of complex social phenomena fail to consider the devastating impact that the history of cultural genocide has had on Native communities. How do we engage the reality that Aboriginal histories, values and ways of life have been annihilated and that surviving populations have been left to struggle with the communal and intrapsychic realities of that inter-generational trauma? Are these lived experiences taken into consideration within mainstream healthcare sites or are Native dilemmas explained away through the use of democratically racist theories of *cultural deficiency* and individual failings? Problematically, mainstream healthcare workers tend not to support "alternative" or native healing practices, nor do they tend to consider these wide-ranging socio-historical pathologies when judging and disposing of their native "problem" patients.[44]

Similarly, gays, lesbians and transgendered people have also found intense discrimination and inequity to thrive within Western healthcare systems. Importantly, studies indicate that the fear espoused by gays and lesbians in this regard are not unfounded as significant numbers of hetero-sexual physicians, 40% in one study, admitted that they are often uncomfortable providing care to gay and lesbian patients.[45] Moreover, many homosexuals assert that, although their healthcare providers do not openly state their discomfort or disapproval, their behaviour reveals how they really feel. Common responses by heterosexual clinicians are: shock, nervousness, difficulty maintaining eye contact and difficulties engaging in dialogue—which in turn could lead to misdiagnosis or inadequate treatment.[46] Often-times, medical professionals may simply not be knowledgeable about the specific health needs of gays, lesbians and transgendered people. As discussed above relative to the issue of healthcare for Aboriginal peoples, these and other similar problematics mark the lives of the oppressed, but they do indeed have specific impacts for bodies that are differently marked and positioned. Again, the intersections of oppression being what they are, it is fundamentally important to further this discussion by looking at the salience of skin color as it relates to the specific role of visibility in oppressive relations of power. For example, while homosexuals often hide their sexual orientation from healthcare providers in fear that they will be rejected, ridiculed and disrespected if open about their sexual orientation, racially minoritized peoples are marked by skin color and so are unable to avoid such discriminatory treatment.[47] Again, this is not an attempt to establish a hierarchy of oppressions. Rather, it is a specific attempt to highlight the role of "difference" in relation to the fluid nature of power and privilege.

In furthering this discussion, studies in the fields of psychology and psychiatry have found that the very definition of mental health will vary dependent on intersections of race, class, gender and sexual orientation.[48] Definitions of mental illness and standards of mental health change over time relative to the values and belief systems of the privileged. For instance, until the 1980 revision of the *Diagnostic and Statistical Manual for Mental Disorders*, the American Psychiatric Association listed homosexuality as a mental illness.[49] Similarly, in the antebellum South, the mental illness known as "draptomania" was employed for Blacks who displayed an "uncontrol-lable urge to break out of slavery." Various researchers have shown that race and ethnicity directly impacts whether patients are labeled as mentally ill and, if so, the types of disorders with which they tend to be diagnosed. One such study found that mental health professionals were more likely to diagnose Blacks than Whites as violent, even when the cases that were being evaluated were identical in all other ways.[50]

When looking at existing investigations into racism in the field of mental health, it becomes clear that research and writing in the area of race-based psychological problems only began to take shape in the latter half of the 1990s. The field has begun to grow alongside the landmark studies by Jackson et al. (1996), which interrogated psychological distress among

Blacks in the United States, Klonoff, Landrine and Ullman's (1999) article on psychiatric symptoms among Blacks and, perhaps most notably, the introduction of a model for the systematic study of the physiological effects of perceived racism among African Americans by Clark et al. (1999).[51] However, while these works are noteworthy because they have at least cleared the table to discuss psychiatric and psychological issues relevant to peoples of color, they still engender certain problematics that hinder the advance of anti-racist research. As in the work of Nader, Dubrow and Stamm (1989), who addressed cultural differences and the treatment of trauma, or the work of Halligan and Yehuda (2000), who disregarded race in their comprehensive overview of risk factors for PTSD, the issues of racism and racial oppression are too often muted and/or omitted in these works.[52] Seemingly in concert with his recognition that race and racism have been sidestepped in favour of a heavy ethno-cultural emphasis in research, Scurfield (2001) notes that such endeavors mark only the beginning of what should be a greater emphasis on racism in psychiatric and psychological explorations:

> There are only three chapters in the collection of international contributors in Marsella, Friedman, Gerrity and Scurfield that substantially discuss racism and its relationship to PTSD...Many clinicians and researchers do not routinely inquire about possible exposure to race-related stressors, such as racial discrimination or assault that occurs solely or primarily because of the client's racial status or appearance. Exposure to stressful and traumatic race-related experiences may be a critical etiological factor in a client's presenting problems.[53]

Similar to other aspects of our democratic socio-economic systems, healthcare is marked by omissions and carefully managed negations. Simply put, within these contexts, the concerns, needs and experiences of the oppressed are commonly placed on the backburner of the socio-economic agenda. As illustrated thus far, the relations of power work to re-inforce and sustain hierarchies within a framework of White privilege and in no place are these disparities more greatly felt or more earnestly realized than within the walls of Western justice: the legal system.

Our legal systems are deeply enmeshed with oppressive socio-economic and political factors that do away with the possibility of true neutrality: "The notion of *blind justice* is a fairytale taught to children on the *White* side of the color-line. Consider these historical examples: the legalizing of the slave trade, the criminalization of Black literacy and the internment of Japanese Canadians during World War II. Importantly, however, while such examples speak of very dark chapters in our nation's histories, they are merely part of the larger contextual picture. When examining our modern-day justice systems, new manifestations of racism and new forms of discriminatory treatment are found to mirror the racist attitudes and oppressive behaviours found in North American society in general. Systemic racism significantly influences the operation of the justice system and impacts greatly on the lives and liberties of racially oppressed peoples.

Ungerleider (1993) argues that racially heterogeneous democracies with inequalities in the distribution of wealth and power will experience tension and conflict in the relations between police agencies and the communities they serve. These relations are extremely fragile in that police are effectively the physical embodiment of White power.[54] Racialized communities often argue that they are over policed, under protected, subject to the misuse of police powers, blamed for their victimization and under-represented within police organizations. As a direct result, racialized peoples are marked as targets in the criminal justice system.[55] For example, it is hard to dismiss the celebrated case of professional basketball player Dee Brown, who was stopped by police solely because he was a Black man driving an expensive car. The case stood as such a pointed example of racism in policing practices that as a result the Ontario Court of Appeals issued a groundbreaking ruling that recognized and validated the existence of racial profiling by police. In response, the Canadian Race Relations Foundation (CRRF) declared that this decision would pave the way to more serious discussions on how to end racial profiling and racial discrimination altogether.

While we agree with the spirit of the CRRF's statement, we would suggest that before any substantial reform can begin, we must first be willing to acknowledge that such "color-coded" rules of engagement are not specific to police alone. Rather, it is essential that we come to recognize that the ideology and practice of racial profiling has become commonplace among judges, lawyers, jurors and other officials throughout the justice system. We make this specific point because it is fundamentally important to establish that such racist beliefs and discrim-inatory practices are commonly held and exercised by powerful White people who are very "well intentioned." However, these "good intentions" are still undoubtedly constituted in and through democratically racist formations that impact and frame one's ability to carry out fair and equitable treatment under the law.[56] Just as evidenced in such North American criminal justice cases, data from the United Kingdom also reveal that police disproportionately stop, arrest and charge Blacks. Furthermore, and again paralleling North American trends, there is an over representation of Blacks in British prisons.[57] US statistics clearly illustrate the disproportionate nature of this dilemma with striking clarity:

- The ratio of Black to White in American prisons is seven to one
- Of every twelve Black males in their twenties, one is in prison
- Of all Black babies born, one in thirty will die a victim of intentional or non-negligent homicide
- Among Black males and females aged 15–44, the leading cause of death is homicide[58]

Russell (1998) points out that although explicitly racist double standards in policy have been removed from the American criminal justice system, racist practice still figures prominently in how justice is framed and dispensed. For example, when we look at police crackdowns on drug sales and the racial disparities in arrest and conviction rates that follow, might we not also ask why such major crackdowns so rarely occur in relation to blue-collar crime? Why the pointed disparity between efforts to uncover drug trafficking on the streets as opposed to drug activity in office suites? It becomes hard to side step the obviously glaring reality that racial minorities tend to be involved in street-level drug activity while Whites tend to take part in office-level crime. Clearly, the targeting of street-level crime occurs for various reasons: (a) the efficiency of such crackdowns; (b) the limited legal resources of street-level criminals leading to greater conviction rates; or (c) a desire to get at the violence that is associated with street-level crime.[59] Whichever the case, such policies and practices may result in arrest patterns that are racially disparate—with one kind of law enforcement for Blacks and another for Whites.

In further exploring this racially charged problematic, Russell (1998) looks at the federal crack-cocaine law in the United States. This law hands out a mandatory five-year prison term for possession of five grams of crack cocaine, while an offender would have to possess five hundred grams of powder cocaine to receive the same five-year prison term. It should be noted that powder is more expensive and a purer form of cocaine, while crack is cheaper and more widely accessible on the streets. Looked at in this light, it becomes difficult to ignore the reality that the difference in penalty between street and suite crime in this case carries a disparity ratio of 100:1.[60] Russell states that in 1995, 88% of the people serving time in US prisons under this law were Black: a statistic that clearly demonstrates how race plays a signif-icant part in today's criminal justice system.

So where do these discussions lead us? Earlier in this chapter we discussed how democratic racism allows people to maintain conflicting value sets that support racist beliefs and behaviours while also developing values of justice, fairness and equality. However, as we have shown thus far in this section, any such beliefs belie the truth of racial oppression and the materiality of racism. That being said, we end this chapter with a brief examination of how racism manifests in the beliefs, values and assumptions of people in these democratically framed social spheres. In doing so we hope to unravel some of the commonly voiced opinions and comments about racism that attempt to explain away, minimize or deny its effects on the realities of racialized peoples.

First and foremost, many racially privileged people assert that racism couldn't possibly exist in a democratic society. However, equality of opportunity does not mean equality of access. Even though overt racism is openly disavowed and disapproved of, manifestations of covert racism tend to be explained away, excused and denied. As a point of dire concern for many oppressed peoples, the difficulty of "naming" often places us in the vulnerable position of seeking to justify our pains to our oppressor. Problematically seeking to prove the locus of that pain is intrinsically difficult and potentially violating. The violating experience of racism, as a "real" fact of racially minoritized people's lives, is not something that should be defined and/or measured by "our" ability to prove it—the onus of such proofs must not fall to us. Often it is very difficult for us to pinpoint covert expressions of racism in that we have no measures to assess them and no language with which to talk about them.

Our lives are confined/shaped by forces that are neither accidental nor occasional, and so they always tend to exist beyond our control.[61] Relative to this "ascribed" quality, social oppressions impact the circumstances of life in ways that construct the intensity, duration and intrusive nature of the experience as always relative to the specifics of situational context. For example, experiences of racism and sexism are always framed relative to visual markers of skin color and gender that cannot be easily hidden or altered. Similarly, experiences of classism, while framed by similar "ascribed" visual characteristics of poverty are subject to change because the possibility of upward and downward economic mobility makes class memberships potentially alterable. Along these lines, it is argued that because there is a saliency to visual aspects of identity, the "invisibly" oppressed, in their ability to "pass," can often access advantages that are usually reserved for those in positions of privilege. Bishop (1994) talks about her experience of being invisible rather than visible:

> When I travel or eat in a restaurant with visible minority friends, I am grateful
> that I am not visible. Some racist incident, small or large, happens at least every half

hour. It is harder for them to see some of the things that I face and they do not, like insults from those who assume I am heterosexual, the high internal price of hiding and lying, or the fear that I will be separated from my partner in the event of injury or illness.[62]

We do not engage this distinction between visibility and invisibility to suggest a hierarchy of oppressions. Rather, we feel these distinctions to be an important entry point to understanding how individuals experience oppressions in different ways and, in turn, how those oppressions circumscribe our lives differently.

We learn to establish reference groups—out-groups with whom we feel a sense of alienation and in-groups with whom we feel a certain affinity. Through our daily experiences of oppression, we learn to recognize those "others" who are also positioned as deviant, "less than" and violable, and they come to represent a "solidarity reference group." Over time, as we mature in Western contexts, our chain of oppressive and inclusive interactions will indicate/frame potential strategies for survival. Some strategies for survival will reflect a need to identify with and engage in solidarity interactions with our fellow oppressed and other strategies will move us to identify with our oppressor. As clarified by Summers-Effler (2002):

> Because there are different ways of gaining emotional energy, and there are overlapping/competing opportunities for each of these ways, the process of weighing outcomes in terms of emotional energy is complex. A woman may be rewarded with emotional energy for behaving subordinately; in this case she would lose some emotional energy from submitting to subordination while simultaneously gaining more than is lost through reward. Likewise, a woman can be rewarded with emotional energy for experiences of feminist solidarity, but she may lose emotional energy from conflict within her family that results from taking a feminist stance. Either pattern of behaviour reflects the greatest *perceived* potential for the woman to maximize her emotional energy based on her history of interactions.[63]

Summers-Effler also suggested that the "perception of potential emotional reward" stands as the ultimate gauge as to which strategies are employed by the oppressed. Similarly, we echo Karumanchery's (2003) assertion that those who *go along to get along* do so because they either consciously or subconsciously feel that "passing" functions to eschew the likelihood of further alienation and rejection. In reflecting on this tendency to "pass," we are reminded of Boler's (1999) suggestion that emotions can be used as a form of social control. We would also assert that it is through our constitution within normalizing discourses that our "identification" with privileged perceptions of reality frames "passing" as one of the best routes toward maximizing our emotional energy reserves. What we should be careful to recognize are the lengths to which so many oppressed are willing to go in order to experience the relief, acceptance, belonging and "relative safety" that come with being "normal." For them, the potentiality of experiencing such "transient emotions" supercedes and obfuscates the realities of the less visceral, but still cumulative, long-term emotional consequences that accompany such "denial-based" strategies for survival. It is in such moments as these that we see peoples of color phasing out those aspects of culture and heritage that they deem to be too obtrusive for their oppressor. However, it is extremely crucial to recognize that while some momentary benefits to emotional energy may be made in these particular interactions (e.g., acceptance, recognition and the ability to manage daily interactions), the cumulative effects of long-term emotional trauma and energy depletion are not so easily displaced.

Problematically, even though "passing" might ease the experience of immediate transient emotions such as pain and humiliation, it does little to combat the internal conflicts that arise through the patterned day-to-day violations of oppression. In these respects, as a strategy, "passing" must be understood to be ultimately self-defeating and self-denying. So while the "salience of visibility" is clearly a factor when we examine disparities in employment, housing and other material discriminations that speak to access and belonging in oppressive spheres, it is crucial that we do not place visibility as the central locus of pain for the oppressed. We still feel it important to re-iterate that visible markers of difference preclude the ability of the oppressed to "pass" in potentially violent situations and that this visibility engenders an inescapable materiality to the experience of oppression. However, in doing so, we are careful not to sidestep the impact of less material oppressive effects nor the realities of psychological harm that all marginalized peoples "experience" via the internalization of such violence.

To move forward in this discussion, the specifics of historical context are fundamentally important to any understanding of how various groups experience oppression differently. Given the history of colonization, the oppression experienced by Jewish, Black, Native, Asian and South Asian peoples in North American contexts take different forms. For example, the particular nature of Native land rights and struggles, the history of Jewish dispossession and dislocation and the long history of Black slavery and colonization have framed oppression for these groups relative to their specific histories. It shapes each group's struggles differently; they take up different issues and are hurt differently in different moments. For example, the meanings and interpretations of different racial slurs/insults will always be taken up relative to the socio-historical contexts in which they formed. Which is to say that oppressive relations will always engender different levels of severity for people dependent on positionality and power. The same words and/or actions will have entirely different impacts on different groups because of the socio-cultural and historical meanings that infuse them.

As addressed earlier, the issue of "difference" again arises as funda-mental to these discussions. Commonsense beliefs that race and other socially constructed differences do not impact people's lives serve to belie the intrusive and invasive nature of oppression. Such approaches to race and racism are invariably bolstered by the problematic conflation between equality and equity. Again, at the present stage of social formation, it is impossible to treat people of color equitably when that equity is framed in a search for equality of treatment. We make this distinction because in West-ern contexts, equality is always framed relative to the "normalcy" of the White standard. When we hear "all people should be treated the same," we should ask in return "The same as what, the same as whom?" It is fundamentally important to recognize that we experience the world from specific social locations and via specific sites of power which are unequally and differently produced, regulated and manifested. We can no longer afford to abide claims that disregard and deny the direct link between human difference, inequity and the materiality of oppressions.

CHAPTER SIX
The Banality of Racism: Living 'Within' the Traumatic

I speak of trauma because it clings to skin, gender, sexuality and every 'otherized' feature of our oppressed lives. The voice of our oppressor tells us what ordinary is, what normal is, but that normalcy is subtly infused and framed in his 'Whiteness', in his freedom and in his safety. We have been blinded to the reality of our situation— blinded to the reality that ours is an abnormal existence. We live *within* a traumatic event, scrupulously policed and disguised by a 'normalizing gaze'. Our pain emerges in quiet moments when no one can hear and our tears flow in dark rooms when no one can see. This is the suffering that circumscribes our lives and these are the traumatic intrusions that imprison our minds and our souls.

—Leeno Luke Karumanchery, *The Color of Trauma*[1]

It was in the context of studying the phenomenology of hope, in the late 1960's, that I first interviewed...survivors of the Nazi Holocaust. To my profound, yet retrospectively unsurprising, anguish and outrage, all of my interviewees without exception asserted that no one, including the mental health professionals, listened to them or believed them when they attempted to share their Holocaust experiences and their related, continuing suffering. They and later their children, concluded that nobody who had not gone through the same experiences could understand. Many thus bitterly opted for silence.

—Yael Danieli, *History and Conceptual Foundations*[2]

How do you frame a life that is built on fear, violation and panic as common, everyday states of affair without understanding that existence to be oppressive? It is a peculiar human capacity that allows us to recognize and lament the abhorrent nature of individual suffering while turning a blind eye to the multiple atrocities that torment, violate and oppress generations. In North American contexts we are inundated by racialized/racist discourse in every moment and in every space. So how do we formulate our understandings of self and *other* when our very bodies, minds and souls rebel against what we 'know' to be 'real'? In fact, if we believe that racism is a social construct, if we truly need not feel pain in the racist moment and if we know

Brown skin is beautiful—then why do we have to keep reminding ourselves of these facts—these things that we "know" to be true? Why is it that our claims to an "intrinsic" beauty, strength and virtue are not normalized in the everyday rather than indicative of a productive ambivalence in the moment? Do the privileged have to constantly re-affirm their self-worth in order to feel normal and ordinary, or are those images embedded in dichotomies relative to our deviance and depravity?[3]

We began this chapter with the words of Karumanchery and Danieli because they both speak to a very pointed issue—the "reality" of oppression, the "reality" of pain and the ongoing nature of racialized suffering. We can sit behind the privileged doors of academia and discuss/reflect: What is "the real"; how is *it* real? How are we participants in our own oppression? From a theoretical viewpoint it might be feasible to discuss the possibilities of resistance relative to consciousness and our ability to critically interrogate our own positionality and participation in the moment—but how much practicality does that have in the "real" world? How would that critical consciousness play itself out relative to the ongoing effects of dispossession, deprivation and discrimination that arise in the everyday?

Psychological distress is very much a part of everyday life for the child of color who is isolated, denigrated and mentally tortured. It is very much a part of life for the adolescent who is exhausted at the thought of dealing with another racist incident where s/he is forced to feel like an outsider, trapped under a spotlight that allows everyone to see and know what s/he really is. It is very much a part of life for the racialized adult who wakes up every morning to a reflection that is the "wrong" color—a re-flection that will inevitably cause her/him to know pain, humiliation and fear. It is a part of racialized parents' lives when they realize that their child will know the same fear, humiliation and pain through which they struggled.[4] So, if psychological trauma is an affliction of the powerless as asserted by Herman (1997), then *we* all suffer from it in some way and in spaces and places that we least expect.[5]

As discussed previously, conventional psychological theory commonly asserts that traumatic events are extraordinary, not because they are rare, but because they have the ability to affect our normal adaptations to the everyday world. According to the *Comprehensive Textbook of Psychiatry*, feelings of intense fear, helplessness, loss of control and threat of annihilation are the common denominators of psychological trauma.[6] On reviewing this short list, we find ourselves systematically trying to pigeonhole moments from our lived experience (particularly those from childhood and adolescence) into one or the other criteria and, not surprisingly, we find that they fit all too well. It would seem that racialized pain and emotional confusion are the constants that circumscribe our lives. After all, as asserted by Delgado, what options are left to us within racialized/racist contexts? Racially minoritized children who find themselves rejected, attacked and isolated on a regular basis have little recourse but to react, but that defensive reaction can take shape only in two forms: hostility or passivity—neither an effective strategy. Hostile reac-tions always serve to pathologize the victims of violence as angry, bad and aggressive children, while passive reactions function to internalize the violence until they are "robbed of confidence and motivation [and] withdraw into moroseness, fantasy and fear."[7] The severity of psychological harms cannot be quantifiably measured relative to any single hierarchy of pain. Any attempts to do so relegate our struggles to relativistic comparisons of trauma and suffering: "My hurt is worse than yours, so yours doesn't matter." Nevertheless, Herman identifies (a) being taken by surprise, (b) being trapped, or (c) exposure to the point of exhaustion as several identifiable experiences through which the likelihood of harm is increased. As a corol-lary to these indices, she adds that the probability of extensive psychological damage will increase if such events involve physical violence or injury.[8] Bearing these indicators in mind, let us look at how racial violence translates into the everyday experience of our lived oppression.

"You are too sensitive." This is a rhetorical observation/claim/denounce-ment/tool that we (the racially oppressed) hear throughout our lives. It is a functional mechanism through which our oppressors seek to place respon-sibility for oppositional/anti-racist moments firmly at our feet. But, as asserted by Freire, such moments—be they violent or simply oppositional—are never initiated by the oppressed. Rather, their existence as oppressed is a result of the violence of oppression; their natural opposition to that violence is quite understandable and basic to oppressive situations. Simply put, if there were no situation of violence to begin with, then there would be no oppressed to stand in opposition to his/her oppressor.[9] So as we move be-yond the obvious privileged denials of responsibility within racist scripts and structures, the rhetoric of sensitivity speaks to a very pointed issue within an anti-racist critical consciousness: hyper-arousal as symptomatic of trauma.

After traumatic experiences, the normal biological systems that promote self-preservation begin to function in preparedness for the recurrence of the event. It is important to note that regardless of the probability of the event's recurrence, the invasive nature of the moment pushes the oppressed into permanent alert mode. This state of "hyper-arousal" manifests itself in several physiological ways: (a) extraordinarily sensitive and disproportionate responses to situations or moments that are interpreted to be similar to the original moment; (b) a pronounced shock reflex; and (c) impaired sleep.[10] As suggested by Kardiner and Spiegel (1947) in relation to their study of WWI veterans and stress-related illness, "the nucleus of the [traumatic] neurosis is *physioneurosis*."[11] Like Karumanchery (2003), we are pointed in our use of the term physioneurosis because it speaks directly to the physical responses that we develop within racially charged environments. Rejection, isolation and the demarcation of prohibitive social boundaries are a part of the everyday experience for the racially oppressed. Thus, the development of psychological/physiological reactions of anxiety and preparedness relative to oppressive environments is quite understandable. More than just simply linguistic in nature, such social alienations are expressed through multiple sign systems and symbolic gestures like a rejected handshake, an empty seat on a bus or a smile-turned-frown when you enter a room. Ultimately, on a fundamental level, they are all part of the complex interplay between meanings and socially constructed boundaries.

Racialized subjects need not be told which incidents are racist to recognize and internalize them. Whether or not we have the words to frame an incident as racist, the experiences speaks to oppression and we live through our violation/violability in the moment. For the racially privileged, racialized children's responses to the moment are often interpreted as excessive and extraordinarily sensitive and their responses often take shape in aggressive behaviour that allows others to mark them as troublemakers and bad kids. It is a cyclical dilemma that promotes further feelings of rejection and often pushes racialized children toward silence and the internalization of their oppression.[12] However, like Freire, we assert that such reactions are reflective of an oppositional response to racism in the moment and relative to a lived history of oppression.

Terry Eagleton proposed that children make the best theorists because they have not yet been educated into accepting the normative nature of social practices.[13] Bearing his assertion in mind, we would propose that in these oppositional moments, children of color are able to read the symbolic meaning of their rejection relative to the mediating factor of skin color as it has played out in their lives. It is through this theoretical reading that they interpret racism, so their understanding of alienation, rejection and isolation in such moments is informed by a framework contextualized by their psychological and physiological experience. In interpreting these moments relative to the rhetoric of "oversensitivity," we must remember that psychological responses to humiliation and isolation form through one's awareness that others perceive and treat him/her as different and inferior. As discussed earlier, awareness of oppression will often result in the stigmatized individual's development of physiological and psychological manifestations of hyper-sensitivity and anticipation of pain.[14] We read aggressive responses in these moments as a reactive manifestation of the cumulative traumas in which we are made to feel powerless.

Relative to our shared social representations of group, relation, community and belonging, we all follow standardized ideological and discursive frameworks that position and discipline us as to who we are, what we are and what we are worth. Culture infuses us with meaning through the everyday practice of the social world. Therefore, the ideas we hold to be true and the actions that we take are all fundamentally shaped in/by/through the socio-historical frameworks in which we have been raised. In this respect it is important to note that the pains of our youth cannot be compartmentalized and separated from our other various experiences of oppression. Rather, they must be recognized as the intersecting and interlocking racial traumas of our individual and collective lifetimes. The social knowledges that inform our external and internalized oppression tend to be explicit, precise, overt and detailed—to us—to the oppressed. As asserted by Herman, rather than the "normal" baseline level of "alert but relaxed attention," the traumatized person has an elevated "baseline level of arousal in which s/he is ever on the physical alert for danger."[15] When we (the authors) began our dialogues in the development of this work, we engaged our own lived experiences of racism. In those discussions, we were surprised by the clarity with which we remembered specific racist moments as they occurred throughout our lives. We would contend that such "race specific memory" is a common state of affairs among racially oppressed people and that these memories are continuously drawn upon in the framing of our everyday experiences. As put forth by Shalev et al. (1991) relative to the acoustic dimensions of PTSD, we would assert that this preparedness, or hyper-arousal, does not allow the oppressed to "tune out" the "repetitive stimuli" that others ignore or look past in their everyday lives. Rather, we respond to each repetition as if it were a new and potentially dangerous incursion into our "semi-safe space."[16] Moreover, we learn to track and interpret these repetitions, incursions and scripts as they develop.

The psycho-physiological problematics that arise relative to chronic/hyper-arousal engender both extensive and lasting changes to the oppressed individual's ability to function outside a state of generalized anxiety and tension. We learn to live in anxiety because we spend our lifetimes seeing, hearing and feeling these moments—not because they exist in our minds alone, but because they are repeated over and over in our daily lives. What the eyes and ears of privilege would note as oversensitivity and what the oppressed frequently internalize with self-doubt, we very pointedly mark as a self-preservational state of constant concern that functions to keep us from experiencing each new moment with the same surprise and pain as the first. Unfortunately, that preparedness comes with a price. In recent years, research concerning "racial stress" has grown considerably and the mounting evidence seems to suggest that the inhibited, constrained and restricted nature of oppression leads to physiological difficulties such as high blood pressure, higher morbidity and mortality rates, hypertension and stroke. Once thought to be genetically predisposed to such health problems, studies of people of color and particularly North American Blacks, are beginning to show a strong correlation between such physical consequences and social-psychological factors like "name calling." Moreover, related research has shown that a correlation exists between darkness of skin and stress in which levels rise as skin color darkens—a likely reflection of greater or more frequent experiences of discrimination felt by dark-skinned Blacks.[17]

In our discussions of autonomic responses and generalized anxiety as they relate to race and racism, we make a very specific point about the naturalized stress, fear and turmoil that result from the everyday experience of racial oppression. Unlike the survivors of other traumatic circumstances, whose anxiety might recede once removed from the space, place and moment of the trauma, racially oppressed peoples will find it exceedingly difficult to establish safe-space for themselves because race permeates every facet of our world. So, in these terms, the world, in all its material and immaterial forms, is an intrinsically unsafe place for the racially oppressed. We firmly assert that claims to our "oversensitivity" to racism speak less to the issue of sensitivity than to the reality of hyper-arousal that is necessarily born of oppression. Demands for the oppressed to "just get over it" and claims that we have "chips on our shoulders" belie and ignore the reality that we relive our traumas every day in intrusive moments that cannot be mapped through privileged eyes.[18]

Relative to the orthodox interpretation of what constitutes a "traumatic event," it is uniformly accepted that "traumatic intrusions" work to disrupt a survivor's ability to recover from the "event" and resume the normal course of life. However, we must problematize this imagined normality relative to racial trauma in the moment.

I felt small and bewildered and put up a struggle to keep something of myself from vanishing and to maintain a little sense of significance. Though I did not know it then, I was being produced as the *other*, as 'different', but not neutrally different, not just a cultural variation on the theme 'human', but 'different and inferior'. But at this time I only suffered from this at the level of feeling—feelings that had not yet been named, interpreted and become my experience.[19]

In the above passage, Bannerji (1995) makes an important clarification about the emotional and intangible quality of racialized pain as continually recurring, reproductive and intrusive. It is an important point because it takes us to very specific and uncharted territory in understanding the banal nature of racial trauma. Traumatic moments are indelibly etched onto our muted psychology and we carry those imprints as cemented markers of what we have been through. As asserted by Herman above, existing literature on trauma and stress suggests that traumatic events functionally constrain the course of "ordinary development" and recovery by continuously and repetitively re-inserting themselves into the survivor's life.

This process of intrusion and mental re-enactment is understood to invade the survivor's life such that it is re-lived in the present as if constantly recurring, even long after the traumatic event has passed.[20] We assert that racial trauma circumscribes the lives of racially oppressed peoples, so removing ourselves from the temporal space and place of any one specific event is never a realistic option for us as a healing strategy. That is to say, the "ordinary development" of *our* racialized lives is fundamentally based in oppression. As implied by Bannerji, the real question is not whether the racist moment will recur, but whether we will see it coming or "name" it when it does. So, as noted in past research, the seemingly innocuous images, textures, smells, sounds and tastes that inform "intrusive recurrences" will elicit powerful mental reflections and disjointed memories of our initial trauma(s). In these intrusive moments, normally safe environments may come to feel unsafe or dangerous because the potential for recurrence is ever-present and ever-threatening.[21]

A very real and very powerful normative dialectic develops between the racially oppressed and the world relative to each racist moment. These memories arise as fragmented but vivid sensations and images contextualized and focused by the one common denominator—racism: The wordless, inevitable and timeless quality of these events are reflected in our disjointed recollections and re-imaginings of the moment.[22] Different spaces, people, times, situations—the only constant being the racist/racial implications of each moment. So bearing the multiplicity of the intrusion(s) in mind, the traumatic and oppressive effects gain a heightened aura of materiality and certainty. As mentioned earlier, the moments' multiple manifestations pose considerable problems for the oppressed person's ability to live without constant repetitive intrusions. How does s/he react to the words "Oh, I have a really great joke"? How does she feel when s/he sees a car full of White guys? Who will s/he choose to have relationships with and if s/he is with a White person, when, where, how and why will those memories re-surface? The questions are endless and fraught with new permutations because the moments themselves are always being re-formed and re-inscribed within our psyches.[23]

Traumatic racialized memories speak for the oppressed in the absence of verbal narrative and cognitive clarity. In their form, imagery and action, the indelibly encoded nature of these intrusive memories will often manifest through affective re-enactments of the racist moments themselves. Through the generally innocuous everyday behaviours that speak to the markers of trauma, in many ways, we act out our oppression in ostensibly self-disciplining fashions.[24] Freire (1970) took up this problematic in his assertion that oppression is functionally domesticating.[25] Firmly constituted and entrenched within our oppression, we have internalized powerful images of Whiteness and *otherness* that are all innately coded by and through the traumatic moments that have framed our memory. We often take on the "privileged" task of condemning our own cultural heritages, while conversely painting the Euro-American/White dream in idealized terms. Moreover, while many of our fellow oppressed can be heard to deny the impact of racism on their lives, their subconscious and often conscious choices to "pass" reflects a very different oppressive reality that is carefully managed and regulated. When we are "allowed" to enjoy a sense of freedom and "anonymity," we do so by engaging social codes that enable us to access and retain what amounts to a relative "state of grace": Don't be too loud or they'll find you—If you're not nice enough, you'll be next. These are the silent complicities that arise in our desire to avoid re-living the pain and struggle that we know so well. There is a stark discomfort that frames these experiences as we opt for silence while others suffer. It is the type of internalized guilt that the oppressed commonly endure because moments of complete surrender are "par for the course" in the game of psychological domination and oppresssion.[26] Herman (1997) asserts:

> Terror, intermittent reward, isolation and enforced dependency may succeed in creating a submissive and compliant prisoner. But the final step in the psychological control of the victim is not completed until she has been forced to violate her own moral principles and to betray her basic human attachments...this is the most

destructive of all coercive techniques, for the victim who has succumbed loathes herself. It is at this point, when the victim under duress participates in the sacrifice of others, that she is truly 'broken'.[27]

Our fear targets us, our skin marks and *otherizes* us without hope of escape and our dependence on our "relative freedoms" adds to our submissiveness even while that compliance gains us only tentative freedoms. Importantly, all of these factors speak to our personal adaptive struggles in the moment and in the everyday. These are concessions that the oppressed must make to forestall the ever-present reality of further trauma, but in our complicity we internalize the everyday markers of weakness and *otherness* that inscribe our souls. It moves us to absorb the guilt over our inaction, even while we engage the humiliation of 'knowing' that 'they' have broken our will and taken our last vestiges of autonomy. The question of "Why?" will rattle about inside our psyches like a rusty saber, thrusting and slicing with each intrusive memory, each re-enacted moment. In many ways, our actions/ in-actions work to integrate our traumatic memories into an acceptable and tolerable synergy between what we know and what we can accept. Unfortunately, what we know is rarely acceptable.[28]

As asserted earlier, traumatized people will find themselves re-living their traumas in physically overt ways as well as in the more subtle psychological manifestations discussed above. Such physical re-creations or re-enactments of the traumatic moment take form in both overt and covert manners. Terr (1988), in a study of post-traumatic memory among abused children, found traumatic experiences could and would, be re-enacted in play.[29] Moreover, Terr (1990) asserted that the post-traumatic play of children would often be so literal that one might be able to guess the trauma without further clues.[30] This point is of interest here in that it raises the question: How might one go about interpreting and assessing the racially traumatized child's "markers of harm"? Unlike sexually abused children, there are no "forbidden games" to interpret and unlike survivors of a singular/past trauma, racialized youth continue to live through the "real" repetitions and intrusions of trauma that others fear. How do we interpret a child's response to the real repetition of racial trauma in her daily life when it surfaces as passivity? In reality, such responses might well act as a marker of trauma, but such innocuous behaviour is too frequently ignored as a "bad mood" or more problematically, a "bad attitude." On the other hand, reactionary and oppositional responses to racism are often interpreted to be signs reflective of "problem children" and "troubled youth." As an extension of the problematic, the pathologizing of the child is often conducted by those closest to the children in their everyday experience of the world (e.g., teachers, caregivers, clinicians and even parents).[31]

As children and even as adults, our efforts to avoid this "locus of suffering" will reflect the desperation and intense desire to escape the helplessness and loss of control that circumscribes us in and through our oppression. So, our actions, as suggested by Russell (1990), while seemingly engaged on conscious levels, may be better understood to be particularly "affective" rather than "cognitive" reactions to our everyday suffering.[32] That is to say that in our repetitive engagements with racism and in our ongoing negotiations in those moments, a "repetitive compulsion" arises as a subconscious attempt to gain mastery over the moment. Somehow, reliving the moment will help the mind repair the damage done to it. We find this perspective in trauma theory to be very useful in the study of "intrusion" relative to intra-psychic symptoms such as traumatic memory, dreams and denials—as well as of the more physical manifestations such as re-en-actments—as they relate to race. As spontaneous attempts to find some middle ground between "living" and "living in fear," such subconscious engagements with trauma seem to suggest a fundamental desire for closure. However, regardless of that motive, the reality of "traumatic racial memory" is that, whether consciously sought or subconsciously avoided, the oppressed are continuously "buffeted by terror and rage."[33] The result: we will often find ourselves limiting the likelihood of "intrusion" by minimizing our exposure to people, places and things that carry a racist potentiality. For racially oppressed people, these strategies arise in our demarcations of whom we will date, with whom we will socialize, where we will vacation and in what type of neighbourhood we will live. In socio-economic terms, these subconscious strategies will silently guide what levels of education we will pursue and to what types of jobs we will gravitate. As racially oppressed, our normal everyday choices are marked by these traumatic intrusions: whether they are consciously engaged or not, they find a way to re-surface.[34]

There is a common state of political, intellectual and physical paralysis that often overcomes us when we collide with these new, unexpected reminders of our oppression and our inability to do anything in the face of it. Regardless of the strategies that we employ in preparation for such moments or the critical knowledges that we bring to them, the intrusion of constrictive childhood memories of racism will often take us emotionally, psychically and physiologically back to those times when we felt small and helpless. In effect, in those moments we are transported back to the confines of our childhood powerlessness and we experience a return to the fear, horror and panic of those initial traumas. Importantly, this constrictive state has several different manifestations. As discussed briefly above, helpless or constrictive states of inner surrender are reflected in children who develop difficulties in planning for their future.

Because children of color comprehend, interpret and engage culture and the pejorative nature of social context as they develop their sense of worth and/or ability, they will often develop a sense of helplessness with respect to fighting the system. As a result, racially oppressed people will often reflect this sense of powerlessness by opting to "go with the flow" and avoid socio-economic spaces and places in which they can expect to re-experience racial trauma. Disciplined to engage such self-defeating, conscious/subconscious directives to "give up," the racially oppressed will often employ these strategies when confronted with seemingly overpowering and uncontrollable events. Dei et al. (1997) addressed the development of such "counter-initiatives" in the problematic but common disengagement of racially minoritized children who are "pushed out" of the educational system.[35] Such powerful examples of socio-economic manipulation develop alongside purposeful limitations or alterations to life and self, all in the effort to gain a sense of safety or control over an otherwise helpless existence.

In this perspective, when we address such alterations to life, we speak to the various issues of self-worth and social stigma that arise as common everyday struggles for the oppressed. These are our "hidden secrets": the moments when little Black girls wore towels to imagine their long flowing White hair or the unspoken duality of racialized men who are disciplined to want White women because the image of White beauty is emblazoned into our psyches. We perform these dances in private spaces where the outside world cannot see our pain acting as a staging ground for our public displays of duality. These are our struggles to "pass" under the radar of our oppressor, to be that which we can never be—free. However, while notions of "passing" are often associated with a desire to be one of the privileged, they are also deeply entrenched in feelings of fear and *otherness*—realizations that you are a target. We learn to see that we have no control and these moments speak to the innate differentials in power that exist between us and our oppressor. In these moments, we run headlong into the deeply encoded cultural forms and knowledges that constantly engage the image of racial/cultural inferiority; in turn, we conclude that our innate inability to succeed has been preordained and that we are marked for failure. In this fashion, we recognize and tap into the established sources of meaning that underlie our oppressor's words and actions and in so doing we interpret the signs and symbols represented in the dialogue as etched within a "truth" of race and inferiority. In the disciplining of our racialized bodies, we are framed, positioned and pathologized in ways that naturalize and legitimize the "truth" of biological determinism within us and leave indelible prints of pain and tension in our cerebral landscape. Our discrete constitution within this racially charged social sphere impels us to reflect the racialized consciousness that speaks to and through us in the everyday.[36]

We engage our childhood memories in these racist moments within a self-referential impulse that is particularly poignant relative to our experiences of paralysis, interplay and oppression. In each new moment, we suffer through more than the traumatic nature of the temporal moment itself, but rather through the intrusive memory being re-enacted and re-inscribed into each new moment. When a person finds herself in a situation of complete and utter hopelessness, where any form of self-defense is futile, then it is always possible that she, depending on the traumatic nature of the event, will retreat into a state of total surrender. In such cases, defense shuts down entirely—and the traumatized person will commonly experience moments of paralysis, disassociation from the temporal moment and other physiological "shutdowns."[37] The problem is that through our lived experience of racism and racial oppression, we commonly find ourselves disciplined, or as Chopra (1997) suggests, imprinted in very specific ways. As is so often the case, these imprinted "shut downs"—while modes of self-defense for the traumatized person—ultimately act as a barrier to further healing.

> All of us were imprinted one of two ways: either the world is dangerous with moments of safety, or the world is safe with moments of danger.[38]

What Chopra asserts in philosophical prose, Horowitz (1986) and Janoff-Bulman (1985) confirm in their various interrogations of trauma and recovery: the clear imperative being that traumatic events can fundamentally impact an individual's sense of self in relation to others and, more generally, in relation to her sense of safety in the world.[39] Racism's traumatic nature invariably affects our sense of safety because we never know when or where "it's" going to happen, so we must always be prepared in a state of hyper-arousal—just in case. When our sense of security is shattered in spaces and places and by people who are supposed to be comforting and protective, the consequences to our basic sense of equilibrium are multiple. We must remind ourselves that the violations of such moments speak to far more than the words being uttered; they speak also to the context, histories and positionings that they have on our bodies and minds. To the eyes and ears of privilege, such incidents may appear ineffectual; however, the contextuality of those moments carry fundamentally violating potential for the oppressed, in particular when occurring in what is supposed to be safe space. These are the moments in which we most commonly find ourselves paralyzed and helpless in spite of our experience, knowledge and preparedness. These are the moments that we remember because they shatter the basic constructions of self, friendship and community that we sustained until that point.[40]

The racially oppressed speak in clear testimony to the loss of security engendered in/through such moments. When one person utters a racial epithet or formulates racist theory and rhetoric in the moment, the subconscious and intrapsychic turmoil that erupts within the oppressed does so by extrapolating the implications of the moment beyond that one racist body. Racist events carry the potential to produce severe breaches of social and communal bonds. They rupture the racialized person's basic connection to human relationships and on a subconscious level the moment is always interpreted to be more than an individual act of cruelty and betrayal. It is in these moments that we find ourselves wondering: "Is everyone else thinking the same thing?" "If it can happen here and with this person that I trusted, could it happen anywhere?" We make these extrapolations because we recognize that there is a social aspect to the moment and that there is likely a social group influence in the event. Importantly, in this recognition of the social aspect of the incident, we also have an understanding that rather than suddenly becoming an issue, it always was an issue and that this moment just brought "it" to the fore. Therefore, this is a violation, not of intimate human connections formed through bonds of friendship, but a breach of our basic connections to community and the other.[41]

Again, these breaches are particularly traumatic when arising within sites of friendship, love and trust that, to that point, had been safe space (i.e., when trusted companions say or do something racist for the first time). When such moments occur, we are thrown into a state of existential crisis that damages all of our most basic assumptions about friendship, loyalty, trust, compan-ionship and the general safety of the world. In other words, our "faith in a natural or divine order"—where life makes sense and things like love and friendship can be known—is shocked and upset. The moment undermines "the belief systems that give meaning to [our] experience" and as a result we are made to feel alone and intrinsically vulnerable.[42] We (the oppressed) negotiate a multiplicity of shifting identities and one moment is all it takes to send us on a "Diasporic" journey from insider to outsider, from being in familiar and comfortable ground to being a stranger in a foreign land. These common Diasporic dilemmas are reflected in the intergenerational culture clashes and internal conflicts that arise between family, community and world. However, we would posit that these instances are more than figurative erasures; they are also symbolic-literal denials of home. Importantly, it is in these instances of psycho-social surrender where we attempt erasures of ethnicity, culture and race, that we may trace the emergence of the "dislocated and disconnected self."[43]

Karumanchery (2003) asserts that the great majority of these "disconnective moments" originate in traumatic childhood events. We make this specification because, in relation to racial trauma in Western contexts, the first moments almost always occur in our relationships and interactions as we are learning to code race into our dialogic self. Our initial connections and interactions with people (e.g., parents, friends, neighbors and teachers), help to form the foundation of our personalities. Therefore, the traumatic nature of racist childhood events carry the innate ability to sever those connections. Once these bonds are frayed or severed, the child is thrown into an intrapsychic struggle to understand why he is not good enough to be loved, accepted and befriended. This basic loss of "self" is fundamentally important to the ways in which the oppressed learn to position themselves in relation to other people and in relation to their sense of self-preservation in moments that are otherwise very innocuous. We internalize these pointed moments of otherness and *otherness* and they in turn establish what we should and should not expect within our racialized existence. Ultimately, however, these are not statements on an inter-play between people but rather, statements on internal self worth. We see this dialectic playing out in our pointed demar-cations of where, when and with whom we can be safe.[44]

There is a very particular subject effect here. It is an internalized re-action that sees the oppressed implicated as active contributors in the maintenance of our own oppression. We see the world through the oppressor's eyes and interpret the interactions and actions of the *other* as he would. We find ourselves bent to the will of our oppressors and turned against ourselves because the locus of the oppressor's worldview is the only point of "true" convergence for our damaged and constricted sense of reality. In our desire for safety and in our alienation, we take on the task of becoming as much like the oppressor as we can, because that is the forbidden site of safety to which we aspire. The intrapsychic scars are similar for us all in that our "surrender" is a breach of faith and autonomy that takes place on an intensely intimate level. In an interesting parallel, the work of Bowker,

Arbitel, McFerron (1988) and Walker (1979) speak to similar cases of intimate betrayal and sacrifice as they relate to battered women who fail to protect their children from physical mistreatment. They assert that the coercive relationship between the woman and the abuser will commonly involve some form of sacrifice on her part.[45] Following Karumanchery (2003), we draw similarities between these two abusive situations in that the notion of captivity and the prolonged/repetitious nature of the abuse requires interro-gation. Extrapolating from these works in relation to our discussions, racism vacillates along a continuum that places us within a sphere of ever-present and episodic violability. We are faced with daily traumas arising in racism's discursive claims to the "truth" of our general inferiority and the degeneracy of our histories, cultures, heritages and skins. We are maneuvered into positions where we bear our abuse in silence in the hopes of escaping future pain. In this way, our demoralization and submission becomes solidified in our inability to speak out and resist our oppression.[46]

The identity formed within the traumatic moment is intrinsically different from the identity as it was beforehand. Insider–outsider–insider–outsider. Once the initial racial trauma has occurred, we will regularly shift between positions as the dialogical intricacies of a Diasporic identity force us to constantly confront our multiple "*I* positions." The oppressed are constantly shifting between who they feel they are, who they feel they must be and who they are allowed to be. In our experiences of isolation and shock in the moment, we are informed as to our positionality and how we are rele-gated to exist in a borderland of power, culture and community—where we must always anticipate feeling like an "outsider." Fundamentally important here is the issue of autonomy and initiative. Essentially, in all of these situations, the wants, needs and desires of the oppressed count for nothing; thus our positionings are established in relation to the actions and intentions of others. Rather than participants in a dialogic partnership, the oppressed are part of a "monologue" disguised as a dialogue. It is through this monologue that privileged voices work to deny the oppressive nature of our existence, while the proof of racial oppression flourishes all around us. As discussed above, the traumatic nature of racism works to infuse dominant ideologies into our oppressed psyches such that we commonly engage in intra-psychic struggles to disassociate ourselves from our cultures and heritages.[47]

Skin, as the key signifier of cultural and racial difference in the stereotype, is the most visible of fetishes, recognized as 'common knowledge' in a range of cultural, political and historical discourses and plays a public part in the racial drama that is enacted everyday in colonial societies.[48]

Again, as asserted by Karumanchery (2003), we are disciplined to see ourselves as different from the inside out. Our skin becomes a social marker of everything that we can never be, made in direct relation to Whiteness. While we interpret our experience of race as made from without, our ugliness, our alienation, our isolation, all push us to disassociate ourselves from our race, culture and heritage—from ourselves. However, what is hidden in our perception of privilege is that parallel to our image of "White normalcy" is the realization that pain, cruelty and trauma are reserved for us and those *others* like us. These moments engage the dynamics of a life script that is designed to oppress—and designed to create a pensive and fearful oppressed bloc. As discussed, traumatic experiences of social stigmatization will also commonly deter the racially oppressed from planning for the future or looking to the future with hope and expectation.

Our national and cultural identities are not intrinsically concrete. Rather, they intersect in a shifting terrain of meanings and re-negotiations. However, even as geographical lines change and our Diasporic cultural lines blend, these same national and cultural images seem cemented in static notions of color, language and ethnicity. Case in point, because Western cultures are most commonly equated with Whiteness, in these contexts, racialized bodies are formed and negotiated as inherently unequal and certainly less desirable than their White counterparts. In order to effectively combat these power-fully oppressive influences, the oppressed must be able to access some form of social and cultural support structure. In those situations where such supports are not forthcoming (e.g., supports such as family and community), we find that the oppressed and racialized children in particular are often unable to cope with and/or combat the racialized traumas that arise in the everyday. Without the cultural capital to employ in our engagements with the mainstream, our general sense of duality leaves us to develop a positive self-concept in a world that makes it nearly impossible to do so. As a result, many of us internalize these "everyday traumas" into our identities until some other system of support is found—if it is found.[49] In a study of racially oppressed mothers, Delgado (1982) explains:

> Some, as a defense against aggression, identified excessively with Whites, accepting Whiteness as superior. Most had negative expectations concerning life's chances. Such self-conscious, hypersensitive parents, preoccupied with the ambiguity of their own social position, are unlikely to raise confident, achievement-oriented and emotionally stable children.[50]

In our pointed desire to avoid the dangers of pathologizing communities, families and parents, we feel it important to reiterate that the symptoms of dysfunction, as noted by Delgado, are symptoms of traumatic experience; the pathogen must be noted as existing *a priori* to and productive of the dilemmas faced by oppressed peoples. To single out familial or community relationships as the root causes behind the emotional and cog-nitive stability of racially oppressed peoples is to avoid and ignore the obvious impact of racial trauma on their social and intrapsychic identity development. The dialectic interplay between home and the "outside world" infuses us with relational notions of self that are developed and mediated through the dynamics of difference and *otherness*. The dialectic speaks to the ongoing nature of racism as a "fact of life" for people of color.

> A single traumatic event can occur almost anywhere. Prolonged, repeated trauma, by contrast, occurs only in circumstances of captivity. When the victim is free to escape, she will not be abused a second time; repeated trauma occurs only when the victim is a prisoner, unable to flee and under the control of the perpetrator. The barriers to escape are generally invisible...They are nonetheless extremely powerful...Captivity which brings the victim into prolonged contact with the perpetrator, creates a special type of relationship, one of coercive control...In situations of captivity, the perpetrator becomes the most powerful person in the life of the victim and the psychology of the victim is shaped by the actions and beliefs of the perpetrator...His most consistent feature, in both the testimony of victims and the observations of psychologists, is his apparent normality...How much more comforting it would be if the perpetrator were easily recognizable, obviously deviant or disturbed.[51]

So why have we included this quotation about racial oppression, pain and the nature of our oppressor when in many ways it is a simple repetition of earlier points? Simply put, because these comments were drawn from Herman's (1997) seminal work on trauma and the aftermath of violence, they were not written with racial oppression in mind and yet they speak clearly to the dynamics and problematics discussed throughout this work. In this work, Herman relates instances of prolonged and repeated trauma as occurring only in circumstances of captivity, such as prison, concentration camps, institu-tions of organized sexual exploitation, families (in relation to domestic abuse) and in other regulated bodies of power and difference such as brothels or religious cults. However, nowhere in her treatise does she discuss the issue of race and racism. For the same reasons of normality she discusses above, our oppressor is never seen in relation to deviance from the norm. That is precisely because the norm in racially constructed societies places our oppressor as the model for that normality. It is only upon critical reflection that we realize that normal should be understood in relation to equity and social justice. And, in effect, our lived experience within oppressive conditions is a state abnormality in the truest sense of the word. Herman asserts that the most powerful determinant of psychological harm is the character of the trauma itself in direct relation to the number of people affected and/or the intensity and duration of harm.[52] How then do we determine the impact of racial trauma in Western contexts, when it extends to all racially marginalized peoples who are "held" for the entirety of their lives in a state of oppressive captivity? The notion is deeply disturbing in theoretical terms, but when placed within the context of real people's lives, the disturbing quality grows in [un]fathomable and [un]nameable ways.

The various methods used by our oppressors to enslave our "will to truth" and to manage our lives as oppressed, are incredibly similar to those used in more obviously tyrannical systems of domestic and political violence. The notion that oppressive discourses are transmitted through the State and social apparatus and internalized within the oppressed, is reflected in Herman's (1997) suggestion that the transmission of coercive methods can be traced from "one clandestine police force to another."[53] The systematic use of coercive techniques is "universal," as they relate to abusive relationships, whether in intimate situations of domestic abuse or in larger forms of political and social violence. The common denominator in all of these abusive relationships is the oppressor's ability to "season" or break the oppressed. Importantly, that process of "seasoning", carefully planned in political situations, does not appear to require the same formal organization in social contexts. That is to say, domestic abuse and larger scales of social oppression appear to develop strikingly familiar techniques for domination without the necessity of formal instruction.

As shown thus far, the invention and re-invention of these coercive techniques develop through the systematic and repetitive infliction of psychological trauma and the constant threat of violence. Importantly, the violent nature of racism is key to our work in that the necessity of anti-racism is often downplayed by critics who see violence only in its grossest most obvious terms and so sidestep the reality of racism as intrinsically violent. To clarify, while we often speak of racism in terms of violence within anti-racist contexts, those discussions tend to reflect an understanding of the pain and devastation caused in those moments. On the other hand, we must take care to reflect understandings of racism in the moment as a dialectic between symbolic and material violence. This particularly insightful perspective on the nature of the racist moment is useful in our discussion of coercion relative to abusive relationships.[54]

Methods of psychological control are designed to terrify the object of their abuse and while that violence is a universal method of instilling terror, it need not be employed in order to achieve the desired effect. Rather, the threat is all that is necessary to keep the oppressed in a constant state of fear.[55] The threat of violence, as veiled and inscribed within each racist moment and experience, is far more frequent than the actual moments of physical violence, but that physical "reality" is experienced as ever-present in our lives. As part and parcel of these coercive controls, the threat of violence and the threat of the re-emergence of the racist moment act to subtly constrict the ability of the victim to ever feel at ease. The sense of dread that develops within abusive environments is re-engaged and re-inscribed with each inconsistent and unpredictable racist moment. It is an ever-present reality for the oppressed because each moment of intrusion that sparks in our memory as we grow older will be inscribed with these incidents of fear and assault. Each moment is inscribed within an internal dialectic that speaks to the violence/pain of racism with little more than the threat of it. In other words, we experience that pain even in those moments when the threat is all we have. Fear is generated in these moments and re-visited with each intrusive episodic memory, but more than simply generative of fear and insecurity, the oppressed are pushed into a carefully regulated experience of accommodation and compliance. Threatened with the prospect of further pain and hardship, we often distance ourselves from the aspects of heritage, culture, family and community that target us.[56]

The frequent and unpredictable nature of racism's traumatic intrusions tells the oppressed that we are being watched at all times and that we should always be careful—because the moment can recur at any time and in any place. The "domino effect" that often takes place in the wake of such moments is particularly telling during childhood experiences of racism— where some children choose to join in the moment, while others opt to stay silent in the face of it. Ultimately, in these experiences of isolation, the commonly repeating message sent to the oppressed is that: "You are alone, you are helpless and you have no options, so live with it because it is never going to stop." We are positioned in very specific ways within these moments, but our reactions arise in relation to the larger experience of ongoing oppression and not simply in response to the moment. Fanon asserts:

> Guilt and inferiority are the usual consequences of this dialectic. The oppressed then tries to escape these, on the one hand by proclaiming his total and unconditional adoption of the new cultural models and on the other, by pronouncing an irreversible

condemnation of his own cultural style…Having judged, condemned, abandoned his
cultural forms, his language, his food habits, his sexual behaviour, his way of sitting
down, of resting, of laughing, of enjoying himself, the oppressed *flings himself* upon
the imposed culture with the desperation of a drowning man.[57]

Fanon's words, like those of so many other theorists, pedagogues, activists
and students who have taken up the pen to write about the plight of the
oppressed, echo with the pain, frustration and desperation of a lifetime spent
in shackles. In re-visiting his writings on the "African Revolution," we are
reminded of the sense of "absolute resignation" that so often and commonly
inscribes the experience of colonized, oppressed peoples. Similar to the
subject of Fanon's narrative, our voices trace the same surrender to the
inevitable and our narratives carry the same "weight," the same earnest
tone—we too fling ourselves at our imposed culture with the desperation of
the drowning.

CHAPTER SEVEN
Weaving the Tapestry: Anti-Racism Theory and Practice

Through the natives' strange questions it is possible to see, with historical hindsight, what they resisted in questioning the presence of the English—as religious mediation and as cultural and linguistic medium...To the extent to which discourse is a form of defensive warfare, then mimicry marks those moments of civil disobedience within the discipline of civility: signs of spectacular resistance.
      —Homi K. Bhabha, *Signs Taken for Wonders*[1]

No perspective *critical* of Imperialism can turn the Other into a self, because the project of Imperialism has always already historically refracted what might have been the absolutely Other into a domesticated Other that consolidates the Imperialist self...A full literary inscription cannot easily flourish in the imperialist fracture or discontinuity, covered over by an alien legal system masquerading as Law as such, an alien ideology established as only truth and a set of human sciences busy establishing the native as 'a self-consolidating other'.
      —Gayatri C. Spivak, *Three Women's Texts and a Critique of Imperialism*[2]

How often have we heard the political rhetoric that suggests that public resources cannot and should not be allocated toward the needs and/or demands of special interest groups? This book began with a clear mission to "re-think" commonsense understandings of how we experience racism and the resulting implications for strategy and resistance. Moreover, we have voiced a clear desire to help develop a revolutionary consciousness that might operate outside the auspices of power and privilege. Simply put, we want this work to play a part in developing a "civil disobedience": an insurgent call to "intellectual arms" that might, in turn, grow into an "organic" revolutionary movement. In seeking to equip individuals with the knowledge and skills to confront everyday racism and to work for social change, we hope this work has legitimized the oppositional and subjugated voices of minoritized peoples. However, it is important that we recog-nize, as asserted above by both Bhabha and Spivak, that it grows increasingly difficult to nurture insurgent knowledges when the language and systems we would employ are inscribed through the power and privilege of our oppressor. In this chapter, we pose questions and explore possibilities for social change that are based on the politics and theory of an integrative anti-racism framework. As discussed in the introduction, the anti-racist project is a tapestry and we engage an integrative anti-racist praxis as an important thread in that tapestry. Many of the strategies and practices discussed in this chapter require amelioration from within sites traditionally controlled by "privilege," but we feel that they entail a radical re-visioning of the status quo that speaks to our transformative social agenda.

Remaining reflective of and attuned to the oppressive nature of our contemporary political and institutional formations, the pointed questions asked in this chapter focus on the asymmetrical power relations that run between and among social groups within society. We seek a re-distribution of power to ensure fair representation, not only of the actors themselves, but also of the subjects of knowledge production. In this light, we also seek to cultivate a project of transformative possibility in which all people can challenge and resist the structural forces that continually re-produce social oppression and inequality. The theoretical orientation in this chapter highlights the saliency of race in order to focus our attention on the specific problematics of difference and power. We no longer want to speak through our oppressor: we no longer wish to take up the muted categories of multiculturalism and diversity made available to us by their grace. Rather, as race and racism are central to how social spaces are claimed, occupied and defended, we employ a critical anti-racism in an effort to delineate the causes and/or factors that contribute to racial oppression and, in turn, to offer alternative solutions to that problematic. Our politics of research and study is not simply to generate knowledge but to produce new knowledge and perspectives that will help oppressed peoples rethink their subjectivity in North American contexts. It follows, then, that the purpose of this chapter is twofold: First, we pay particular attention to the public discourse against anti-racist politics, practice and educational reform; second, we take a critical look at how anti-racist praxis might fit into Western Diasporic contexts.

Our basic contention here is that anti-racism is a powerful and feasible tool for social change. While we do not see anti-racism as the only tool to social change, we are emphatic that these models hold the possibility of transforming society in light of the issues raised in this book. Throughout this text we have argued that racism is endemic in society. We concur with Omi and Winant (1993), Fine, et al (1997) and many others in their contentions that our society is racially coded and that we live our fears, anxieties, desires and pleasures in racial terms. We must confront the cancer of racism and its myriad forms if we are to interrogate the ways and processes through which race is claimed, denied and acted upon. To deal with racism it is important that we develop political and academic strategies that explain how and why the concept of race continues to hold political, economic, material, symbolic and psychological consequences for social groups. Admittedly, there are several approaches to equity and social change that may be applied within this framework. For example, an anti-racist model may emphasize the "saliency of race" in anti-oppression work while acknowledging the intersections of race and other forms of difference. We argue that depending on the historical context, race becomes a salient marker of difference and disparity. Elsewhere, Dei (1999) explains this notion of "saliency" as a political and pragmatic choice to take an anti-racist entry point. It reflects the reality that our histories and educational backgrounds position us to read oppressions differently.[3] As Fanon noted:

> Face to face with the White man, the Negro has a past to legitimate, a vengeance to extract...In no way should I dedicate myself to the revival of an unjustly unrecognized Negro civilization. I will not make myself a man of the past...I am not a prisoner of history; it is only by going beyond the historical, instrumental hypothesis that I will initiate the cycle of my freedom.[4]

In highlighting the "saliency of race" we acknowledge that we all have multiple subject identities, but we further argue that there are differing social consequences for the various components of our identities (class, gender, race, ethnicity, culture). In fact, even as we articulate the fluidity of identities and their relative saliencies respective of social context, we are also mindful that race may cut across all contexts. The problem, as we see it, is that the very notion of intersecting/multiple/fluid identities may give the appearance of a balance between "impermanent identities," but such interpretations risk "trivializing each identity by regarding it as transitory."[5] To reiterate an important point that has been touched on throughout this work, "salience" does not mean we look at oppression separately. Rather, it speaks to focus— we still work within an understanding of oppressions as connected. The saliency of race is an "and/with" rather than an "either/or" analysis that stresses the centrality of race and the connection of race with class, gender, ethnicity and sexuality. We feel this to be a strategic way of maintaining the gaze on race, which has so often been ignored and/or silenced in both public discourse and in the imagination of our oppressor.

A policy model for social justice work may target specific groups by acknowledging a severity of issues for certain bodies, but it is important not to confuse such strategies with "interest group politics." It is both a strategic and pragmatic approach that maintains a deserved focus on a particular oppression in order to deal with it comprehensively, all the while recognizing that it does not stand alone in a hierarchy of oppressions. Thus, a policy can be enacted which addresses multiple oppressions by targeting a particular oppression as the focal point of response and political direction.[6] So, for example, in terms of educational policy, it is important that schools and local boards are able to enact anti-racism policies without having them negated or dismissed by arguments that call for the development of broader "equity-based" programs. In making this point, we distinguish between "discourse" (as in discursive analysis) from "social policy" (as in political practice). We do so because policy models may adopt a multi-centric approach to change (i.e., focus on race, gender, sexuality, class and multiple centres of action) while drawing on the connections between these identities. In such a case, we distinguish between policy and discourse in that there are unique histories at play here and a severity of consequences for certain bodies.

As discussed earlier, in our very politicized stance, we highlight the inseparability of oppressions. Also, addressing the pointed issues of race and racism necessarily entails dealing with and reflecting the intersecting and interlocking of other oppressions as well. Therefore, the struggle against racism requires that we maintain a simultaneous gaze on sexism, classism, homophobia, heterosexism and other forms of social oppressions. We know, for example, that there are racialized sexisms, just as there are sexualized racisms. Similarly, class intersects powerfully with questions of race, gender and sexuality. We contend forcefully that oppressions are experienced simultaneously, but we must take up the lessons of history illustrating that when oppressions are strung together some forms of oppressions are least discussed. There is a discomfort in speaking about racism and so we will often find ourselves struggling to bring "race-talk" out from "the margins of the margins." Therefore, in our political decision to focus on race and anti-racist work, we assert that we must have the ability to name all oppressions explicitly within a politics of change. Racism must be up-front in our discussions in this work. We take this political and oppositional stance against the bland and problematic talk of plurality of oppressions, holding that such discussions ignore the situational and contextual variations of oppression and the historical denials of racism.

As educators and community workers, we cannot afford to either create or assume a false separation between our issues and the subjects that we study. Neither can we separate theory from practice. Our theory and practice should speak to our personal and collective implications in the subject matter of inquiry. Similarly, our theory and practice should be informed by the lived and historical experiences, interests and aspirations of our subjects. In this light, we assert firmly that something is missing within many of our academies of learning: The perspectives and knowledges of subordinate groups in society, the voices of the *other*. The virtual absence of these voices is indeed problematic because debates in our academies critically concern marginalized peoples. But equally troubling is the attempt to maintain a distance from the subjects of inquiry, as if such academic detachment makes for a comprehensive understanding of the phenomenon of study. Anti-racism is an explicit academic stance of personal involvement and implication in the problem of racism.

The notion that a critical educator must put the ideals and values of his or her subjects of study at the centre of academic and social inquiry is extremely important. For some, this stance has allowed us to critique the dominance of Eurocentric knowledge production. But we are grounded in what we write about when we show how the subject matter of academic investigation affects our lives as individuals, as subjects and as members of communities. We live in a world in which scholars from minoritized backgrounds have had to deal with constant negations, erasures, misrepresentations and inaccuracies in the reporting and explaining of their human condition, history and social realities. We have become acutely aware of how knowledges are produced, disseminated and used, both internally and globally; thus we recognize the dangers that accompany claims to objectivity and dispassion. We would argue that knowledge production for the sake of knowledge is no knowledge at all. The processes of knowledge creation must be fair to the subjects of study. Knowledge producers must always be mindful of the welfare of our subjects. There is no academic freedom without matching responsibility. Responsibility means using knowledge to address fundamental questions of social injustice and power inequities in society.

The anti-racism discourse and practice that we advocate has far-reaching implications for our global community. Increasingly, our societies are having to confront the challenges of dealing with difference and diversity in populations. Increasing international migrant flows and re-settlements are working to change the demographic makeup of schools, particularly in large metropolitan centres. In these times of Diasporic evolution, the individual and collective rights of racial, ethnic, religious, linguistic, cultural, socio-economic *others* have posed significant challenges for the mainstream with respect to its responsibility to adapt to and reflect our contemporary realities. In looking again to the educational system as a microcosm through which important cultural values, signs and symbols are transmitted, we see very explicit examples of how official rhetoric about education may not necessarily match what is actually taught and practiced. For the most part educational systems transmit shared cultural values that function to produce an educated pool of "workers" who are tailored to the needs and requirements of a job market and who subscribe to the attributes of *individualism, competitiveness, achievement, quality, meritocracy, excellence, standard, hard work* and *objectivity.*

While the market is glorified through this commodification of the educational system, personal ownership of knowledge becomes heralded while individual rights supersede notions of collective responsibility. The underlying systemic function, as education works to serve the needs of the market economy, is that discussions of "educational excellence" and "quality education" become separated from issues of equity and social justice. So as schooling becomes detached from local communities, the values of communal membership, social responsibility, culture and history become de-emphasized and muted. The results, as seen in today's curriculum, are that the contributions of *other* peoples to world civilization have become devalued, if not negated. Furthermore, a "blame the victim" stance has manifested in the popular understanding of educational failure as attributable to a lack of student ability and effort. In such positions, interrogations of the structures for teaching, learning and administration of education become truncated.

In the discursive politics of anti-racism, it is important to see the minoritized both as individual subjects and as members of a collective. Understanding identity and subjectivity is crucial to articulating this sense of the individual as also belonging to a group/collective. In drawing this distinction, we move beyond the pointed issue of claiming rights and responsibilities in that we feel it is also a matter of presenting a more nuanced reading of subjectivity and identity. Along these lines, an interesting and astute observation was made by Brettschneider (1999) when noting that "identity" in the postmodernist frame has been oppressive even while the postmodern stance has asserted a move away from such oppressive politics. He asks: "what do you do if you want to end oppression and do it still within the context of identity?"[7] As we have noted, "identity" and "subjectivity" are key to any political engagement and we feel that the nuanced meanings we bring to these concepts have important implications for anti-racist politics.

With these notions of "identity" and "subjectivity" in mind, we re-assert that there is no universal nor isolated subject. Rather, we contend that marginalized groups have their own cultural frameworks of meaning that developed long before the mainstreams of Western culture sought to inform their identities.[8] Identities are not just imposed, they must be understood to be both claimed and resisted. Today, marginalized groups are increasingly claiming their legitimate positions as subjects rather than objects to be acted upon. These groups do not see themselves simply as individualized subjects with atomistic autonomy, nor do they see themselves performing as "culturally stripped universal agents."[9] There are communal notions of self, subject and identity that become tied to collective histories and heritage. In fact, as Brettschneider further notes, "when the specifics of your community's oppression have been marked, at least in part, by the fracturing of bonds, relations, connection to history and group knowledge, then further fracturing actually represents further oppression."[10] Therefore, we cannot negate modern "subjectivities" without paying a heavy price to the successful pursuit of a politics for transformative social change.

While a postmodern discursive praxis may require that we challenge the biases and exclusions of historical constructions of subjectivity and identity, such challenges must not then position us to negate the very existence of the subjects themselves.[11] To claim an identity is also a political undertaking, so we must struggle to liberate our identities and multiple positionalities from the oppressive constraints that have been ascribed to them.[12] Within supposedly democratic nations that articulate qualities of fairness and justice, we cannot simply insist on our rights and responsibilities as autonomous subjects. Rather, we must remember that we are also members of identity groups and identified social groups, so we enter new political spaces not just as citizens but as members of racialized collectivities. In such spaces, these identities and subjectivities assist in shaping our politics, desires and aspirations. Within the emerging contestations, contradictions and ambiguities of these new political spaces, we must also begin to analyze power in its multiplicities given that our identities exist along multiple grids of power.

In this analysis, we employ an integrative anti-racism in order to work with the categories of race, class, gender, sexuality, ability, culture, language, religion and all other forms of difference through a race-centric lens. Race, class, gender and sexuality are constructed and experienced simultaneously, so the ways in which we experience racism differ dependent on the intersections and interlocks of these various other oppressions. To clarify, interlocking analysis entails working with all the concepts of oppression (race, gender, class, sexuality, age, (dis)ability, language, culture and religion) without engaging in the politics of competing oppressions or marginalities.[13] Yet, there is no universal standpoint on what would constitute an effective interlocking analysis. Any claim to the contrary is to engage in essentialist politics stemming from a position of a unilateral fragmentation around difference. We cannot offer a universal standpoint approach on interlocking analysis, in part due to the difficulty of working with all oppressions/ concepts at the same time. There are pertinent questions to be broached: (a) What are the implications for theory building when we pay attention only to the commonalities or the differences in social constructions of oppression? (b) Are there more politically relevant differences in our claiming the mantra of race, gender, class and sexuality as simultaneous oppressions? (c) Do we do justice to all our social identities when we claim to analyze the categories of race, gender, class and sexuality within an interlocking/intersectional paradigm? (d) What are the philosophical and theoretical challenges posed by the political position of maintaining a critical gaze (on race) in an integrative anti-racism?

While the categories of race, gender, class (and to some extent sexuality) have received primacy in interlocking analyses, we further need to ask why other forms of difference (for example, religion, culture, language) are seen as secondary. Greenebaum (1999) argues that the ability to name one's oppression is a mode of power and that those who produce the categories of race, gender, class, sexuality occupy positions of power.[14] She further cautions that dominant discourses on oppression cannot conveniently focus on material/economic inequality.[15] Such focus can be problematic if it is realized that there are powerful emotional, spiritual and psychological consequences to oppression.[16] The aura of *otherness* is dangerous at all times. So if, as Greenebaum claims, the "concept of intersectionality was created to show the complexities in women's lives," then it is troubling in an integrative theory to downplay other forms of difference that impact social existence.[17] In order to address this problem, an integrative anti-racism analysis acknowledges race as the central axis of power (difference) and a focal point/lens through which other forms of oppression can be looked at or understood. The saliency of race in an integrative anti-racism analysis recognizes the situational and contextual variations of oppressions as well as the fact that politics, desires and interests shape our academic practices. A race saliency approach also alludes to the power of skin color privilege, racism and White supremacy and to the fact that oppressions may be similar but yet not equal nor identical in their consequences.

As Bourne (1987) noted, "the politics of equal oppressions...is ahistorical in that it equates oppressions across the board without relating each to its specific history."[18] So bearing these issues in mind, we contend that, while everyone can be victims of race prejudice, for racially minoritized groups, the issue of "racism" is a historically, culturally and politically specific complex of disabilities. Racisms are attuned not only to feelings and attitudes, but also to the institutional and systemic conditions that support and justify the denigration and oppression of peoples on the basis of race and "difference." As discussed in Chapter Five, in order for anti-racism to offer change, the discourse and practice must speak directly to institutional racism by extending the discussion beyond racial prejudice. Racism lives through the applications of prejudice and power—unearned power. We make this particular clarification because power from unearned privilege may appear to be strength—when actually all that such power allows is the privilege to dominate or escape complicity.

While both White supremacy and the racism of dominant society are institutionalized and sanctioned, subordinate groups can indeed work oppositionally within the tropes of White racism. However, we would maintain that, while such challenges to power and privilege are a necessity, we must be careful to ask from where those challenges arise. It is only when minoritized communities challenge their own members for working with the tropes of dominance that transformation truly occurs. For, as Connolly astutely observes, when oppressed communities are marginalized for working with the very tropes of privilege, then oppression functionally recurs and strengthens. Interestingly, when minoritized groups react to the oppression they experience and act in resistance, the dominant would often call that response and resistance racism or in contemporary terms—"reverse-racism."[19] The challenge for the minoritized continues to be how to voice transformational praxis even while power of privilege persistently intercedes in the imagination of possibilities for conceptualizing change.

Respective of these privileged challenges and their tendency toward maintenance of the status quo, critical anti-racists must not be afraid to ask how these societal institutions and settings respond to the multiple needs and concerns of a diverse body politic. The aim must be to ensure that excellence becomes accessible and equitable within these societal/institutional settings. So, within this framework, how might we move beyond the bland/seductive politics of inclusion and tolerance to a pointed discourse of institutional transparency and accountability that is both oppositional and pragmatic within our institutions? Can we build a common view of justice that guides and guards human interactions without vilifying theory and dismissing philo-sophies in the call for practical tools for social action? Moreover, how might we work with different models of social justice that do not fall into the problematics of an equality versus equity debate?

Critical anti-racism may help provide us with some answers to these important questions. The history of community activism and communal roots for anti-racist work shows how local groups have struggled with these concerns.[20] Through the advance of community politics, commonsense ideas about difference have been challenged and/or resisted. Moreover, in this new Diasporic landscape, it is no longer tenable to argue that those who accentuate difference are actually the problem. In other words, frameworks that seek to problematize the salience of "difference" itself have been refuted in political practices for social change. In fact, to paraphrase Sleeter (1993), rather than negate the importance of difference we must disassociate the negative meanings that are attached to it. We must resist the construction of difference as a hierarchy and instead espouse the idea of difference as strength. Difference can be a circle of knowledge in which every subject within the circle has a contribution to make.[21] Importantly, we assert that, while we live in a world today that is much about "difference," we must not act in ways that simply claim differences for the sake of intellectual politics. This means we must move beyond celebratory modes of difference to distin-guish between the heralding of diversity and the creation of divisiveness.

Anti-racism work for social change acknowledges our respective privi-leges and complicities. Owning up to our complicities means that we begin to cast our gaze on multiple sites of oppression, acknowledging differential privileges that permit us to see and not see oppressions. Acknowledging complicity calls for a degree of self-criticality. It means being self-reflexive and developing a critical ability to reflect and act, without claiming inno-cence and moral distancing.[22] We should also find ways to deal with risks and consequences that come with doing anti-racist work. The intellectual, physical, emotional and psychological attacks on anti-racism work/workers are vivid forms of symbolic and physical violence. There is the constant questioning of one's credibility and legitimacy in pursuing anti-racist poli-tics. Thus, rather than seeking to define/manage who does anti-racist work, it is perhaps more important and legitimate to examine whether potential allies/partners are prepared to take the risks and accept the consequences that come with doing anti-racism work?

In dealing with many of these questions we must situate equity within the broader definition of education; that is, seeing education as the varied ways, strategies and options through which people come to know their world and act within it.[23] So in writing this work and truly in our conceptualization of this project, we engage education as more than schooling and the institutional setup of knowledge production, dissemination and use. Rather, just as we hope this work functions as a dialogue between writer and reader, we feel that true libratory educational praxis engages the interplay between our knowledge of self and world—whether in the workplace, church, schools, homes, families or communities. Such inclusive conceptualizations of education also demand that we work toward a broader definition of equity (race, gender, class, sexuality, language, religion, culture, age, physical ability) that also recognizes the severity of issues for specific disadvantaged groups. Rights have accompanying responsibilities. Which is to say that, in asserting that citizens have the right to education (as broadly defined), we must also acknowledge our collective responsibility to critically question our societies.

For educators, the ability to teach is a privilege, but in a broader sense, it is a privilege that runs parallel to the responsibility of teaching relative to the complete history of ideas and events that have shaped and continue to shape human growth and development. This requires that one acts relative to one's own subjective agency. There are several sites for such anti-racist political action. Anti-racism practice begins where one is, that is the self and then proceeds to multiple sites: school, home/family, local community, workplace, union halls, courts and the justice system. At this juncture we will focus on the school system to examine the reasons and possibilities of pursuing anti-racism as educational strategy for change. We see all stakeholders, as well as individual subjects who occupy educational sites, as the agents of change. While it is important to speak about human agency, we must correspondingly acknowledge the structural constraints to such agency. As we have done throughout this work, we ask critical questions about the structural and organizational processes for delivering education to all learners: For example, what do you understand by power and privilege? What are the challenges of being a minority in a White-dominated society? What does it mean to be "different"? What are the strengths of having "difference"? What is the relationship between race, the social contexts of schooling, work, family and the self?

In choosing the school as a site of action, we are cautious of the words of Butler (2000), who maintains that she has "some difficulty with…putting most of our anti-racism education eggs in the public school basket."[24] There are other (maybe more strategic?) sites for anti-racism work (e.g., mainstream media, legal system, government policy making at all levels of government, "charitable organizations," social services, police training, the arts, corporate culture, etc.). She goes further to ask how anti-racist work might be made more comprehensive.[25] In writing this text, in this way, we are hoping to engage a very particular strategy for change and the advancement of critical consciousness. We are aware that anti-racism applies to a variety of contexts, not just the school system. However, at this juncture we are being strategic in suggesting the school as a site of change.

As racially minoritized subjects living in Toronto, we are aware of the many changes taking place in Ontario's education! But the more things appear to change, the more they remain the same. The demographics of our schools and the broader society are changing almost faster than our ability to recognize. Let us ponder some inter-related arguments: Changes in schools have not kept pace with the changing demographics of race, religion and ethnicity. For example, looking at our high schools, one would note that over one-third of the students in Metro Toronto public schools were born in approximately 174 countries outside of Canada; over 40% speak a mother tongue other than English.[26] Bearing that in mind, we must begin to question whether our schools have really registered this demographic fact. Similarly, at the college level, it is painfully clear that diversity is a serious concern to staff and faculty in many of our institutions. At the university level, minority representation makes up less than 5% of educators.[27] Many departments are "lily White." For example, in 1991 only about 5% of the new student-teachers in Ontario's nine university faculties of education classified themselves as visible minorities. Similarly telling, in 1997 Metro Toronto School Boards reported that racial minority students made up over 50% of the overall student population.[28]

We maintain that moral, political, economic and social arguments can be advanced to address this difference and diversity. At a wider level, difference and diversity must be critically addressed if we are to have a complete history of ideas and events that have shaped human growth and development. Research on educational performance of students shows the severity of issues for certain student bodies. For example, African Canadians, First Nations and Portuguese students have higher dropout ratios.[29] As briefly discussed in Chapter Five, these groups are particularly streamed in that they have a 42% dropout rate as compared to 30% for the general population. Students from these groups are disproportionately enrolled in special educa-tion and non-university stream programs. But this is not to say these are the only groups with educational concerns. In fact, Asian students, while widely perceived to be "doing well," also have educational mischaracterizations to deal with. For example, notions that Chinese learners are "the" model minority contribute to the streaming of these youth into narrow fields of academic choices such as science and math-related occupations.[30]

On the surface, what can we discern from statistics and quantitative measures? While they are often useful in directing the course of research, it is important to also recognize that there are ephemeral or "human sides" to the stories that we hear—aspects of the lived experience that statistics cannot explain for us. Beyond the statistical figures, there is a human dimension to the disengagement of certain children from their schooling experiences.[31] Particularly for students of color, there are often trade-offs to academic success that surface in relation to navigations of self-identity, history and social esteem. What this tells us is that we cannot avoid a critical examination of the institutional structures in favour of a simplistic approach to individualizing social problems and issues. We must highlight the systemic barriers to academic success and explore how the structures of teaching, learning and administration contribute to the problems productive of youth disengagement from school. Sites of formal education present interesting challenges for anti-racist politics; indeed, there are disturbing educational reforms currently rising throughout Western contexts. As a perfect case in point, let us address the changes presently taking place in Ontario's educational curricula.

Elsewhere, Dei and Karumanchery (1999) discussed the extent to which school reform in Ontario has successfully sidelined equity issues, at least in official circles. An important question to broach in this specific context is: How does the new Ontario curriculum speak to us as racialized minorities? [32] Hatcher (1998) maintains that such "modernist" policies of "school improve-ment" tend to promote an approach to schooling reform that does not consider the unequal effects of race, class and gender on the lives of students. Hatcher goes further to frame four main characteristics of such reforms: (a) an *abstract universalism* that downplays the specificities of local school situations; (b) a *decontextualization* that devalues the importance of students' experiences, histories, cultures and identities as they relate to the learning process; (c) a *consensualism* that avoids dealing with conflict and controversy; and (d) a *managerialism* that privileges a top-down approach to the administration of schooling.[33] In their promotion of a deracialized approach to schooling, such reforms fail to address the structural, political and historical dimensions of change. In these features of market-based reform, we see some of the inherent problematics of a "corporate managerialist model of education."[34] As asserted by Dei and Karumanchery (1999), today's fiscally conservative governments have forced many communities to face reforms that effectively undermine public schooling. Such curricula primarily present an outcome-based approach to schooling change that fails to recognize the differential experiences of the learner; what it takes to teach a student; what it means to develop expectations of a teacher and a learner; and the implications of having a limited vision for education. This ideological "return to basics" has functioned to cover-up various discourses that maintain privileged interests.

These "special interests" suggest that the specific implications of the new curricular changes for diverse students have been taken off the discussion table. The common axiom of "standards matter the most" carries with it heavy baggage. How we speak of "standardization" in the midst of difference, diversity and inequity speaks to how we understand the "realities" of diversity and difference for students, their families and their social development. The whole idea of a "common curriculum" suggests that generic terms are to be applied to students irrespective of race, ethnicity, gender, sexuality, linguistic proficiency or cultural differences. We recognize that there is a dire need for differential allocation of resources in schools because students enter into the schooling environment as differently positioned. It is an undeniable fact that schools with a large number of new Canadians require additional resources (e.g., funding for additional programs such as heritage and English as a second language). However, currently, fearful of the brand of "special interest politics," such allocations of resource are few and far between.

Karumanchery (2000) argues that an integrative anti-racist approach to schooling interrogates the ability of oppressed and minoritized groups to resist the traditional positions of marginality assigned to them, as well as the more contemporary positions that develop relative to such modernist reforms. However, pivotal to this framework is an understanding that the responsibility to resist oppression cannot rest with the oppressed alone. Rather, a great deal of accountability in these matters must also be placed in the hands of privilege. [35] However, to paraphrase Stuart Hall (1988), there is a "Great Moving Right Show" going on in Ontario and not everyone is amused by this show.[36] Educational changes and reforms have been designed in the interest of capital and global markets and these reforms are not situated in a critical understanding of social difference and change.[37]

To interrogate the growing problematics of these "bottom-line money management" reforms, it is crucial to examine how such changes reflect the further racialization and marginalization of students. For example, with the advent of the "commonsense revolution," high school students in Ontario may now be categorized and segregated relative to educational and earning potential—either (a) college or (b) vocational. The "academically" streamed students would find themselves "pushed" toward university, while those *other* students would find themselves "pushed out" in and amongst students relegated to a field of lower potentiality. We must ask ourselves, "who is being slotted into these groupings"? Ontario students now require 30 credits to graduate and of those, 18 are compulsory. Problematically, while course grades are made part of the permanent record (in the apparent desire to illustrate success and potential), do we ever ask how those records should be read? Remembering that statistics are always up for interpretation, do the failures reflect inability or failure of students, or do they reflect students' struggle to engage their schooling experience? It is, at best, a slippery slope.

There is a need to re-cast schooling and education in order to assist racial, ethnic, linguistic and cultural minority students to develop a sense of entitle-ment and belonging in their schools. As already argued, the dominating emphasis on "standards" fails to critically interrogate the existing structures and processes of schooling. Due to the link between structures and standards, anti-racism pays particular attention to the delivery of education (e.g., teaching, learning and administration). These structures are pivotal in determining the "standards" of education. Anti-racism challenges the ongoing trend of de-coupling "excellence" from discussions about "equity" in education. The problematic assumption that somehow those who speak about equity are not concerned about standards, quality and excellence in education is a farce. Current anti-racist politics must begin to use the few spaces and position of power that minorities have secured as principals and vice principals in our school systems to subvert White dominance in our institu-tional settings. Notwithstanding the pervasiveness of structures, how can we use those spaces and power bases to rupture for fundamental change?

We know that race is an unsettling issue, and even more so—a taboo issue for those in spaces and places of privilege, but in reflecting on issues of anti-racist educational praxis we must start to acknowledge the politics of affirmation and denial as they pertain to race and difference[38] Subjects in schools are de-racialized, de-classed and de-gendered.[39] The universal definition of the student allows for the reproduction of dominant Eurocentric knowledge. Within this cult of individualism, the everyday rationalization of racist behaviour in schools and society allows people to comfortably use soft words such as "ethnicity" and "culture" to pathologize minorities and their communities. The failure to draw that important conceptual distinction between pathologizing families and asking parents and communities to take additional responsibilities for the education of their children is at the root of the problem. Anti-racist practice must challenge the stigmatization and labeling of minorities. But even more specifically, it must deal with racially differential treatment that promotes the culturalization of race.[40] There is a dire need to subvert the use of code words (e.g., merit/standards/excellence) that pathologize children and families rather than addressing the inadequacies of the system. Anti-racist practice must evoke individual rights and collective responsibility while challenging the existing power hierarchies that position race, gender, class and sexuality as differences to be ranked and streamed. The bland talk of inclusion does not take into account the problematics of existence at the margins.

We assert that, if for no other reason, the push for anti-racism as a moral and political issue addresses "difference" outside the tailored frameworks of demographics and to the question of educating students relative to the histories and experiences that have shaped and continue to shape human growth and development. We need "difference" to be represented in schools if the diversity of human experiences and knowledges are to address the lack of curricular sophistication and the problem of representation in schools. Schools are contested spaces and, as such, it is intrinsically problematic to approach schooling and, particularly, curriculum as socially, politically and ideologically neutral. Anti-racism change calls for new program initiatives that will pay attention to the material/economic, spiritual, psychological, emotional and cognitive needs of learners. Such paradigm shifts to educational models will require that the cultural resource bases of local communities are incorporated into the schooling environment and, moreover, that they will necessitate the promotion of local languages, the representation of multiple knowledges and attention to the paramount issue of representation. On the issue of physical representation, anti-racism politics demand that institutions establish clear guidelines and accountability procedures for faculty, staff and student diversity. School administrators must put in place specific guidelines/timetables and develop transparent processes for faculty diversification at the elementary/secondary, college and university levels of the educational system.

We would encourage the development and implementation of local community organizations that might take collective initiatives to establish an arms-length Council for Minority Education. Such community-based strategies might effectively ease the responsibility of charting the course of minority education from regional and national levels to the local level. Such community councils could be representative of our diverse minority communities. In supporting local communities in the use of legal recourse to address inequities in education and schooling, we see such initiatives as less an issue of educational reform than as an issue of basic "human rights." Education is both an individual and a collective right. Simply put, the system must be held accountable if it is failing disadvantaged youth—particularly considering that as tax-paying citizens, members of local communities should expect equitable educational services. We would also encourage the development of other community-initiated alternatives to mainstream/ conventional education in that local community groups, particularly the racially minoritized, cannot rely on the school system to address their educational needs.

History teaches that our minoritized communities cannot simply hope to mainstream our youth to academic and social achievement, nor can we relegate the educational opportunities of our youth to a system that has proven to be uninterested and uninvested in their success. Our local communities need to take control over the education of our youth. In that declaration, we would encourage the development of community-focused schools. However, the provision of material and non-material support from the community will be crucial to sustaining these alternative learning environments.[41] These learning environments could be critical in developing interests in multiple subject fields, including the arts and humanities, science, technology and mathematics among minority youth. We connect these educational issues at multiple fronts. Within the academy the differential experiences of students along lines of ethnicity, gender, class and sexuality play out in the multiple sites of schools, colleges and universities. Anti-racism politics also connect diverse communities, drawing on the similarities and the differences that permeate different communities. Similarly, this politics connects issues among the diverse racial and ethnic populations in different social spaces (e.g., within Ontario, making connection between Toronto, Sudbury, Windsor; and also making Canada-wide connections between, say, what is happening in Ontario, Nova Scotia and New Brunswick; and across trans-national spaces, sharing and comparing notes on educational issues).

As we began this chapter with a clear recognition of the partiality of knowledge, we would re-assert that we must continue to "inquire-invent-inquire-reinvent," on route to a more equitable and just system. In this chapter and in Chapter Five, we have spent some time discussing the material consequences of racism and the denial of "difference." We feel it is important to again look at the emotional and psychological effects of this oppressive milieu. To that end, let us address some of the issues taken up in this chapter—issues of community and representation—in order to address how such initiatives are both needed and how their implementation might positively effect the lived experiences of racially oppressed children.

CHAPTER EIGHT
Cultivating Culture: Consciousness and Resistance

Discovering the futility of his alienation, his progressive deprivation, the inferiorized individual, after this phase of deculturation, of extraneousness, comes back to his original positions. This culture, abandoned, sloughed off, rejected, despised, becomes for the inferiorized an object of passionate attachment...there is indeed the intuition experienced by the inferiorized of having discovered a spontaneous truth. This is a psychological datum that is part of the texture of History and of Truth... Because the inferiorized rediscovers a style that had once been devalorized, what he does is in fact to cultivate culture.

—Frantz Fanon, *Toward the African Revolution*[1]

Individuals cannot separate where they stand in the web of reality from what they perceive. In contemporary critical social theory this statement lays the foundation for the concept of 'positionality'. Positionality involves the notion that since our understanding of the world and ourselves is socially constructed, we must devote special attention to the differing ways individuals from diverse social backgrounds construct knowledge and make meaning.

—Joe Kincheloe and Shirley R. Steinberg, *Changing Multiculturalism*[2]

In working through the preceding chapters, we hope to have opened spaces to interrogate the world in new and insurgent ways that might help to untangle the web of reality that has been stretched over our eyes. As we have seen in the foregoing chapters, racism and the racist moment carry enormous potential to breach the sustaining bonds of "self" that fundamentally connect us to the world in which we live. This feeling of connection to others is basic to our sense of place in the human condition. So as racism serves to distort the symmetry of those relationships within ever-widening spheres of hierarchy, our sense of connection to ourselves and the world around us, by necessity, must begin to rupture. So let us work to rediscover a "style" that has been denied us. Let us re-define ourselves and our positionalities in ways that reflect the possibilities of empowerment, while celebrating and rewriting the nature of our Diasporic identities.

In our discussions, it has become clear that the systematic fracturing of our racial, cultural and communal solidarity effectively prevents us from accessing what would otherwise be powerful social supports capable of sustaining us in our efforts to fight those ruptures. We would contend that a firm sense of "commonality" could in fact temper the episodic intrusions of past traumas, as well as mitigate the influence/fear of similar moments occurring in the future. While racism functions to isolate the oppressed within self-disciplining positions of regulation, fear, disengagement and disconnection, "group solidarity" re-creates the sense of belonging and safety that has been made unavailable to us. Recognizing that the development of a critical anti-racist consciousness is intrinsically important to our ability to reclaim that sense of commonality, we assert that the journey toward resistance is nurtured through the process of "becoming" as are the possibilities of re-writing our oppression.

As we move from *spaces of Whiteness* to *places of Color*, our eyes become opened to the commonality of our experiences, the commonality of our oppression and the commonality of our struggles. In other words, we start to recognize the patterned interactions and relations of power that frame our oppression. In such moments of critical awakening, we find that we are not only able to place racism as a part of our reality, but that we also recognize its hidden structures, systems and meanings. We find ourselves moving from our adhesion to a racist and racialized reality that is defined by others, to a critical consciousness of reality as defined and framed in our recognition of oppression in historical contexts. Up until this point in our experience of *otherness*, we were made to struggle not only through our desire to be our oppressor, but also through our desire to distance ourselves from the markers that signaled our "differences" and deviations from the norm. As discussed in Chapter Four, this relative visibility directly impacts our ability to oppose and to resist our oppression because we are identifiable and, therefore, easily policed. This "problematic" visibility works to guarantee a "self-disciplined duality" that prevents us from developing a critical gaze into our constitution as oppressed. Simply put, this duality speaks to an existence at a crossroads where we can never truly feel at home. So where do we begin to find that sense of place and space when at every turn the possibilities of developing theory, policy and practice are discouraged and those of us who do resist are singled out for all of the communal, social and economic repercussions that accompany the label of "troublemaker"?

We are talking about the politics of knowledge and the strategic implications of how we position and engage that knowledge. Simply put, what we "know" and how we "know" are at least as important as what we do with that knowledge. The contemporary race for theory has become particularly fierce in recent years. Throughout this work we have endeavored to speak from marginalized sites, to extrapolate from the narratives of the oppressed and to engage our "lived experiences." Problematically, in our academies such work always runs the risk of being branded atheoretical, if not theoretically challenged. This is in part because of the high premium placed on the ability to theorize and the insidious attempts to deny the validity of the knowledges shared by certain bodies. Our intention in this chapter is not to contest such positions, but to problematize such conceptions of theory as having little or no bearing on the lived realities of peoples whose academic and political interests are to subvert the social order. We hope to offer an understanding of social reality and resistance as understood from the vantage point of the marginalized and subordinated.

Elsewhere, Dei (2000) argued that the worth of a social theory should not solely be measured in terms of its philosophical grounding.[3] We would further contend that theoretical work must not be validated from sites of privilege such that marginalized voices and experiences are muted in academies in much the same fashion as they are in the mainstream. We contend that relevance of a theory and practice should be seen in its ability to offer a social and political corrective: the power of theory to bring change in everyday political practice. Similarly, Fanon (1963) argued that decolonization can only be understood as a historical process that ultimately culminates in changing the social order; that it is an initially violent encounter of two forces, "opposed to each other by their very nature, which in fact results from and is nourished by the situation in the colonies." In his arguments for decolonization, he called the whole colonial situation and its aftermath into question in order to make the critical connection between "what is" and "what ought to be." What we are alluding to here is the need to combine discussions about "what is possible" with "what exists." We make this distinction because, in interrogating "what exists," we are able to offer a practical critique of the social order within an awareness of our limitations.

Like Thiophene (1995), we are arguing for a process that invokes an ongoing dialectic between hegemonic systems and the possibilities of peripheral subversions.[4] We recognize that the process of validating what is "knowledge" in the academy can be a colonial exercise in and of itself and that is why we are more interested in heralding knowledges and strategies that might assist learners in the development of insurgent "countercultures." For far too long we have been aware in the academy that the "authority of

Western knowledge" processes colonizing tendencies in such a way as to accede a false status to the colonial subject while at the same time ensuring that local knowledges are negated and/or de-valued. In this recognition we encourage the oppressed to break with the ways in which the human condition are defined and shaped by dominant European American cultures and to assert an understanding of social reality as informed by local experiences and practices.[5] We make these assertions because, within the historiography of colonized peoples, important bodies of knowledge have been, for the most part, made inaccessible. Such knowledges can be a means of staking out an identity for colonized peoples outside of the *otherized* identities that have been and continue to be constructed in Western ideology.[6] We must learn to challenge and resist the continual subordination of our *other* lived experiences.

Given the ongoing postmodernist critiques of the inadequacies of grand, meta-theories in offering a critical and comprehensive understanding of the complexities of today's society, we take into full account the fact that academic and political questions are continually changing to reflect our social realities.[7] Case in point, much anti-racist research points to the notion of solidarity and community as a fundamentally important starting point to addressing the realities of social oppression. Through comparative story-telling and a sharing of experiences, we begin to recognize the fundamentally empowering nature of group solidarity in that standing alone in the face of racism is often anything but empowering and that the discovery of commonality in group settings teaches us the simple but forceful message that we are not alone and that our experiences are the experiences of "a people."

Yalom (1985), in relation to the healing potential of "group psychotherapy," referred to this sense of empowerment through solidarity as the experience of "universality." He specified that this experience was especially penetrating amongst victims of trauma who had felt particularly isolated by shameful secrets.[8] This assertion speaks to the experience of the oppressed in relation to our duality, and it recognizes the intra-psychic dilemmas faced by any of us who would rather have *just denied it*. Karumanchery (2003) argues that racism impacts our intrapsychic ability to frame ourselves in relation to others without interjecting "*I* positions" that reflect isolation, alienation and self-pathology and that, therefore, the importance of finding a sense of commonality is crucial to our healthy recovery en route to "becoming." The solidarity and sense of safety that arise in these "common places" are simply not available to the oppressed when they are in group environments or one-on-one situations in the "everyday-mainstream world." In fact, this would account for the often-noted "need for *them* to stick together." After all, how often do we hear White voices claiming such "Black Group Dynamics" to be just so much "reverse-racism?" We would contend that the search for safety is an incessant voice in each of us and that, for the racially oppressed, that voice is best heard in the safety of community.[9]

The impact of racism is dulled not only within environments where the notion of "group suffering" diffuses the concentrated nature of the moment, but also within the sense of "universality" that develops in such solidarities. We may begin to transmute our experience from *the moment as personal attack* to the moment *as part of a larger system of racial oppression*, impacting one and all in the same moment. It is in such moments of critical clarity that we begin to glimpse ourselves as part of the great *otherhood* of oppressed peoples and not as lone victims of racism and discrimination. It is important to note that this notion of critical awakening through commonality extends beyond the "dialogue between physical bodies" and to the dialectics of the metaphysical and the symbolic. This symbolic push toward a reclamation of self and peoplehood appears to arise most powerfully within the political missions arising in oppressed solidarities that have undergone the same traumas (e.g., The Holocaust and the Jewish people, American slavery and the African American). Within this perspective, the saying "It's a Black Thing" takes on new meanings.[10]

It is only in the safe haven of these communal spaces that we find ourselves able to reflect on the innate differences of entitlement and experience that are ascribed to and inscribed within our experience of being *other*. It is in these safe spaces that we are able to reflect on our sense of Diasporic struggle. Ayo, an African Canadian woman speaks to the dilemmas of identity growing up in relation to her discovery of a normalized Blackness:

> And then when I was twelve, my dad took us to Sierra Leone and I hadn't been there
> since I was five. Cause 12 is just before adolescence—identity stuff is kicking in and
> I know my parents didn't consciously know that they were doing me this huge thing.
> But yeah, I spent like four months there and it was like 'That is the norm'. Like
> wow! I looked like everyone else. That was not normal where I was from and I
> really didn't want to go back. I was like, 'Just leave me here, I want to stay'. Yeah,
> so there was a moment in time when I fit in somewhere so I think it was an
> important thing to have that experience.[11]

For so many of us, like Ayo, when we think of home, we are forced to recognize that our *otherness* makes the home that we have known all our lives, anything but a "place" that reflects and embraces us. We see in this re-writing of self, a story that resonates the fundamental difference between space and place. It is for us that such travels signal a "homecoming" that in many ways helps to highlight the oppressive "reality" that holds sway over us. It reminds us that this home that we have always known exists as an *otherized* locus for pain, displacement and dislocation. Once thought to be the bane of non-Western immigrants in orthodox Diasporic theory, racialized "indigene" also must face the hard truth that in many ways "home" will always be somewhere else. It is through these realizations that we come to grips with both our Diasporic selves and the fact that our sense of *otherness* in the Western world speaks to an oppressive "colonized" experience and not to any innate flaws of self, character or culture. That being said, are such re-connections with racial/ethnic identity and cultural groups always the catalyst for these dynamic revisions of self?

Importantly, for many of us, our experiences of commonality and belonging are "the" factor that pushes us toward exploring our racialized experience. However, for many others, that "moment of critical awakening" occurs in places that offer new readings of "the world": sites that offer us an "apolitical" experience of normality. We specify this as an apolitical experi-ence because, as proposed by Karumanchery (2003), for many racialized peoples, travel offers an opportunity to see a world where Whiteness is not the norm. Moreover and more importantly still, in those opportunities for a "return to a homeland," we find ourselves able to experience life from the view of "a regular person." In respect, these moments are less an experience of political awakening than they are experiences of awakening to the true nature of our humanity. Within group dynamics where an individual is accepted without constraints and regulation, a process of spiritual mirroring occurs. In relation to group therapy, Herman (1997) employs this notion of mirroring to describe how "as each participant extends herself to others, she becomes more capable of receiving the gifts that others have to offer."[12] Therefore, in these moments when we are at home with "our people," we find that we are able to see ourselves as beautiful, normal, capable and every other positionality refused us in Western contexts.[13]

We must remember that the experience of racial oppression plays into our ability to make informed and critically conscious choices in relation to the moment. As is always the case for those as yet unable to deconstruct "it," our multiple identities are framed by, in and through their multiplicity and as such, the moment becomes inscribed with varying meanings. "Am I being too sensitive?" "Maybe they're right." "If you hear it often enough it must be true." In many ways, our participation in these Diasporic groups can provide us with a politicized interpretation of our "raced identities" in reaction to racism and in the face of our dislocation in the Diaspora. For many of us, sharing the experience with *others* who also feel the impact of racism can act as a pre-condition for personal empowerment in what would otherwise be an entirely helpless condition. In fact, the response of these communities, as part of a mutually rewarding and supportive collective, can have powerful influences for us: influences on our sense of self, our sense of belonging and our recognition of the power of collective action in the face of racism. To reiterate, these experiences speak to the importance of politicized environments in relation to the development of a critical anti-racist consciousness.

Through various entry points, we can find our way into healing relationships within groups that could afford us a sense of commonality. In these engagements with "in-group dynamics," strong connections can be made to a solidarity of experience, support and a sense of safety that we have never known. Importantly, throughout the pages of this work, we have come to recognize that this sense of commonality is intrinsically important to how we engage our traumatic past and our racist present. In these settings of solidarity, in-group members inform each other not only about their experiences, but also about their politics, all within an inclusive and safe environment. This is an illustration of how group members can help each other to share and bear the pains of past moments, as well as how that collective knowledge and theorizing engage personal strategies for resistance.

Interestingly, in terms of traditional trauma therapy, the first principal of recovery is the empowerment of the survivor. In critical anti-racist theory, that same sentiment is reflected in Freire's (1970) call for the oppressed to fight for their own liberation. As seen in the previous sections, however, that empowerment and that liberation are attained through great difficulty and often at great cost. The deeply seeded nature of racism constitutes our bodies, minds and souls and so at the core of our experience, we are disciplined to accept our oppression and to live it in relation to the lives of those with privilege. In other words, we live, breathe, work and struggle in moments that are beyond the White ability to experience, imagine or reconstruct.[14] When we hear mainstream statements such as—"I understand racism because I went to China" or "I'm not racist because one of my best friends is Black," or "If I weren't White, I think I would..."—we are reminded of John Howard Griffin's attempt to engage the Black experience by "coloring" his skin and "passing" for a few days (i.e., while Griffen's study undoubtedly arose in and through the best of intentions, the underlying supposition that one could come to "know" the Black experience in such a facile and finite manner was at best flawed and at worst, dangerous).

Whether meant rhetorically or in an earnest desire to be an ally, these types of problematic statements function to mute pain and deny the salience of race and difference. Such interpretations of the racial experience and the reactions of mainstream society in general, have a profound effect on how the racially oppressed integrate their traumatic experiences relative to the coping mechanisms they employ in their everyday experience. In effect, they are forced to carefully negotiate their positions and voices in all circumstances and moments where safety is an issue—if not consciously, then subconsciously. It is specifically with the issue of safety in mind that we parallel Karumanchery's (2003) contention that truly beneficial relationships must proceed with an eye toward engaging and healing the traumatic within a carefully managed dialogue of partnership. We say "managed," because "leading" the oppressed toward a libratory praxis always runs the danger of superficial conversions, so we must be cognizant of our efforts as leaders.[15]

Both Herman (1997) and Danieli (1998) assert that recovery from trauma can only take place within the contexts of relationships that engender a sense of safety and convey a clear acceptance of the survivors' autonomy within the relationship.[16] Relative to that framework, we engage Freire's (1970) notion that working on the side of the oppressed must be truly "pedagogical" in the sense that the processes of healing, consciousness raising and politicization take place through action *with* the oppressed.[17] Aside from the personal and solitary efforts that the oppressed make toward those ends, the efforts of caring, dedicated and personally invested partners must be understood to be fundamentally helpful to the overall process of "becoming" and "healing." Several important points arise in these discussions of in-group solidarity and politicized partnerships. First, as previously discussed, the notion of commonality is intensely important here in that the theoretical and experiential underpinnings of these relationships reflect a mutual starting point in and of pain. In and through these partnerships, we find ourselves able to re-establish the bonds of connection that were shattered through our previous traumatic experiences of racism. Because we feel safe in these working relationships, our intra-psychic energies need not be expended in self-defense, as they are within our *other* everyday interactions. Rather, within the frame of these relationships, we find ourselves able to sidestep our positionings as *other* in order to re-establish our basic capacities for trust, autonomy and initiative.[18]

It is only within this type of safe dialogical environment that we are able to recognize that we do, in fact, have autonomy and an ability to resist in the face of our oppressor. Through the "universality" experienced within these relationships, we find ourselves able to interpret the dialogue between ourselves and our new partners in the project, not as monologue but as a dialectic in which both are active, engaged and mutually supportive. In other words, these communities validate our experiences through their politics—a cooperative environment that allows their experiences, knowledges and politics to engage ours without attempts to control us. In many ways, these environments of safety are engendered through the liberatory praxis of the community in their rejection of both moral and political neutrality. The implicit dedication to resistance and the explicit devotion to in-group solidarity functionally establishes this "space" as a "place" in which the reality of our oppression, pain and trauma will not be questioned or muted. Rather, the mutually expressed call for social justice places us in a position of solidarity reflective of a fundamental acknowledgment of our pains and victimizations. It is relationship that fosters both theoretical and intellectual partnership within an awareness of empathetic solidarity.

Another prominent theme arising within these in-group formations is the impact that mentoring relationships have on our sense of "the possible" in terms of engaging racism as generally oppressive and as specifically destructive. One of the major impacts of racism on the oppressed is its ability to infuse the individual with a sense of utter helplessness over our life circumstances. The healing impact of positive role models and the powerful, validating influence of a critically conscious and politically active mentor must not be underestimated. Such politically charged relationships do more than direct our attention toward a more self-reflexive consciousness; they also allow for the powerful convergence of a mutually supportive dynamic between external and individual autonomies.[19] This dialectic speaks to the importance of taking part in critical dialogues that are directive rather than instructive. These mutually supportive relationships act as a crucible, through which "we" may burn away the irrelevancies that cloud "our" eyes to the "truth" of "our" oppression. Whether or not we consciously engage these relationships with an eye toward addressing our personal experiences of racism, there is an intense potential for healing because these partners enter as allies who not only believe our experiences of *otherness*, but understand their nature as well. In such safe environments (safe because we know that "we are not alone"), these partners enter into dialogue with us while placing all their experience and knowledge at our disposal. Importantly, we would note that when placed in structured settings (e.g., classrooms), these mentoring models will develop relative to the power dynamics inherent in the teacher/student dialectic. Simply put, the mentor/ teacher/professor occupies a relatively static position of power in this dialectic and, in that clear assertion alone, we are reminded of our initial warning that such spaces need to be engaged within a carefully managed dialogue of partnership. As students in search of knowledge, acceptance and safety, we enter into such relationships recognizing this innate power structure and voluntarily submit to the dynamics that arise therein.

For the oppressed, no other act can be more fraught with a sense of peril, because loss of control and helplessness are the daily experiences that infuse our lives. Importantly, there is, in any such setting, the potential for the abuse of power and, as asserted earlier, this could easily become an instructive, controlling relationship rather than a dialogic and freeing enterprise. The oppressed are always vulnerable to manipulation and exploitation in these spaces because (a) the universal experience of childhood dependence on a parent is invoked, leading toward feelings of transference that further exaggerate the inherent power imbalance of the relationship[20] and (b) the condition of oppression itself imposes an unauthentic view of the world in which the oppressed often become controllable, helpless and emotionally dependent.[21] Entering this relationship, the mentor—in philosophy, politics and pedagogy—creates an environment for us. But whether that space is instructive or liberating depends on the political praxis of the mentor.

In the foregoing sections of this chapter, we have spoken to the enormous importance of restoring the individual's sense of connection to the world through the experience of commonality within group solidarities. The experience of "commonality" constitutes an integral component of the healing process of "becoming." However, it is important to recognize that other intersecting themes of reclamation and resistance also exist. One such theme is illustrated in the decided movement of some oppressed peoples toward a greater critical consciousness and recovery through personal empowerment. In the course of "becoming," we recognize a gradual shift: a shift from perceptions of their existence as unpredictably dangerous to a more tempered view of the world as reliably safe within context. I specify "within context" because as discussed, a "complete healing" or "total revision of the traumatic" is unlikely to occur given the reality of racial oppressions' ongoing proclivity. It is more likely that, in the development of our critical consciousness, we might learn to walk beside the narrative of our pain.

The racially oppressed are always perceived to tread a thin line between consciousness and oversensitivity. We draw a distinction here between the use of the terms "oversensitivity" and "hyper-arousal" as discussed earlier: hyper-arousal as linked to the problematic "reality" of the traumatic and oversensitivity is linked to a problematic perception of "reality." The notion of over-sensitivity suggests a self-violation of sorts. It is an expression of mainstream discourse that creates a space for the oppressed to be taken up as complicit and at least partially responsible for their oppression in the "everyday." As discussed previously, this distinction between "real" and "imagined" violence arises out of an entire socio-historical complex designed to further support hierarchy, power and privilege, while "blaming the victim." However, as asserted by Karumanchery (2003), the first step to addressing these "inverted perceptions" of racialized existence is to understand exactly what that experience entails. So for the oppressed, in particular, the initial enterprise of our forays into the "real" must be to establish first what the "real" is, because the dire problematics of everyday racial trauma cannot be properly treated if not first diagnosed as such. Throughout these narratives, we can see the oppressed engaging in two specific diagnostic activities en route to a greater critical consciousness and personal empowerment: naming of the problem and the restoring of personal control.[22]

There is a pathology here, but it does not rest within the Diasporic body. In our self-reflexive diagnoses of the concrete and not so concrete circumstances that constitute and encompass our lives, we often interrogate the socially constructed nature of racial oppression as a starting point to engaging the dilemmas of the moment. This is a pivotal step that clears cognitive ground from which we might engage the insurgent development of resistant knowledges. Karumanchery (2003) asserts that these initial theoretical moments will often move the oppressed to begin interrogating their experiences as racialized and oppressive and that the common denominator in these interrogations is a clear, if not pointed, engagement with the relationship between power and difference. In these critical awakenings to the "relations of power," we can see an intrinsic shift in how the world is perceived and, more importantly, how individuals are perceived in relation to their world. In these moments, there is a movement away from self-defeating notions of personal deficiency and the socially inscribed desire to see "reality" through the eyes of our oppressor to a more politicized perception of power, difference and positionality. This is particularly striking when the oppressed begin to self-reflexively recognize and interrogate their passive interaction within the moment. What we find particularly interesting is that these "moments of clarity" tend not to arise in starkly racist circumstances, but rather within everyday moments that normally act to circumscribe us within our racist milieu.[23]

The banality of these "reality checks" speaks volumes as to our growing perception of racism as "far more than *lynchings* and *racial slurs*." We make this specific point because revelations in the moment do little in the way of engaging the more subtle violations that subversively frame our oppression. Racist moments that disguise themselves within the "everyday" pose a far greater challenge to our cognitive ability to recognize and theorize our oppression. The problematic that arises, as seen throughout Chapter Six, is that without the ability to pathologize the social frameworks that ground, construct and constitute our oppression, we have no way to interrogate our symptomatic responses in the moment. Knowledge is always potentially empowering, but also, it is essentially about empowerment in relation to directional movement and the strategic allocation of resources. There is an importance to the contextualizing of the dynamics of power and difference, relative to experiences of racism. As seen throughout this work, there is a sense of relief and/or release in the simple recognition that there is, in fact, an external locus for the various feelings of anxiety, hyper-arousal, depression and general despondency that so often outline the condition of racial oppression. This "clarity" is not only about recognizing the moment as racist, but also about recognizing one's positionality in the moment. Whereas beforehand it would have been all about us, now the critical analysis allows for a more cognitive response to the moment and reflection on how we are being written and constituted, both in the moment and in general. At the emotional level and without a critical gaze, we "know" that we feel *otherized* and isolated, but the words escape us, the knowledge escapes us and, as a result, we can neither act nor defend ourselves. But within and forever after, the experience when it all suddenly comes into focus, we find ourselves able to place that "un-nameable feeling" in context and address it from a cognitive position and without the same immateriality with which it has always been associated. In other words, we are no longer imprisoned by the wordlessness of the moment.

As reflected in the previous discussions of "universality," talking about the politics of race and the reality of racism allows for the marginalized to enter into meaningful dialogue about the intrapsychic, emotional and behavioural distortions that occur within oppressive systems. The prolonged and repeated nature of racial trauma will result, as described throughout these pages, in a complex of disabilities that mires the oppressed in the constant task of negotiating pain in the face of the "un-nameable." In this light, conceptual frameworks that regulate traumatic experiences and episodic intrusions through a political lens provide a basis for the formation of therapeutic strategies for resistance.

Recognizing the harmful and wide-reaching nature of racism provides the oppressed with a reasonable cognitive method of tempering the emotional effects in the moment. *Naming racism as racism is important.* But by the same token and for much the same reasons, we would follow Karumanchery (2003) in arguing that naming racism as traumatic is equally important in that it provides a clear and traceable pathology for the persistent social and internal difficulties faced by the oppressed. Such a framework for racism in context is important, if for no other reason than to help combat the internalized feelings of isolation, rage and frustration that arise in the "not knowing why." Acknowledging the "reality" of racism and the "real" physiological and psychological effects of its influence on our lives is ultimately empowering and on a very basic level. Without recognizing and acknowledging the cause of our difficulties, how can we expect to properly engage strategies for resistance? The metaphor is simple: Racism is an illness and our traumatic responses are symptoms of that illness. Importantly, naming racism as the issue is the major key in the development of strategies for resistance. Or in following the metaphor, diagnosing our experiences as racially traumatic brings us closer to finding a route toward healing.[24]

In discussing social change and insurgent resistance, the concepts are so radical and engaged on such grand scales that there is extensive room for variations in strategy. Rather than any one "right" method, we must engage multiple sites and strategies for change. However, when we speak of returning control to the oppressed, we are making a very pointed issue about the necessity of re-examining ourselves in our oppression and in our living of/out that oppression. Which is to say that in our movement toward a greater personal liberty we cannot afford to remain tied to our old processes of living, because they are intrinsically constituted by and constitutive of our oppressed duality. We, in effect, are works in progress—the question is whether we take one step forward and two steps back, or whether we consistently move forward in our progression. Problematically, our duality, as an internalized discursive effect, pushes us to understand our oppression from the perspective of our oppressor. So, in effect, our resistance is regulated in our ability to discipline ourselves. Importantly, our ability to move forward to a greater critical consciousness is closely related to the traumatic effects of a lifetime of racism that has diluted and muted our sense of power and control. We have taken this particular approach to theorizing issues emerging from our lived experiences of duality and isolation in order to interrogate the powerful configurations embedded in Western contexts and to focus our gaze on the validation and use of indigenous and communal pursuits of agency, resistance and subjective politics. Anchored in indigenous notions of a collective and common consciousness, we feel that an insurgent politics for change directly contests "colonial" conceptualizations of the *other* as "foreign" or "alien."

Our approach recognizes the importance of locally produced knowledge emanating from cultural history, daily human experiences and social interactions. In these pursuits of agency and resistant politics, we argue that power and discourse are not possessed entirely by the colonizer, but rather that discursive agency and power of resistance has resided in/among colonized groups. Bhabha (1994) rightly observed that an anti-colonial discourse "requires an alternative set of questions, techniques and strategies in order to construct it."[25] Similarly, we critique the reading of the history of Southern peoples strictly in demarcated stages (e.g., periodization pre-colonial, colonial and post-colonial epochs). We are proposing a counter/oppositional discourse to the denial and repudiation of the repressive presence of colonial oppression and an affirmation of the reality of re-colonization processes through the dictates of global capital. We are also working toward a celebration of the oral, visual, textual, political and material resistance of colonized groups, a shift away from a sole pre-occupation with victimage. The idea/notions of "nation," "community" and "citizenship" are not simply imagined constructs, but they have real meanings for the oppressed and those meanings carry profound conesquences for agency and resistance. Without a sense that we can make a difference and without the critical support structures to frame our oppression, we will find it difficult to make that leap from awakening to a politically effective critical consciousness. In relation to that journey, one of the guiding principles of psychological healing lies in the ability of the oppressed to restore that sense of power and control to themselves.[26]

Orthodox psychological treatment of trauma would assert that the first task of recovery is to establish the survivor's safety and then to move toward other areas of healing. However, with respect to an anti-racist strategy for recovery or "becoming," we follow Karumanchery's (2003) suggestion that the knowledge that one has been traumatized stands out as a key factor in that road to healing. The everydayness of our violations makes that critical understanding of paramount importance to the process. We assert that this initial awakening must take place before all others and that once seen for what it is, the oppressed may take on the task of re-integrating this new sense of safety and autonomy into our experience and knowledge of the world. Because we tend to feel unsafe in our oppressed bodies, our emotions and our thinking feel out of control. Regaining that control is of fundamental importance in healing, because that initial drive to learn about what it was that had isolated and frozen us in the moment is pivotal in the development of our anti-racist voice. It begins in small ruptures: questioning why our child-world was so immersed within White norms and White perceptions of reality, why we laughed in moments that were fundamentally painful, why we chose to "go along to get along." In regaining a sense of control, our next step takes us to a point where we might access this knowledge that had been "kept" from us all our lives and then attempt to regain control over our body, mind and environment. We then might begin to reach out to heritage and community as support structures that allow us to (a) regulate and control our environment and (b) re-develop a sense of both autonomy and safety.

In this discussion, we have drawn on several powerful theoretical revelations. First, we recognize the depth of the impact that racism has on the racially oppressed throughout childhood and adolescence. Not only were we made to feel ashamed and isolated, but for so many of us those feelings of *otherness* translated into a duality that reflected in our conscious and not so conscious attempts to "pass" as much as possible—to live up to and emulate our oppressor. These are not easy things to admit, but they are an important part of the healing journey. The processes of remembering pain and mourning loss have always been traditionally valid and empowering moments in the process of healing from trauma because they allow "survivors" to admit that "that" part of their life is gone and that they are now able to move forward in recognition of that loss. Moreover, we learn through these recognitions of pain and hardship what type of life we now wish to live and, consequently, the environment in which that life is to be lived. This is an obvious reclamation of both autonomy and power in that we critically assess the historical context of our lives to determine where, when and with whom these moments tend to occur and, in turn, where, when and with whom we are likely to find the safety and resources to best extricate ourselves from a re-currence of those pains. Where mainstream rhetoric might suggest that this is either reverse racism or weakness on our part, we assert that as a decision made in political earnest, such moves are part and parcel of a rational and empowering decision to heal and thrive within racist contexts. It is an anti-racist strategy and being able to name that strategy for oneself can be an incredibly empowering experience.

CONCLUSION
Transcending Racism, Transcending Trauma

I have retained this unsettled sense of many identities—mostly in conflict with each other—all of my life, together with an acute memory of the despairing feeling that I wish we could have been all Arab, or all European and American, or all-Orthodox Christian, or all Muslim, or all Egyptian…

—Edward Said, *Out of Place*[1]

If psychiatry is the medical technique that aims to enable man no longer to be a stranger to his environment, I owe it to myself to affirm that the Arab, permanently an alien in his own country, lives in a state of absolute depersonalization… The social structure existing in Algeria was hostile to any attempt to put the individual back where he belonged.

—Frantz Fanon, *Black Skin/White Masks*[2]

'Back where he belonged'—it has a peculiar ring to it. So too do Said's impassioned thoughts. The common denominator between the two voices is a sense of needing to fit in, to be a part of something that does not thrust one into an intra-psychic crisis of meaning and contested identities. The words of these dislocated and racialized authors resonate with the same intensity of personal struggle as those stories and narratives shared in this work. They are the multivoiced polyphony of the oppressed; existing in spaces that should read as 'homeland' but instead fluctuate between positionings of *other* 'foreigner' and 'outsider.' In our never-ending struggle to reconcile our contesting voices, we find that such negotiations of Diasporic identity find refuge and connection only in the return to places and spaces where our notions of self can develop in relation to others and not 'others'.

However, in reflecting on the preceding chapters, we believe that racialized experiences of the everyday can be interpreted as learned interactions that follow general patterns of development and deployment. These monologues are organized such that it is difficult for the racially marginalized to resist their oppressed positions. However, we would suggest that employing a critical anti-racist gaze that speaks to the spiritual, the emotional and the psychological might enable us to engage as yet untapped resources in anti-racist resistance theory, pedagogy and practice. Importantly, we would specify that we do not see newly arising strategies as capable of reversing the traumatic effects of racism. The possibility of some sort of "complete healing" is never really an attainable goal for us in that personalities formed in coercive environments generally develop deeply seated problematics with basic trust, autonomy and initiative. However, that being said, healing through the process of becoming is always a possibility and we would assert that through the process, we might learn to walk beside the narrative of our oppression rather than being constituted through it.

As shown earlier, the development of a critical consciousness, the restoration of connective solidarities and healing relationships will all work to heal the oppressed en route to a greater self-world concept. We see the application of anti-racist initiatives as a further strategic tool for the oppressed and, specifically as a defensive tool for those not yet circumscribed by our oppressive social sphere. In concluding this work, we would like to address, at least in general detail, some of the qualities of racialized/racist moments that we might resist through the development of a greater critical consciousness. If anything has become evident in our engagements within these pages, it is that power exists in contested spaces and that its tenuous hold on psycho/social/political authority remains both in and outside the purview of the oppressed, but always relative to the historical frameworks that bind us. As social change cannot be reduced to any single cause or group of causes, it is important to recognize that in these discussions of agency and social justice "everything" is important and nothing is paramount. Because lasting social change—that is to say, an "organic" transition to a more just society—will occur slowly, such change will occur relative to various dimensions of change all occurring simultaneously.

We began this work with several very specific theoretical foci in mind. The most important of those interests being that the unsettled and indeterminate nature of "reality" might lend itself to insurgent and as yet untapped strategies for survival through resistance to, and re-formulations of, oppression in the face of racism. We engaged three main theoretical tenets: (a) that the race concept is socially constructed, (b) that discursive fields function within that socially constructed "reality" to constitute meanings and establish the nature of the body, mind and emotional life, and (c) that as racially oppressed, we come to know our own voices, language and "selves" through the contradictions and tensions of a hyphenated existence.

In the preceding chapters we have addressed the methods, meanings and "monologues" through which privileged positions are infused into social contexts. From an anti-racist perspective, we feel that this theoretical grounding is a necessary entry point to all discussions of resistance in the face of racism. We would specify that, while this work was/is based in a philosophy of hope, it was necessary to engage in a tight interrogation of the social-psychological contexts in and through which racial oppressions arise, because those interrogations provide us with insurgent insights. Furthermore, in line with this "positive" directive, we also contend that one of the main tasks of critical research is to delineate the factors contributing to oppression in the hopes that such interrogations might produce alternative and insurgent strategies for change.

As asserted by Dei (1996), contemporary anti-racist frameworks require non-reductionist, historically specific analyses that touch on the internal elements of the racial and racialized experience. In this sense, Dei maintains that anti-racist theory and practice must expand its epistemology to engage critical inquiries of both the systems that organize and constitute the lives of marginalized people, as well as the internal structures of identity that frame their dialogic relationship with that system. Chief among these considerations is the notion of "becoming." As taken up in Chapter Eight, we put forth that discussions of the racialization of identity should distinguish between racial identity as ascribed from without and racialized identity as a conscious internal act of becoming or assuming an identification.[3] In our corresponding assertions that racial identities are tied to the social construction of race, we engage the production of identity as fundamentally dynamic and contextually specific.

In designing this project, we were influenced by a myriad number of works spanning various disciplines and subject matter. We felt that the interplay has allowed for dynamic intersections of thought and strategy. One such intersection spoke to the question of the inevitability of pain, anxiety and hardship faced by racialized peoples. We take on the perspective that racism is painful because—in living through the experience of it—we know it to be so. But what if our work began to focus on re-writing our experience of race and racism as painless, or at least possibly, less painful? What if we were able to resist that hurt? This was the basic premise of our work as we set out to frame and develop this book. Within the framework of this text, we are looking to interrogate the importance of naming the racist moment in ways that would speak to the specificity of that experience. We feel that— similar to the political/psychological importance of naming moments of "date rape" and "spousal rape" in those specific terms—naming the racist moment as violating and painful would lend some currency to racialized people's experience and knowledge of those moments. It is our hope that such efforts to "name" might help to move us beyond self-defeating searches for validation from sites of privilege. In following the starkly poignant work of Karumanchery (2003) we contend that the painful, isolating and fundamentally damaging experience of racism can only be appropriately addressed if we stop using euphemisms and address the real issue and name it for what it is—TRAUMA. So again, we firmly assert that in order to understand the productivity and functionality of racial oppression, it is first vital that we deconstruct how our oppressors speak in/through/to us—how they traumatize us.

It was only after the concept of post-traumatic stress disorder was legitimated in the 1980s relative to survivors of war, that essentially the same psychological syndrome was seen reflected in the lived experience/trauma of survivors of rape, domestic abuse and incest.[4] As Karumanchery (2003), we assert that racism is a violating, pervasive and destructive force in our society and as such, it functions to traumatize racialized peoples. However, even with the new work being done in the aftermath of September 11th, there continues to be a stark absence of materials relating specifically to issues of race and racism. Case in point, the fourth edition of the *Diagnostic and Statistical Manual of Mental Disorders* (DSM-IV) includes several brief narrative discussions of psychiatric symptoms and disorders related to culture, as well as a glossary of culture-bound syndromes, but factors involving racism are entirely slighted.[5] As noted by Scurfield (2001), while numerous race-specific syndromes arise in relation to such everyday phenomenon as race-based assault, race-hate speech and racist environment, these avenues are not explored in the DSM-IV.[6] He goes on to assert that the specific omission of racial trauma is particularly glaring among the approximately 16 environmental stressors mentioned in the text of Adjustment Disorders, as well as the roughly 36 stress factors in the acute and post-traumatic stress disorders (PTSD) texts.[7]

We suggest that Scurfield's reading of PTSD in relation to race/racism is problematized by the conspicuous absence of critical anti-racism theory, as well as by his neglecting to interrogate the various discursive, symbolic, linguistic and ideological stressors that impact racialized existence. Everyday, in every moment and in every space and place, we are exposed to, disciplined in, constituted through and managed by racial stressors. This is a difficult notion to translate without a praxical understanding of race and racism as socially constructed and as everyday aspects of racialized existence. The psychological impact of a racialized existence has been described in various sociological works:

> Human beings...whose daily experience tells them that almost nowhere in society are they respected and granted the normal dignity and courtesy accorded to others will, as a matter of course, begin to doubt their own worth. Minorities may come to believe the frequent accusations that they are lazy, ignorant, dirty and superstitious. The accumulation of negative images...present[s] them with one massive and destructive choice: either to hate one's self, as culture so systematically demand[s], or to have no self at all, to be nothing.[8]

In recognizing the absences, disavowals and omissions that are clearly evident in present psychological work, the dire need to infuse such research with an anti-racist theory and politics becomes even more evident. While they have begun to broach otherwise untapped areas of racial research, they also display the intense problematics of doing clinical race-work without a basis in anti-racist praxis and without an eye to the traumatic nature of "the everyday." We draw this distinction because the notion of "perceived racism" appears to crop up in much of this type of clinical psychological work. Does the "perception" of racism somehow imply that there is no quantitative "reality" to the experience and therefore no relevance?

Such entry points, at best, work to mute the exploration of the lived experience of racialized peoples and at worst, they serve to pathologize the oppressed by implying their symptoms are somehow self-inflicted or indicative of "cultural" adjustment disorders. We make this very clear distinction because, in many ways, the nature of racial and racist experience is the point of contention here. As has been framed throughout this text, the insidious and pervasive nature of race and racism is of paramount importance relative to how racial trauma is to be taken up. Orthodox psychological tenets will assess exposure to race-related stressors along a continuum that rates discrete/markedly memorable events, subtle exposures and duration of harms. In contrast, we engage a critical anti-racist perspective that frames those stressors as part of a larger ongoing complex of oppression and trauma that infuses every aspect of racially oppressed people's lives. Again, we make this distinction because—regardless of the impact on the individual, family or community—the chronic and pervasive effects of a racialized existence may not meet the DSM-IV's present diagnostic criteria for adjustment and stress disorders.[9]

Importantly, before continuing we would make a very pointed distinction between the work that has been done relative to Racism and PTSD thus far and the work that we are proposing to begin here. Until very recently, traumatic events were believed to exist outside the range of common human experience, so research has tended to focus on race either as a cultural phenomenon or in relation to the very specific aspects of the multigenerational transmission of trauma. Beyond the extensive research and writings on the holocaust and multigenerational trauma (see Bar-On, 1989, 1994; Hass, 1990; Kogan, 1995; Danieli, 1980, 1985, 1989), the relationship between race and PTSD has been addressed relative only to the traumas of indigenous peoples in their own lands and as slaves taken from their lands. Raphael, Swan and Martinek (1998) addressed the legacy of colonialism relative to the traumas of Australian Aboriginal peoples, much as Cross (1998) did relative to African Americans and as Brave Heart and Yellow Horse-Davis (1998) did in relation to North American Aboriginal peoples.[10]

These works, while important in clearing space to discuss the experience and ongoing cumulative effects of historical context and content, do not work to uncover the pervasive impact of cumulative trauma on racialized individuals and peoples who do/did not experience that "great externally visible" upheaval. New definitions are necessary because, as we have seen in the history of other such omissions, we often find little room for the exploration of experiences deemed unimportant by the privileged. As Wellman (1977) reminds us, "a paradox of White consciousness is the ability not to see what is very salient."[11] These omissions beg the question: What about trauma as experienced by migrant peoples and the various *others* whose histories are touched by neither captivity nor forced relocation? After all, we must not forget that the birthmarks of North American racism arose long before the advent of slavery in the antebellum South. So what about trauma as experienced by people whose everyday lives are marked, muted and managed through a socially constructed "prison of the mind"?

As asserted by Delgado (1982), we must recognize that color acts as a badge of inferiority that becomes internalized in the individual and passed on to future generations. The psychological trauma of racism cannot be relegated to any one series of events or moments. Rather, it must be considered relative to the pervasive-expansive socio-historical contextuality of racial formation and oppression as it exists today. By addressing racial trauma only in relation to historical events and historical evils such as Black slavery or Aboriginal dispossession in the Americas, present researchers can sidestep the problematics of their own involvement and complicity in the ongoing dynamics of oppression. Present definitions of what constitutes trauma must be re-assessed and re-focused to reflect the "realities" of race and racism, regardless of the obvious ramifications of placing the privileged in the uncomfortable position of negotiating their place and role in the cycle of racial trauma. The alternative is the resulting "conspiracy of silence" that continues to re-inscribe racially oppressed peoples with a profound sense of isolation and mistrust.[12]

As noted by Danieli (1998) in relation to Holocaust survivors, "social silence" and systemic disavowal of pain and loss will only force the oppressed to conclude that nobody cares to listen and that nobody can understand. Moreover, the social apathy that arises relative to interrogations of race and racism serves only to impede the possibilities of intrapsychic healing for the oppressed.[13] Privileged silence and misdiagnoses are major factors as to why this type of work has not found an anti-racist voice. Racialized trauma is an everyday part of our lives, and so we would assert most emphatically that the time has come to re-write our understandings of what constitutes trauma. As can be seen in the DSM-IV it has been only very recently that traumatic events have gained acceptance as existing within the range of common human experiences. After all, it was only through the immutable push of the North American feminist movement that PTSD became seen as a part of the problematics that circumscribe women's everyday lives through rape, battery and other forms of sexual and/or domestic abuse. We take the position that the study of psychological trauma can be a political and emancipatory enterprise because it holds the possibility of calling attention to and addressing the lived experience of oppressed peoples. No longer linked solely to *extreme situations* such as dispossession, imprisonment, slavery and combat neuroses, "everyday trauma" has gained a greater acceptance in psychological inquiry, specifically because of its banality and ability to overwhelm and damage what Herman terms "the ordinary human adaptations to life." What we need to do now is apply these newly arising formulations of trauma in order to reflect the everyday violations that intrinsically deform our sense of the safety of the world.

What does it mean to build an identity based on marginality and alienation? How do we frame this lived experience of racism that occurs and recurs frequently and unexpectedly throughout our oppressed lives? How do we frame an existence that is constantly formed and re-formed with basic understandings of danger and abnormalcy? How does our silence in the moment reverberate within us? Bearing in mind the infinite permutations of constriction, disconnection, vulnerability, psychic torture and insecurity that result from these moments, how do we frame our racialized lives, if not in relation to trauma? The politics of this work speak specifically to the need for theory and practice to address the central dialectic of psychological trauma and the conflict between the will to deny horrible events and the will to proclaim them aloud. It is only after the truth is recognized that we can begin our recovery and our reclamations of self. The alternative is a silence that invariably returns in symptom rather than in verbal narrative.[14]

The contextuality of the lived experience lends itself to a pointed intervention of theoretical frameworks that propose a "command of consciousness" and a fixed autonomy to human agency and design. Intrinsically problematic "Cartesian" notions fuel the fires of a radical humanism that ultimately works to pathologize the oppressed for our inabiltity to "transcend race" and outstrip our subjugation. What these narratives have demonstrated is the necessity for anti-racist theory to recognize and articulate what Foucault called "the operation of mechanisms of power." Anytime we discuss the moment in order to investigate and interpret the interplay within racial contexts, we must clear space to address the ever-present threat of dispute and disparity that exists within those power relations. As Foucault posits:

> In effect, between a relationship of power and a strategy of struggle there is a reciprocal appeal, a perpetual linking and a perpetual reversal. At every moment the relationship of power may become a confrontation between two adversaries. Equally, the relationship between adversaries in society may, at every moment, give place to the putting into operation of the mechanisms of power. The consequences of this instability is the ability to decipher the same events and the same transformations either from inside the history of struggle or from the standpoint of the power relationships. The interpretations which result will not consist of the same elements of meaning or the same historical fabric and each of the two analyses must have reference to the other. In fact it is precisely the disparities between the two readings which make visible those fundamental phenomena of 'domination' which are present in a large number of human societies.[15]

In engaging Foucault's reading of the *mechanisms of power*, we would interpret the interplay within racist moments as attempts at "interpretive domination," functioning to limit the articulation of resistant/reformative readings. That is to say that the psycho-social contexts in which racially oppressed identities and experiences are formed will minimize the pervasive nature of "racial agency." However, like Karumanchery (2003), we would extrapolate from this interpretation to address the intrapsychic complex in which individuals function as adversaries unto themselves. We are reminded of Sechi's (1980) discussion of "roots and authenticity," in which she writes: "I was made to feel that cultural pride would justify and make good my difference in skin color while it was a constant reminder that I was different."[16] In such contexts, individuals read the same historical fabric of their experience from intrinsically different perspectives. Dependent on our positionality in the moment, we may read our circumstance from multiple sites and through multiple lenses. So until the existing internal struggles are no longer extant, interpretive differences between the cognitive, behavioural and affective self will find voice as intrapsychic struggles to limit, circumscribe and control opposing formulations.[17]

Building on Herman's contentions relative to the problematics of resolving trauma, the historical contextuality of the racialized/racist moment will often displace the paradigms of social action and agency made available to the oppressed and defined by a reliance on logical action and reaction. Our strategies for resistance are constructed within and relative to moments of defiance that emerge only in opposition to our historically cemented erasures and violations. We feel that this point needs to be clarified because we look to develop such strategies *only* because there is a need for them. That need is circumscribed by the existing significations, symbols, meanings and contexts that burn like embers just below the surface of our oppression. The result is a seemingly paradoxical space in which the oppressed, cognizant of our oppression, must forever prepare for battle if we are ever to know peace. The realities of marginality and the challenges of difficult knowledge all reflect the historical chains that bind us—against and parallel to our will.

As put forth by Bhabha (1994), solidarities founded in victimization and suffering may relentlessly and sometimes violently rise in opposition to that oppression. Our resistance in these moments reflects that simple truism.[18] This proposed process of re-inscription and negotiation arises as a product of the subject's agency and directed movement toward revelations of truth relative to symbols of the "social imaginary": a "rediscovery of the world of truth denied subjectivity at the level of the sign."[19] However, this "return of the subject" and her attempt to revise and re-inscribe the inter-subjective realm, takes place in spaces that we would contend are regulated both internally and externally. As Herman (1992) reminds us, these re-inscriptions and revisions take place within spaces that are necessarily charged both historically and emotionally; it is a "mindscape" that places cognitive efforts to transcend race, racism and the moment as problematic at best. To again use Hall's phrase, this is not a zero-sum game: the resolution of racist trauma must be understood as anything but final and recovery is never complete.[20] The multiple impacts of trauma often continue to reverberate throughout the survivor's lifecycle long after measures have been undertaken to curb their effects and hold over the individual.

In Karumanchery's (2003) study of racially minoritized anti-racism workers, a recurrent theme that arose in each narrative was the subject's inability to move beyond the problematics of silence. When asked about her personal strategies for resistance, Magda, a 30 year-old Black woman, was pointed in her decision to speak out against racism, but was also forced to acknowledge the inevitable silences that frame her in the moment:

> Well you know I've chosen to speak out in all moments but I don't. In my mind, I'm always...Like three years ago I said, 'This is the last time I'm going to stand for it...whatever...anything racist, anything unfair, anything unjust, life's too short and I'm just not going to stand for it anymore. But over the past three years, there have been many accounts where I haven't said anything. And I see it happening or hear it happening. In my head I'm thinking...I don't know. I don't think I have totally made peace with it and that's really a big part of my work, why I'm doing this. I'm trying to work that out. I'm trying to say what I didn't say, or say what I'm not saying when I should.[21]

As asserted by Danieli (1998), societal reactions have a profound effect on how survivors integrate their traumatic experiences and coping mechanisms into everyday life and particularly within moments that are reflective or reminiscent of the initial trauma.[22] But again, these societal reactions are part and parcel of oppressive formations that function to blind and constitute both oppressed and oppressor alike. In relation to the scripted interactions that take place in these moments, racialized people's disciplined responses in the face of racism speak to several different dynamics. We cannot overlook the problematics of "internalization" that plague the oppressed in that we have learned to see ourselves through our oppressor's eyes.

The dilemma for the oppressed is that in our perception of the world through the eyes of our oppressor, we will often see the world as fair, just and equitable. Therefore, because we have been blinded to the reality of our situation, we are, in turn, blinded to our existence as an existence of abnormalcy. Let us clarify. As explained by Karumanchery (2003), in terms of racial oppression, the White existence supercedes all other frameworks as the norm. It proceeds from this point because our frameworks of understanding advance from that premise (e.g., norms of speech, appearance, dress, culture, etc.). Therefore, when we experience racial oppression, we are experiencing an abnormal condition through the eyes of our oppressor... because what we experience is not experienced by the White person (i.e., the White person hears "Honky" and there is little reaction, but when the Black person hears "Nigger," or the Indian person hears "Paki," there are immediate connections to history, context, experience and pain). It is either that we are abnormal and that our responses to normal situations are abnormal, or it is that the situations and conditions in which we live are themselves abnormal, but normalized as part of our everyday experience.[23]

Contemporary readings of race and culture offer insurgent interpretations of anti-racism and resistance. Through those interpretations, the study of social identities and the privileged relations embedded therein have come to the fore as key battlegrounds in anti-racist theory and practice. Today, while our understandings of race and racism are generally pinned within interpretations of culture, politics, language and history, alternative readings of the processes of racialization are turning to the fluid sphere of "the self" as a fundamental locus for anti-racist research. Anti-racist scholars are finding that personal methods of resistance, whether internally organized or externally performed, speak to the multiple ways in which we define ourselves in relation to, and in opposition to, a socially inscribed and ascribed *otherness*. In this light, a closer scrutiny of our multiple "*I* positions," voices and identities can serve to expand personal strategies for resistance and engage more praxical anti-racism. As pointed out by Dei, the consequences for research, social and political policy change and educational exclusion are obvious, but less apparent are the consequences for the oppressed. The "traumas of the everyday" invariably damage the oppressed in relation to their self-concept and in relation to their relationships with others. Bearing that in mind, the social world carries the potential to influence the healing process for the oppressed. The question is whether that social milieu is supportive or hostile. A supportive environment might be able to mitigate the impact of racism, while a hostile or negative environment will work to compound the initial damage and aggravate further traumatic syndromes.[24]

With the public backlash and mainstream disdain for political correctness and any other philosophies, practices, initiatives or policies related to anti-oppression, the barriers to social justice and equity work of all sorts are expanding in Western contexts.[25] Issues such as racial injustice, the underfunding and outright erasure of social welfare programs, and the ongoing marketization of public schooling are all working to widen the gap between the rich/privileged and the poor/disenfranchised.[26] As discussed in the opening pages of this work, there is a growing indifference and public apathy toward efforts and initiatives that might work to ameliorate these dire social ills. However, as the lines between "the public" and "the private" spheres become increasingly blurred in the shadow of the global market, the call for social change and revolution must be directed toward new sites of insurgency. We can no longer rely solely on efforts to work within the policies and practices of a system that is designed to keep "us" out/down. Again, as we have asserted numerous times throughout this work, we are being carefully policed, and so the nature of our work must, by necessity, be brought to sites of struggle that are beyond the power of privilege to deny, mute or disengage. It is with these problematics in mind that we began this work, and so with these same issues in mind, we offer these suggestions.

"The ordinary human adaptations to life"—we use Herman's (1997) words to describe what it was that racial trauma had the power to damage and overwhelm. However, in retrospect, we are not even sure what that means to us. As racially oppressed, our lives are constituted by a myriad number of signs, symbols, markers, meanings and knowledges that tell us what ordinary is—what normal is—what real is. Living with trauma, living with racism and living with fear are all part of our ordinary human adaptations to a racialized life and we are forced to recognize that Herman's use of the word ordinary is also subtly infused and framed by the word "White." That is the nature of the racialized experience that we are dealing with. We firmly assert that the "ordinary development" of *our* lives are fundamentally based in oppression—it is all we know. And so it doesn't necessarily mean that we will be constricted, disconnected or affected by any of the other various signals of stress or trauma looked for by clinicians or psychologists in relation to conventional trauma theory.

As asserted by Karumanchery (2003), what it means is that *we exist within a traumatic event* that functions as a pre-present-post–framework for our lives. Moreover, unlike the soldier, who removed from the environment of stress finds his subjective anxiety receding, the racially oppressed never find that panacea where the object of her/his fear is forever kept from her/him. Our state of anxiety always remains reflective of hyper-arousal because we must always live within an oppressive milieu. We will always be "too sensitive" even if we don't admit it. Our psychological and physiological normativity is based on anxiety, fear and a self-preservational instinct, so we must engage a fundamentally proactive and political pedagogy if we are ever to re-write the banality of racial trauma in our lives.[27] By this, we mean to say that because traumatic racist event(s) and racist discourses circumscribe our lives, our ability to recover or "move on"—either by developing cognitive resistance strategies or by removing ourselves from the temporal space and place of specific events—is never a realistic option for us. However, that does not mean that the pain, oppression and trauma of the racist moment must be a fundamental aspect of the lives of our future generations.

We believe that if this book helps raise our individual/collective aware-ness and critical consciousness of how the reality of racism is sidestepped by those with privilege, then we will have been part of something truly important. While critical consciousness allows us to analyze our place within the racist experience, it also suggests that we, as living and feeling agents, think reflexively about both our subjectivity and our experience. In understanding our interconnectedness with/within the discursive relations that constitute our lives, we will be better equipped to mobilize our personal and emotional resources toward affecting change as "subjects" and as actors with agency.

NOTES

PREFACE

1   The nature of this text necessitates that *power* remains in contested space. How we define and operationalize the word is dependent upon our theoretical position and as this work does not rely on any one theorist or theoretical conception the word must remain as polemic.

INTRODUCTION
Anti-Racist Tapestries: Threads of Theory and Practice

1   This quote may be found in its entirety in A. Gramsci. *Quaderni del Carcere.* (ed.). V. Gerratana (Turin: Einaudi Editore, 1975), 2: 1363. The translation used in this text, while incomplete, may be found in E. Said. *Orientalism.* (Vintage Books: USA, 1994), p. 25.

2   M. Tigar and M. Levy. *Law and the Rise of Capitalism.* (NY: Monthly Review Press, 1977), p. 6.

3   Throughout this text, we will use a collective 'we'. In employing this voice, we (the authors) are speaking to a community that (a) shares the discursive stances presented here, and (b) believes in the necessity of engaging in concrete political action to bring about social change.

4   J. Sawicki. *Disciplining Foucault: Feminism, Power and the Body.* (NY: Routledge, 1991), p. 2.

5   We are not writing a text on multiculturalism and we are not writing in the hopes of engendering tolerance for the marginalized. In our declaration of audience and purpose, we have clarified our intent to speak to the oppressed rather than those with privilege. The political nature of this work necessitates the use of clear language.

6   G. J. S. Dei, I. M. James, L. L. Karumanchery, S. James-Wilson and J. Zine. *Removing the Margins: The Challenges and Possibilities of Inclusive Schooling.* (Toronto: Canadian Scholars Press, 2000), p. 2.

7   Before asserting claims to neutrality, the critically conscious researcher should reassess the motivations behind the work - the experiences that brought her/him to the work, the goals of the work and the political/personal reasons why s/he chose to do this work rather than engage another project. At the heart of this

problematic is that claims to neutrality not only negate the importance and over-riding influence of the 'human factor' in social research, but also, there is in such claims, an unspoken disregard for subjectivity and the lived experience.

8   R. Arber. 'Defining Positioning Within Politics of Difference: Negotiating Spaces 'In Between'. *Race, Ethnicity and Education*. Vol. 3(1), 2000, p. 47.

9   A number of scholars have written powerfully on the intersections of oppress-sions. See R. M. Brewer. 'Theorizing Race, Class and Gender: The New Scholarship of Black Feminist Intellectuals and Black Women's Labour'. In S. James and A. Busia (eds.). *Theorizing Black Feminisms*. (NY: Routledge, 1993), p. 13–30; A. Calliste and G. J. S. Dei. *Anti-Racist Feminism: Critical Race and Gender Studies*. (Halifax: Fernwood Publishing, 2000); P. Hill-Collins. *Black Feminist Thought*. (NY: Routledge, 1990); G. J. S. Dei. 'The Denial of Difference: Reframing Anti-Racist Praxis'. *Race, Ethnicity and Education*, Vol. 2(1), 1999, p. 17–38; G. J. S. Dei. 'Recasting Anti-Racism and the Axis of Difference: Beyond the Question of Theory'. *Race, Gender and Class*. Vol. 7(2), 2000, p. 39–56; S. Doyle-Wood. 'Masking Terror'. Unpub-lished paper (Toronto: OISE/University of Toronto, 2002); E. Dua and A. Robertson (eds.). *Scratching the Surface of Racism: Canadian Anti-Racist Feminist Thought*. (Toronto: Women's Press, 1999).

10   G. J. S. Dei. 'The Denial of Difference: Reframing Anti-Racist Praxis'. *Race, Ethnicity and Education*. Vol. 2(1), 1999, p. 17.

11   G. J. S. Dei. Anti-Racism Education: Theory and Practice. (Halifax: Fernwood Publishing, 1996), p. 25.

12   See S. J. Ball. 'Education Markets, Choice and Social Class: The Market as Class Strategy in the UK and the USA'. *British Journal of Sociology of Edu-cation*. Vol. 14(1), 1993, p. 3–19; K. Dehli. 'Between "Market" and "State"? Engendering Educational Change in the 1990s'. *Discourse: Studies in the Cultural Politics of Education*. Vol. 17(3), 1996, p. 366–369; D. Ferguson. 'Changing Tactics: Research on Embedding Inclusion Reforms within General Education Restructuring Efforts'. A Paper presented at the Annual American Educational Research Association Meeting in Chicago, Illinois, 1979; S. Gerwitz, S. J. Ball and R. Bowe. *Markets, Choice and Equity in Education*. (Buckingham: Open University Press, 1995); F. Henry, C. Tator, W. Mattis and T. Rees. *The Color of Democracy: Racism in Canadian Society*. (Toronto: Harcourt Brace and Co., 1995); J. Kenway. 'The Marketization of Education: Mapping the Contours of a Feminist Perspective'. A paper given at the British Education Research Association, September 1995; J. Kenway, C. Bigum and L. Fitzclarence. 'Marketing Education in the Post Modern Age'. *Journal of Education*. Vol. 8(2), 1993, p. 105–122; S. Marginson. 'Education as a Branch of Economics: The Universal Claims of Economic Rationalism'. In *Melbourne Studies in Education: Rationalizing Education*. (Melbourne: LaTrobe University, 1992); H. J. Robertson. 'Hyenas at the Oasis: Corporate Marketing to Captive Students'. *Our Schools/Our Selves*. Vol. 7(2), 1995, p. 16–39.

13   We use the competitive language of 'Victory', 'Game' and 'Ballpark' relative to the combative/oppositional language employed by Gramsci, Hall and others in relation to culture as a contested space (i.e., Gramsci called culture 'a war of

maneuver' and Hall referred to it as a 'war of position').

14   S. Hall. 'What is this 'Black'. In Black Popular Culture?' In D. Morley and K-H. Chen (eds.). *Stuart Hall: Critical Dialogues in Cultural Studies.* (London: Routledge, 1996), p. 468.

15   C. Sparks 'Stuart Hall, Cultural Studies and Marxism'. In D. Morley and K-H. Chen (eds.). *Stuart Hall: Critical Dialogues in Cultural Studies.* (London: Routledge, 1996).

16   As noted by Freire, the first step toward social transformation must be the unveiling of oppression by the oppressed. It is only after that coming to consciousness of their situation that they can commit themselves to change. See P. Freire. *Pedagogy of the Oppressed.* (NY: Continuum, 1970), p. 54.

17   A. Memmi. *The Colonizer and the Colonized.* (Boston: Beacon Press, 1967), p. 83.

18   P. Freire. *Pedagogy of the Oppressed,* p. 126–129.

19   Ibid., p. 35. The term *conscientização* refers to learning how to perceive social, political and economic contradiction and in turn using that knowledge/ understanding to act against the oppressive elements of reality.

20   P. Freire. *Pedagogy of the Oppressed,* p. 20–23.

21   D. D. Brunner. *Inquiry and Reflection: Framing Narrative Practice in Education.* (Albany, NY: State University of NY Press, 1994), p. 15–16.

22   There is a distinct difference between the politics of educational methodologies that employ cooperative frameworks and those that rely on what Freire defined as 'banking theories of education'. For more on cooperative and transformative education, see M. I. Alladin (ed.). *Racism in Canadian Schools.* (Toronto: Harcourt Brace Canada, 1995); G. Allen, et al. 'Community Educa-tion and Education Reform'. In G. Allen, J. Bastiani, I. Martin and K. Richards (eds.). *Community Education.* (London: Open University Press, 1987); J. A. Banks. 'Approaches to Multicultural Curriculum Reform'. *Multicultural Leader.* Vol. 1(2), 1988, J. A. Banks and C.A. Banks (eds.). *Multicultural Education: Issues and Perspectives.* (Boston: Allyn and Bacon, 1993); L. Delpit, 'The Silenced Dialogue: Power and Pedagogy in Educating Other People's Children'. *Harvard Educational Review.* Vol. 58(3), 1988, p. 280–298; P. Freire. *Pedagogy of the Oppressed.* (NY: Continuum, 1970); H. Giroux. *Theory and Resistance in Education: A Pedagogy for the Opposition.* (Massachusetts: Bergin and Garvey, 1983); K. McLeod and E. Krugly-Smolska. *Multicultural Education: A Place to Start: Guidelines for Classrooms, Schools and Communities.* (Toronto: Canadian Association of Second Language Teachers, 1997); K. Murtadha. 'An African-Centered Pedagogy in Dialogue with Liberatory Multiculturalism'. In C. E. Sleeter and P. L. McLaren (eds.). *Multicultural Education, Critical Pedagogy and the Politics of Difference.* (NY: State University of NY Press, 1995); G. J. S. Dei. 'The Politics of Educational Change: Taking Anti-Racism Education Seriously'. In V. Satzewich (ed.). *Racism and Social Inequality in Canada.* (Toronto: Thompson Educational Publishing, Inc, 1998); G. J. S. Dei. *Anti-Racism Education: Theory and Practice.* (Halifax: Fernwood Publishing, 1996); G. J. S. Dei. I. M. James, S. James-Wilson, L. L. Karumanchery and J. Zine. *Removing the Margins: The Challenges and*

Possibilities of Inclusive Schooling. (Toronto: Canadian Scholars Press, 2000); S. R. Steinberg. 'Critical Multiculturalism and Demo-cratic Schooling: An Interview with P. L. McLaren and J. Kincheloe'. In C. E. Sleeter and P. L. McLaren (eds.). *Multicultural Education, Critical Pedagogy and the Politics of Difference.* (Albany, NY: The State University of NY Press, 1995).

23   G. Spivak. *The Post Colonial Critic: Interviews, Strategies, Dialogues.* (NY: Routledge, 1990), p. 56.

24   P. Freire. *Pedagogy of the Oppressed.* p. 126–129.

25   Ibid., p. 71.

26   Ibid., p. 72.

27   R. C. Tucker. *The Marx-Engels Reader.* (NY.: W. W. Norton and Company, Inc., 1972), p. 529.

28   Our three stages of social transformation are based, in part at least, upon the work done by Freire. Where we contend that critical education must exist as a precondition to social change, he collapsed the two into his first phase of social transformation. However, we are in agreement with Freire that the last stage must culminate in a collaborative anti-oppressive condition.

29   P. Freire. *Pedagogy of the Oppressed.* p. 66.

30   There is a decided difference between 'knowing the path' and 'walking the path'. In 'doing the work' we make the connection between reflection and action.

31   P. Freire. *Pedagogy of the Oppressed*, p. 52.

32   G. J. S. Dei. *Anti-Racism Education: Theory and Practice.* (Halifax: Fernwood Publishing, 1996).

CHAPTER ONE
Theorizing Race & Racism: Focusing Our Discursive Lens

1   M. Omi and H. Winant. 'On the Theoretical Status of the Concept of Race'. In C. McCarthy and W. Crichlow (eds.). *Race, Identity and Representation in Education.* (NY: Routledge, 1993), p. 3–9.

2   C. E. Sleeter. 'How White Teachers Construct Race.' In C. McCarthy and W. Crichlow (eds.). *Race, Identity and Representation in Education.* (NY: Routledge, 1993), p. 161.

3   A. Wilson. 'I Want a Black Director'. *New York Times*, 26th September 1990, section 1, p. 15.

4   M. Awkward. *Negotiating Difference.* (Chicago: The University of Chicago Press, 1995), p. 5.

5   See M. Omi and H. Winant. *Racial Formation in the United States.* (NY: Routledge, 1994) and I. F. H. Lopez. 'The Social Construction of Race'. In R. Delgado (ed.). *Critical Race Theory: The Cutting Edge.* (Philadelphia: Temple University Press, 1995).

6   See J. Banks. 'The Historical Reconstruction of Knowledge about Race: The Implications for Transformative Teaching'. Paper read at the Annual Meeting of the American Educational Research Association (New Orleans, LA. April 4–9, 1994); O. Cox. *Race Relations: Elements and Social Dynamics.* (Indiana:

Wayne State University Press, 1976); D. T. Goldberg. *Racist Culture.* (Oxford: Blackwell, 1993); R. Miles. *Racism.* (London: Tavistock, 1989); M. Omi and H. Winant. *Racial Formation in the United States.* (NY: Routledge, 1994); A. Rattansi and S. Westwood (eds.). *Racism, Modernity and Identity.* (London: Polity Press, 1994); C. West. *Race Matters.* (Boston: Beacon Press, 1992),

7   M. Omi and H. Winant. *Racial Formation in the United States,* p. 59.

8   While different forms of racism are manifest in society, they have their roots in skin color racism. As well, racism is more frequently and more harshly manifested against those who are furthest from the 'White skin color norm', regardless of whether or not they fit into the Christian norm. See G. J. S. Dei. *Anti-Racism Education: Theory and Practice.*

9   See L. T. Reynolds and L. Lieberman. 'The Rise and Fall of Race'. *Race, Sex and Class.* Vol. 1(1), 1993, p. 110–114.

10   S. J. Gould. *The Mismeasure of Man.* (NY: W.W. Norton and Company, Inc., 1981). New 'sciences' such as 'craniometry' signaled the beginning of a culture of empirically justified racial/racist thought. The study of cranial capacities and racial brain theories were methodologically flawed (e.g., anatomical studies of cranial development were purposely distorted to create the image that Blacks rated lower than chimpanzees on the 'intelligence scale.'

11   Ibid., p. 39.

12   See R. Herrnstein and C. Murray. *The Bell Curve.* (NY: The Free Press, 1994); and P. Rushton. *Race, Evolution, and Behavior: A Life History Perspective.* (New Brunswick: Transactions Publishers, 1995).

13   S. J. Gould. *The Mismeasure of Man,* p. 45. Similarly today, individuals working within the multicultural paradigm stress an interest in 'celebrating differences.' This not only fails to address power relations in society but also bolsters 'us' and 'them' scenarios where 'they' are seen as 'Exotic', *other* 'outside the norm' and thus 'abnormal' and 'less than'.

14   United Nations Economic, Social and Cultural Organization. *Declaration on Race and Racial Prejudice.* (Paris: 20th Session, 1978), p. 4. Cited in A. K. M. Ibrahim. 'Hey, Wassup Homeboy?'. Becoming Black: Race, Language, Culture and the Politics of Identity: African Students in a Franco-Ontarian High School'. Ph.D. Thesis. (Toronto: OISE/University of Toronto, 1998), p. 32.

15   A. K. M. Ibrahim. *'Hey, Wassup Homeboy?' Becoming Black: Race, Language Culture and the Politics of Identity: African Students in a Franco-Ontarian High School.* p. 32.

16   M. Omi and H. Winant. *On the Theoretical Status of the Concept of Race,* p. 6.

17   G. J. S. Dei. *Anti-Racism Education: Theory and Practice,* p. 17.

18   I. F. H. Lopez. *The Social Construction of Race,* p. 192.

19   S. Razack. *Looking White People in the Eye: Gender, Race and Culture in Courtrooms and Classrooms.* (Toronto: University of Toronto Press, 1998), p. 19.

20   Ibid., p. 19.

21   H. S. Mirza. 'Race, Gender and IQ: The Social Consequences of a Pseudo-Scientific Discourse'. *Race, Ethnicity and Education.* Vol. 1(1), p. 122–123.

22   We (the authors) would like to specify our use of *we* in this context because like our oppressors, racially oppressed peoples are also imprinted with these

understandings. We do not stand exempt from their influence and we are constituted, in our duality, to position, frame and pathologize racialized bodies (our bodies), in much the same way as our oppressors.

23   O. H. Gandy. *Communication and Race: Structural Perspective.* (London: Arnold, 1998), p. 37.

24   E. Lawrence. 'Just Plain Commonsense: The Roots of Racism'. In P. Gilroy (ed.). *The Empire Strikes Back: Race and Racism in 70's Britain.* (London: Hutchinson, 1982).

25   G. N. Smith and Q. Hoare. *Selections from the Prison Notebooks*, p. 328.

26   H. Winant. *Racial Conditions: Politics, Theory, Comparisons.* (Minnesota: University of Minnesota Press, 1994), p. 4.

27   K. Marx and F. Engels. *The German Ideology.* (NY: International Publishers Co. Inc., 1970), p. 64.

28   N. Abercrombie, S. Hill and B. Turner. *The Dominant Ideology Thesis.* (London: Allen & Unwin, 1980), p. 7.

29   B. S. Bolaria and P. S. Li. *Racial Oppression in Canada.* (Toronto: Garamond Press, 1985), p. 18.

30   N. Abercrombie, S. Hill and B. Turner. *The Dominant Ideology*, Thesis, p. 7.

31   S. Hall. 'The Problem of Ideology: Marxism Without Guarantees'. In D. Morley and K-H. Chen (eds.). *Stuart Hall: Critical Dialogues in Cultural Studies.* (London: Routledge, 1996), p. 29–40.

32   M. W. Apple. "Constructing the *other*: Rightist Reconstructions of Commonsense". In C. McCarthy and W. Crichlow (eds.). *Race, Identity and Representation in Education.* (NY: Routledge, 1993), p. 34.

33   S. Hall. *The Problem of Ideology: Marxism Without Guarantees*, p. 40–41.

34   After the decline of feudalism, the advent of modernity generated questions about the future of Western society, solidarity and community. What would happen when communities were formed out of contract as opposed to natural solidarity? Would these communities gel together into cohesive units built on equality and mutual aid? Tonnies suggested that there were inherent problems of stratification and inequality in the Gesellschaft. He asserted that artificially constructed human collectivities would foster such disparity and that the disparity might be noted in the problems of our patriarchal, liberal, democracies. However, Tonnies' argument that the Gesellschaft would support the hierarchy of an elite/capitalist class was far too all-consuming as Capitalism is only one specific type of social formation. Other forms of solidarity and community are feasible and do exist. See F. Tonnies. *Community and Society.* (NY: Harper Books, 1957), p. 64–83.

35   B. Fields. 'Slavery, Race and Ideology in the United States of America'. *New Left Review.* Vol. 181, p. 118.

36   M. Omi and H. Winant. *On the Theoretical Status of the Concept of Race*, p. 5.

37   P. Freire. *The Pedagogy of the Oppressed*, p. 59.

38   I. F. H. Lopez. *The Social Construction of Race*, p. 192.

39   R. Miles. *Racism.* (London: Tavistock, 1989), p. 75.

40   See M. Omi and H. Winant. *Racial Formation in the United States*; and R. Miles, *Racism*.

41 G. J. S. Dei. *Anti-Racism Education: Theory and Practice,* 1996.

42 H. Carby. 'The Politics of Difference'. Ms. (September/October, 1990), p. 85. See also M. Omi and H. Winant. *Racial Formation in the United States*; T. Morrison. *Playing in the Dark: Whiteness and the Literary Imagination.* (NY: Vantage Books, 1992); and V. Ware cited in A. L. Ferber. 'Shame of White Men: Interracial Sexuality and the Construction of White Masculinity in Contemporary White Supremacist Discourse'. *Masculinities.* Vol. 3(2), 1995, p. 5.

43 J. L. Herman. *Trauma and Recovery.* (NY: Basic Books, 1992), p. 1.

44 See G. J. S. Dei. *Anti-Racism Education: Theory and Practice*; P. Gilroy, *Small Acts: Thoughts on the Politics of Black Cultures.* (London: Serpent's Tail, 1993); Sara Matthews. 'Re-Thinking White Privilege Work as Critical Anti-Racism'. Masters Thesis. (Toronto: OISE/University of Toronto, 1998); D. Morley and K-H. Chen (eds.). *Stuart Hall: Critical Dialogues in Cultural Studies.*

45 P. Freire and D. Macedo. 'A Dialogue: Culture, Language and Race'. *Harvard Educational Review.* Vol. 65 (3), 1995, p. 382.

46 M. Omi and H. Winant. *Racial Formation in the United States*, p. 69.

47 A. K. M. Ibrahim. *'Hey, Wassup Homeboy?' Becoming Black: Race, Language Culture and the Politics of Identity: African Students in a Franco-Ontarian High School*, p. 42.

48 H. Winant. Racial Conditions: Politics, Theory, Comparisons. (Minnesota: University of Minnesota Press, 1994), p. 37.

49 Ibid., p. 37.

50 Ibid., p. 28.

51 B. Smart. *Foucault, Marxism and Critique.* (London: Routledge, 1983), p. 26.

52 C. Weedon. *Feminist Practice and Post-Structuralist Theory.* (Britain: Basil Blackwell, 1987), p. 29.

53 S. Hall. *The Problem of Ideology: Marxism Without Guarantees*, p. 29–31.

54 L. Althusser. *Lenin and Philosophy and Other Essays by Louis Althusser.* (NY: Monthly Review Press, 1971), p. 146.

55 S. Hall cited in J. Larrain. 'Stuart Hall and the Marxist Concept of Ideology'. In D. Morley and K-H. Chen (eds.). *Stuart Hall: Critical Dialogues in Cultural Studies.* (London: Routledge, 1996), p. 49.

56 Ibid., p. 49.

57 H. Winant. *Racial Conditions: Politics, Theory, Comparisons*, p. 82.

58 For Althusser, the ideological apparatus of schooling has replaced the church as the primary State apparatus working to reproduce the relations of production. He asserted that the volume of time that children are forced (by law), to spend in schools (i.e., 8 hours a day, 5 days a week, for 8 and 13 years) would combine with the processes of indoctrination that assault students with ruling ideologies to prepare/discipline them to play specific roles within the relations of production. See, Louis Althusser. *Lenin and Philosophy and Other Essays by Louis Althusser.* p. 154–156.

59 L. Althusser. Lenin and Philosophy and Other Essays by Louis Althusser, p. 132–149.

60 I. F. H. Lopez. *The Social Construction of Race,* p. 193.

61　Ibid., p. 196.

62　M. Omi and H. Winant. *Racial Formation in the United States*, p. 59.

63　I. F. H. Lopez. *The Social Construction of Race*, p. 192.

64　O. H. Gandy. *Communication and Race: Structural Perspective*, p. 41.

65　Ibid., p. 49.

66　S. Hall. 'Gramsci's Relevance for the Study of Race and Ethnicity'. In D. Morley and K-H. Chen (eds.). *Stuart Hall: Critical Dialogues in Cultural Studies*. (London: Routledge, 1996), p. 420–421.

67　Ibid., p. 420–421.

68　Ibid., p. 421.

69　R. Simon. *Gramsci's Political Thought: An Introduction*. (London: Lawrence and Wishart, 1982), p. 63.

70　See M. E. Tigar and M. R. Levy. *Law and the Rise of Capitalism*. (NY: Monthly Review Press, 1977), p. 310. In their text, Tigar and Levy attempt to trace the origins and development of our present day legal and economic systems. Similar to Marx, their argument centres on the concept that social change is a bi-product of social conflict and shifting material forces, but unlike Marx, they focus on ideological shifts as a hinge point to social formation. They suggest that the evolution from feudalism to capitalism was merely part of an ongoing process of social change; that tomorrow's political, legal and ideological systems will reflect the interests of today's revolutionary social class. They also suggest that in order to understand the development of capitalism, it is important to recognize that ideology acted as the crucible out of which all action arose.

71　Ibid., p. 212.

72　R. Simon. *Gramsci's Political Thought: An Introduction,* p. 59.

73　Ibid., p. 62.

74　S. Hall. *Gramsci's Relevance for the Study of Race and Ethnicity*, p. 420–421.

75　Ibid., p. 423.

76　R. Miliband. *The State in Capitalist Society: The Analysis of the Western System of Power*. (London: Quartet Books Ltd., 1969), p. 44.

77　R. Simon. *Gramsci's Political Thought: An Introduction,* p. 33.

78　S. Hall. *Gramsci's Relevance for the Study of Race and Ethnicity*, p. 424.

79　Ibid., p. 424.

80　G. N. Smith and Q. Hoare. *Selections from the Prison Notebooks*. (NY: International Pubs., 1971), p. 328.

81　S. Hall. *Gramsci's Relevance for the Study of Race and Ethnicity*, p. 431.

CHAPTER TWO
De-Ideologizing Race: Ideologies, Identities and Illusions

1　S. Hall. *The Problem of Ideology: Marxism Without Guarantees*, p. 26–27.

2　P. Freire. *Pedagogy of the Oppressed*, p. 173.

3　C. Weedon. *Feminist Practice and Poststructuralist Theory*, p. 108.

4　See D. T. Goldberg. *Racist Culture*. (Oxford: Blackwell, 1993); and R. Miles. *Racism*. (London: Tavistock, 1989).

5   T. A. van Dijk. *Elite Discourse and Racism*. (Newbury Park: Sage Publications, Inc., 1993).

6   E. Said. *Orientalism*. (NY: Vintage, 1979), p. 32.

7   Ibid., p. 3.

8   Ibid.

9   J. Scott. 'Deconstructing Equality-Versus-Difference: Or, The Uses of Post-Structuralist Theory for Feminism'. *Feminist Studies*. Vol. 14(1), 1988, p. 36.

10 Ibid., p. 36.

11 H. K. Bhabha. *The Location of Culture*. (NY: Routledge, 1994), p. 66.

12 Ibid.

13 Ibid.

14 Ibid.

15 E. Said. *Orientalism*. (NY: Vintage, 1979), p. 206.

16 See E. Said as quoted in H. K. Bhabha, *The Location of Culture*, p. 71.

17 S. Marcus. 'Fighting Bodies, Fighting Words: A Theory and Politics of Rape Prevention'. In J. Butler and J. Scott (eds.). *Feminists Theorize the Political*. (NY: Routledge. 1992), p. 389.

18 M. Foucault. 'Body/Power'. In C. Gordon (eds.). *Power/Knowledge: Selected Interviews and Other Writings 1972–1977*. (NY: Pantheon, 1987), p. 137.

19 S. Marcus. *Fighting Bodies, Fighting Words: A Theory and Politics of Rape Prevention*, p. 389.

20 See N. Frijda. *The Emotions*. (Cambridge: Cambridge University Press, 1987); and A. Ortony. C. L. Clore and A. M. Collins. *The Cognitive Structure of Emotions*. (NY: Cambridge University Press, 1988).

21 J. F. Rychlak. *In Defense of Human Consciousness*. (Washington: American Psychological Association, 1997), p. 295.

22 P. Heelas. 'Introduction: Indigenous Psychologies'. In P. Heelas and A. Lock (eds.). *Indigenous Psychologies: The Anthropology of the Self*. (NY: Academic Press, 1981), p. 7.

23 A. H. Jenkins. 'Individuality in Cultural Context: The Case for Psychological Agency'. *Theory and Psychology*. Vol. 11(3), 2001, p. 353.

24 A. H. Jenkins. 'The Liberating Value of Constructionism for Minorities'. *The Humanistic Psychologist*. Vol. 17, 1989, p. 161–168.

25 Ibid., p. 161–168.

26 J. W. Scott. 'Deconstructing Equality-Versus-Difference: Or, the Uses of Post-structuralist Theory for Feminism'. *Feminist Studies*. Vol. 14(1), 1988,   p. 35.

27 C. Weedon, *Feminist Practice and Post-Structuralist Theory*, p. 108.

28 H. K. Bhabha. *The Location of Culture*, p. 41.

29 S. E. Hormuth. 'An Ecological Perspective on the Self-Concept'. In R. C. Curtis (ed.). *The Relational Self: Theoretical Convergences in Psychoanalysis and Social Psychology*. (NY: Guilford, 1991), p. 94–108.

30 P. Cushman cited in A. H. Jenkins. 'Individuality in Cultural Context: The Case for Psychological Agency'. *Theory and Psychology*. Vol. 11(3), 2001, p. 353.

31 J. W. Scott. 'Experience'. In J. Butler and J. W. Scott (eds.). *Feminists Theorize the Political*. (London: Routledge, 1992), p. 28.

32   K. J. Gergen. 'The Place of the Psyche in a Constructed World'. *Theory and Psychology.* Vol. 7, 1997, p. 735.

33   Ibid., p. 725.

34   H. R. Markus and S. Kitayama. 'The Cultural Construction of Self and Emotion: Implications for Social Behaviour'. In S. Kitayama and H.R. Markus. *Emotion and Culture: Empirical Studies of Mutual Influence.* (Washington: American Psychological Association, 1994), p. 92.

35   T. A. van Dijk. 'Opinions and Ideologies in Editorials'. A Paper for the 4th International Symposium of Critical Discourse Analysis, Language, Social Life and Critical Thought (Athens, 14–16 December 1995), Second Draft, March 1996.

36   See L. Bandalmundi. 'Developmental Discourse as an Author/Hero Relationship'. *Culture and Psychology.* Vol. 5, 1999, p. 41–65; E. Sampson. *Celebrating the Other: A Dialogic Account of Human Nature.* (Boulder: Westview, 1993); and J. V. Wertsch. *Voices of the Mind: A Sociocultural Approach to Mediated Action.* (Cambridge: Harvard University Press, 1991).

37   M. M. Bakhtin. *Speech Genres and Other Essays.* (Austin: University of Texas Press, 1986), p. 95.

38   H. J. M. Hermans, H. J. G. Kempen and R. J. p. van Loon. 'The Dialogical Self: Beyond Individualism and Rationalism'. *American Psychologist.* Vol. 47, 1992, p. 23–33.

39   S. Hall cited in A. K. M. Ibrahim. *'Hey, Wassup Homeboy?' Becoming Black: Race, Language, Culture and the Politics of Identity: African Students in a Franco-Ontarian High School.* p. 75.

40   M. Bakhtin. 'The Dialogic Imagination: Four Essays'. In A. K. M. Ibrahim. *'Hey, Wassup Homeboy?' Becoming Black: Race, Language, Culture and the Politics of Identity: African Students in a Franco-Ontarian High School.* p. 76.

41   J. Kristeva. 'La Revolution du language poetique: L'Avant-garde a la fin du 19e Siele'. Cited in A. K. M. Ibrahim. *'Hey, Wassup Homeboy?' Becoming Black: Race, Language, Culture and the Politics of Identity: African Students in a Franco-Ontarian High School.* p. 76.

42   S. Bhatia. 'Acculturation, Dialogical Voices and the Construction of the Diasporic Self'. *Theory and Psychology.* Vol. 12(1), 2002, p. 63.

43   Ibid., p. 63.

44   H. J. M. Hermans, H. J. G. Kempen and R. J. p. van Loon, *The Dialogical Self: Beyond Individualism and Rationalism*, p. 28–29.

45   G. Spivak. *The Post-Colonial Critic: Interviews, Strategies, Dialogues.* (Great Britain: Routlegde, 1990), p. 39.

46   A. Bammer. 'The Dilemma of the 'But': Writing Germanness after the Holocaust'. In E. Barkan and M. D. Shelton (eds.). *Borders, Exiles, Diasporas.* (Stanford: Stanford University Press, 1998), p. 22–24.

47   T. Öyan (1996) suggests that Diasporic communities distinctly attempt to maintain real or imagined connections and commitments to a 'Homeland' and that in recognizing their intrinsic connections, such communities would therefore act in collectivity. We contend that such notions of Diasporic identity fail to consider the salience of skin color and the dialectics of identity that

construct and position peoples of color as unfamiliar, foreign and dislocated regardless of a sense of being 'Home'. So when we speak of Diaspora, we do so respective of these formations and positionings of racial/racialized identities.

48   S. Bhatia. Acculturation, Dialogical Voices and the Construction of the Diasporic Self, p. 62.

49   H. J. H. Hermans. 'Voicing the Self: From Information Processing to Dialogical Interchange'. *Psychological Bulletin.* Vol. 119, 1996, p. 44.

50   D-C. Martin. 'The Choices of Identity'. *Social Identities.* Vol. 1(1), 1995, p. 6.

51   S. Hall. 'Old and New Identities: Old and New Ethnicities'. In A. King (ed.). *Culture, Globalization and the World System.* (NY: State University Press, 1991), p. 21.

52   L. Grossberg. 'Cultural Studies and/in New Worlds'. In C. McCarthy and W. Crichlow (eds.). *Race, Identity and Representation in Education.* (NY: Routledge, 1993), p. 96.

53   S. Bhatia. *Acculturation, Dialogical Voices and the Construction of the Diasporic Self,* p. 67.

54   J. V. Wertsch. *Voices of the Mind: A Sociocultural Approach to Mediated Action.* (Cambridge: Harvard University Press, 1991), p. 124.

55   E. Sampson. *Celebrating the Other: A Dialogic Account of Human Nature.* (Boulder: Westview, 1993), p. 143; See also S. Bhatia. Acculturation, Dialogical Voices and the Construction of the Diasporic Self, p. 67.

56   S. Bhatia. *Acculturation, Dialogical Voices and the Construction of the Diasporic Self.*

CHAPTER THREE
Theorizing Power: Rupturing Dichotomies

1   M. Foucault cited in N. Hartsock. 'Foucault on Power: A Theory for Women?' In L. J. Nicholson (ed.). *Feminism/Postmodernism.* (New York: Routledge, 1990), p. 168.

2   Ibid., p. 110.

3   S. Matthews. 'Re-Thinking White Privilege Work As Critical Anti-Racism Practice'. Master Thesis. (Toronto: OISE/University of Toronto, 1988), p. 31.

4   A. Lattas. 'Essentialism, Memory and Resistance: Aboriginality and the Politics of Authenticity'. *Oceania.* Vol. 62, 1993, p. 249–263.

5   S. Hall. *The Problem of Ideology: Marxism Without Guarantees,* p. 38.

6   M. Barrett. *The Politics of Truth: From Marx to Foucault.* (California: Stanford University Press), p. 137.

7   J. Sawicki. *Disciplining Foucault: Feminism, Power and the Body.* (NY: Routledge, 1991), p. 20.

8   Ibid., p. 21–23.

9   G. J. S. Dei. *Anti-Racism Education: Theory and Practice.*

10   S. Marcus. *Fighting Bodies, Fighting Words: A Theory and Politics of Rape Prevention.*

11   R. Collins. 'Stratification, Emotional Energy, and the Transient Emotions'. In

D. Kemper (ed.). *Research Agendas in the Sociology of Emotions.* (NY: New York Press, 1990), p. 27.

12   Ibid., p. 27–29.

13   E. Summers-Effler. 'The Micro Potential for Social Change: Emotion, Consciousness, and Social Movement Formation.' *Sociological Theory.* Vol. 20 (1), 2002, p. 43.

14   Ibid., p. 44.

15   See also M. B. Zinn. 'Race and the Reconstruction of Gender'. Research paper No. 14. The Center for Research on Women. Memphis State University, 1991. See also E. N. Glenn. 'From Servitude to Service Work: Historical Continuities in the Racial Division of Paid Reproductive Labor'. In *Signs: Journal of Women in Culture and Society*, 18(1), 1992.

16   P. Hill-Collins. *Black Feminist Thought: Knowledge, Consciousness and the Politics of Empowerment.* (Cambridge: Unwin Hyman Ltd., 1990).

17   A. Lorde. *Sister Outsider.* (NY: The Crossing Press, 1984).

18   See P. Essed. *Understanding Everyday Racism.*

19   S. Bhatia. *Acculturation, Dialogical Voices and the Construction of the Diasporic Self.*

20   J. W. Scott. *Deconstructing Equality-Versus-Difference*, p. 36.

21   Ibid., p. 36.

22   S. Marcus. *Fighting Bodies, Fighting Words: A Theory and Politics of Rape Prevention*, p. 389.

23   J. W. Scott. *Deconstructing Equality-Versus-Difference*, p. 35.

24   C. Weedon. *Feminist Practice and Post-Structuralist Theory*, p. 125.

25   J. W. Scott. *Deconstructing Equality-Versus-Difference*, p. 35.

26   C. Weedon. *Feminist Practice and Post-Structuralist Theory*, p. 108.

27   S. Hall. *The Problem of Ideology: Marxism Without Guarantees*, p. 26–29.

28   M. Barrett. *The Politics of Truth: From Marx to Foucault.* (California: Stanford University Press), p. 27.

29   S. Marcus. *Fighting Bodies, Fighting Words: A Theory and Politics of Rape Prevention*, p. 389.

30   b. hooks. *Talking Back: Thinking Feminist, Thinking Black.* (Toronto: Between the Lines, 1988).

31   Ibid.

32   C. Weedon. *Feminist Practice and Post-Structuralist Theory.*

33   Ibid., p. 389.

34   J. W. Scott. *Deconstructing Equality-Versus-Difference: Or, The Uses of Post-structuralist Theory for Feminism.* p. 37–38.

35   C. Weedon. *Feminist Practice and Post-Structuralist Theory*, p. 164.

36   Ibid., p. 387.

37   R. Delgado. 'Words that Wound'. In R. Delgado (ed.). *Critical Race Theory: The Cutting Edge.* (Philadelphia: Temple University Press, 1995), p. 165.

38   Ibid., p. 159.

39   C. Weedon. *Feminist Practice and Post-Structuralist Theory*, p. 125.

40   H. Frith and C. Kitzinger. 'Reformulating Sexual Script Theory'. *Theory and Psychology.* Vol. 11(2), 2001, p. 210.

CHAPTER FOUR
White Power, White Privilege

1   M. Foucault. 'Discipline and Punish'. In P. Rabinow. *The Foucault Reader.* (NY: Pantheon Books, 1984), p. 206.

2   J. Kovel. *White Racism: A Psychohistory.* (London: Free Association Books, 1988), p. lxxxix.

3   See H. Giroux. 'Rewriting the Discourse of Racial Identity: Towards a Pedagogy and Politics of Whiteness'. *Harvard Educational Review.* Vol. 67(2), 1997, p. 285–320; P. McLaren. 'Unthinking Whiteness, Rethinking Democracy, or Farewell to the Blonde Beast: Towards a Revolutionary Multiculturalism'. *Educational Foundations.* Vol. 11(2), 1997, p. 5–39.

4   As discussed earlier, power and privilege are relational concepts, so cognizant of the intersections of oppression, we do not want to imply that all power and all privilege exist somehow beyond our experience. To this end, we recognize that we are all differentially positioned and that in certain spaces and in certain moments, we access privilege. So in this light, we would specify that we are cognizant of our specific privileges and positionalities of power.

5   P. Kivel. *Up Rooting Racism: How White People Can Work for Racial Justice.* (Philadelphia: New Society Publishers, 1996), p. 10–11.

6   L. L. Karumanchery. 'The Color of Trauma: New Perspectives on Racism, Politics and Resistance'. Ph.D. Thesis. (Toronto: OISE/University of Toronto, 2003), p. 41.

7   A. Lorde. *Sister Outsider.*

8   M. B. Zinn, L. W. Cannon, E. Higginbotham and B. T. Dill. 'The Costs of Exclusionary Practices in Women's Studies'. *Signs: Journal of Women in Culture and Society.* Vol. 11(2), 1986, p. 297.

9   T. Grillo and S. Wildman. 'Obscuring the Importance of Race: The Implication of Making Comparisons Between Racism and Sexism (or Other isms)'. *Duke Law Journal.* 1999, p. 397–412.

10 S. Wildman with M. Armstrong, A. Davis and T. Grillo. *Privilege Revealed: How Invisible Preference Undermines America.* (NY: NY University Press, 1996), p. 8.

11 P. McIntosh. 'White Privilege and Male Privilege: A Personal Account of Coming to See Correspondences Through Work in Women's Studies'. In P. Hill-Collins (ed.). *Race, Class and Gender: An Anthology.* (California: Wadsworth Publishing Co., 1992), p. 71.

12 Ibid., p. 73–75.

13 D. T. Goldberg. *Anatomy of Racism.* (Minneapolis: University of Minnesota, 1990); and D. T. Goldberg, *Racist Culture.* (Oxford: Blackwell, 1993).

14 See R. Miles, *Racism*; G. J. S. Dei. 'Towards an Anti-Racism Discursive Framework'. In G. J. S. Dei and A. Calliste (eds.). *Power, Knowledge and Anti-Racism Education: A Critical Reader.* (Halifax: Fernwood Publishing, 2000); G. J. S. Dei. *Anti-Racism Education: Theory and Practice.*

15 See G. J. S. Dei. Anti-Racism Education: Theory and Practice; M. Castagna and G. J. S. Dei. 'An Historical Overview of the Application of the Race Con-

cept in Social Practice'. In. A. Calliste and G. J. S. Dei (eds.). *Anti-Racist Feminism: Critical Race and Gender Studies.* (Halifax: Fernwood Publishing, 2000).

16   G. Spivak. *The Post Colonial Critic: Interviews, Strategies, Dialogues*, p. 56.

17   I. Grewal and C. Kaplan. *Scattered Hegemonies: Postmodernity and Transnational Feminist Practices.* (Minneapolis: University of Minnesota Press, 1994), p. 138.

18   R. Frankenberg. *White Women, Race Matters: The Social Construction of Whiteness.* (Minneapolis: University of Minnesota Press, 1993); R. Dyer. *White.* (New York: Routledge, 1997); D. Roediger, *Towards the Abolition of Whiteness: Essays on Race, Politics and Working Class History.* (London: Verso, 1994).

19   L. T. Reynolds and L. Lieberman. 'The Rise and Fall of Race'. *Race, Sex and Class.* Vol. 1(1), 1993, p. 109–128.

20   M. Foucault. *Discipline and Punish*, p. 188.

21   Ibid., p. 188.

22   Ibid., p. 189.

23   Ibid.

24   A. Gobineau. *Essay on the Inequality of Human Races.* Translated by A. Collins. (London, William Heinemann, 1915), p. 209; See also H. F. K. Gunther. *The Radical Elements of European History.* Translated by G. C. Wheeler. (London, Methuen and Co. 1927).

25   J. Feagin and H. Vera. *White Racism: The Basics.* (NY: Routledge, 1995); and C. West. *Race Matters.* (NY: Vintage Books, 1994).

26   P. Taguieff. 'From Race to Culture: The New Right's View of European Identity'. Translated by D. Cook. Telos, 98–99. Winter 1993–Fall 1994, p. 99–125.

27   See A. Fremantle (ed.). *The Papal Encyclicals.* (NY: New American Library, 1963), p. 258.

28   See E. Said. *Orientalism.* (NY: Vintage, 1979); and F. Fanon. *The Wretched of the Earth.* Translated by C. Farington. (NY: Grow Press, 1966).

29   M. Foucault, *Discipline and Punish*, p. 195.

30   Ibid., p. 195.

31   Ibid., p. 210.

32   Ibid., p. 210–215.

33   Ibid.

34   G. J. S. Dei. *Towards an Anti-Racism Discursive Framework*, p. 23–40.

35   R. Frankenberg, *White Women, Race Matters: The Social Construction of Whiteness.*

36   See H. Giroux. 'Rewriting the Discourse of Racial Identity: Towards a Pedagogy and Politics of Whiteness'. *Harvard Educational Review.* Vol. 67(2), 1997, p. 285–320; P. McLaren, 'Unthinking Whiteness, Rethinking Democracy, or Farewell to the Blonde Beast: Towards a Revolutionary Multiculturalism'. *Educational Foundations.* Vol. 11(2), 1997, p. 5–39; M. Fine, L. Weis, L. Powell, and M. Wong. 'Preface'. In M. Fine et al. (eds.). *Off White: Readings on Race, Power and Society.* (NY: Routledge, 1997), p. vii–xii.

37   See M. Wray and R. Newitz (eds.). *White Trash: Race and Class in America.*

(NY: Routledge, 1997); R. Post and M. Rogin (eds.). *Race and Representation: Affirmative Action*. (NY: Zone Books, 1998).

38 For a different context, see J. Lorrain, 'Stuart Hall and the Marxist Concept of Ideology'. In D. Morley and K-H. Chen (eds.). *Stuart Hall: Critical Dialogues in Cultural Studies*. (London: Routledge, 1996), p. 47–70.

39 D. Roediger. *Towards the Abolition of Whiteness: Essays on Race, Politics and Working Class History*. (London: Verso, 1994), p. 13; R. Dyer, *White*.

40 P. McLaren. 'Unthinking Whiteness, Rethinking Democracy, or Farewell to the Blonde Beast: Towards a Revolutionary Multiculturalism'. *Educational Foundations*. Vol. 11(2), 1997, p. 5–39.

41 R. Dyer. *White*.

42 See S. Bowles and H. Gintis. *Schooling in Capitalist America: Education Reform and the Contradictions of Economic Life*. (NY: Basic Books, 1977); S. Aronowitz and H. Giroux. *Education Under Siege: Conservative, Liberal and Radical Debate over Schooling*. (Massachusetts: Bergin and Garvey, 1985); J. Gaskell, A. McLaren and M. Novogrodsky. 'What is Worth Knowing?' In E. D. Nelson and B. W. Robinson (eds.). *Gender in the 1990s: Images, Realities and Issues*. (Canada: Nelson, 1995); M. Fleming, N. Habib, T. Horley, S. Jones-Caldwell, K. Moules, L. Waserman and S. Wehbi. 'Gender, Power and Silence in the Classroom: Our Experiences Speak for Themselves'. Women's Supplement, *Lexicon*. March 6, 1991.

43 M. Valverde. *The Age of Light, Soap and Water: Moral Reform in English Canada, 1885–1925*. (Toronto: McClelland and Stewart Inc., 1991).

44 I. Rajagopal. 'The Glass Ceiling in the Vertical Mosaic: Indian Immigrants in Canada'. *Canadian Ethnic Studies*. Vol. 33(2), 1990, p. 91–101.

45 N. Chater. 'Biting the Hand that Feeds Me: Notes on Privilege from a White Anti-Racist Feminist'. *Canadian Woman Studies*, Vol. 14, 1994, p. 102.

46 See M. Wray and R. Newitz (eds.). *White Trash: Race and Class in America*.

47 C. Harris. 'Whiteness as Property'. *Harvard Law Review*. Vol. 106(8), 1993, p. 1759.

48 Ibid., p. 1786.

49 See L. Roman. 'Denying [White] Racial Privilege: Redemption Discourses and the Uses of Fantasy'. In M. Fine, M. L. Weis, L. Powell and L. Mun Wong (eds.). *Off White: Readings on Race, Power and Society*. (NY: Routledge, 1997), p. 270–282.

50 See H. Giroux. 'Rewriting the Discourse of Racial Identity: Towards a Pedagogy and Politics of Whiteness'. *Harvard Educational Review*. Vol. 67(2), 1997, p. 285–320.

51 G. J. S. Dei. 'Contesting the Future: Anti-Racism and Canadian Diversity'. In S. Nanacoo (ed.). *21st Century Canadian Diversity*. (Toronto: Canadian Educators Press, 2000), p. 295–319.

52 See G. J. S. Dei. *Anti-Racism Education: Theory and Practice*; and G. J. S. Dei. The Denial of Difference: Reframing Anti-Racist Praxis, p. 17–38.

53 Ibid., p. 17–38.

54 C. Ungerleider. 'Immigration, Multiculturalism and Citizenship: The Evolution of Canadian Multiculturalism'. Paper presented at the Learned Societies

meeting of the Canadian Society for the Study of Education (CSSE) at Brock University, St. Catharines, Ontario, June 4, 1996.

55   M. Fine, L. Weis, L. Powell, L. M. Wong, *Preface*, p. x.

56   F. Fanon, The Wretched of the Earth, p. 78.

57   J. K. Gibson-Graham. *The End of Capitalism (As We Knew It): A Feminist Critique of Political Economy*. (Oxford: Blackwell, 1996), p. 120.

58   www.foxnews.com. *Study Links Bulimia/Anorexia in Fiji to the Arrival Of TV*. May 20, 1999.

59   P. Jay. *Hitman Hart: Wrestling with Shadows*. A Documentary produced by High Road Productions, 1998.

60   S. Hall. 'Ethnicity, Identity and Difference'. *Radical American*. Vol. 13(4), 1991, p. 9–20.

61   D. Lorimer. *Color, Class and the Victorians*. (Leicester: University Press, 1987), p. 90.

62   J. Kovel. *White Racism: A Psychohistory*. (London, Free Association Books: 1988), p. lxxxix.

63   B. D. Tatum. 'Talking About Race, Learning About Racism: The Application of Racial Identity Development Theory in the Classroom'. *Harvard Educational Review*. Vol. 62, p. 1–24.

64   J. Olsson. 'For White Anti-Racists: Avoiding the Detours in the Journey Towards Justice'. *Women's Education des Femmes*. Vol. 12(4), 1996/1997, p. 19–20.

65   Ibid., p. 20.

CHAPTER FIVE
The Materiality of Racism: Democracy and Dissonance

1   T. Walkom. 'Does Race Really Matter at U of T?' (Toronto Star, Jan. 11, 2000), p. A13.

2   G. J. S. Dei. *Anti-Racism Education: Theory and Practice*, p. 130.

3   N. Karumanchery-Luik. 'Race, Gender and Class: Malayalee Women's Experiences in Toronto'. Ph.D. Thesis. (Toronto: OISE/University of Toronto, 1997).

4   Ibid.

5   L. L. Karumanchery. 'Ethnic Identity Retention: A Cross Generational Analysis of Malayalees in Toronto.' Master Thesis. (Winnipeg: University of Manitoba, 1996).

6   S. Hall. *Gramsci's Relevance for the Study of Race and Ethnicity*, p. 424.

7   F. Henry, C. Tator, W. Mattis and T. Rees. *The Color of Democracy: Racism in Canadian Society*, p. 51.

8   J. P. Portelli. 'Democracy in Education: Beyond the Conservative or Progressive Stances'. In J. P. Portelli and R. P. Solomon. *The Erosion of Democracy: From Critique to Possibilities*. (Calgary: Detselig Enterprises, Ltd, 2001), p. 280.

9   Ibid., p. 280.

10   Ibid., p. 281.

11   D. T. Sehr. *Education for Public Democracy*. (Albany: State University of New York Press, 1997), p. 43.

12   S. Benhabib. 'Toward a Deliberative Model of Democratic Legitimacy'. In A. Phillips (ed.). *Democracy and Difference.* (Cambridge: Polity Press, 1993).

13   R. A. Dahl. *On Democracy.* (New Haven: Yale University Press, 1998).

14   F. Henry and C. Tator. 'The Ideology of Racism—Democratic Racism'. *Canadian Ethnic Studies.* Vol. 26(2), 1994, p. 2.

15   F. Henry, C. Tator, W. Mattis and T. Rees. *The Color of Democracy: Racism in Canadian Society*, p. 17.

16   P. Essed. *Understanding Everyday Racism*, p. 20–30.

17   Ibid., p. 30.

18   H. Carby. 'White Women Listen! Black Feminism and the Boundaries of Sisterhood'. *The Empire Strikes Back: Race and Racism in 70's Britain.* (London: Hutchinson, in association with the Centre for Contemporary Cultural Studies, 1982), p. 212–235; A. Davis. *Women, Race and Class.* (NY: Random House, 1981); P. Parmar and V. Amos. 'Challenging Imperial Feminism'. *Feminist Review*, Vol. 17, 1984, p. 3–19.

19   S. L. Gaertner and J. F. Dovidio. 'Racism Among the Well Intentioned'. In E. G. Clausen and J. Bermingham (eds.). *Pluralism, Racism and Public Policy.* (Boston: G. K. Hall, 1981), p. 208.

20   Ibid., p. 210–213.

21   S. L. Gaertner and J. F. Dovidio. 'The Aversive Forms of Racism'. In S. L. Gaertner and J. F. Dovidio (eds.). *Prejudice, Discrimination and Racism.* (NY: Academic Press, 1986).

22   F. Henry, C. Tator, W. Mattis and T. Rees. *The Color of Democracy: Racism in Canadian Society*, p. 20–21.

23   Ibid., p. 20–21.

24   F. Henry and C. Tator. *The Ideology of Racism—Democratic Racism*, p. 29.

25   M. Frye. 'Oppression'. *Politics of Reality: Essays in Feminist Theory.* (Crossing Press, 1983), p. 1.

26   Ibid., p. 10–11.

27   See G. J. S. Dei. *Anti-Racism Education: Theory and Practice*; J. Cummins. 'Report of the Heritage Language Research Conference'. Ottawa, May, 1984: 112–130; J. Ogbu. 'Variability in Minority School Performance: A Problem in Search of an Explanation'. *Anthropology and Education Quarterly.* Vol. 18, 1987, p. 312–334.

28   I. Elliston. 'Racial Attitudes and Racial Violence in the School and School Community in Metropolitan Toronto, Ontario. A Survey of Personal Opinion'. Metro Task Force on Human Relations; see also the Ministry of Citizenship, 1990, 'Anti-Racism Strategy for Ontario', 1977.

29   See Karumanchery-Luik. 'South East Asian Students' Perceptions and Experience of Racism and Their Relation to School Achievement'. Master Thesis. (Toronto: OISE/University of Toronto, 1992), p. 87–90; L. S. Kahen. 'Experimental Manipulation of Bias in Teachers' Scoring of Subjective Tests'. A Paper given for the American Psychological Association. (NY: September, 1966); R. Rosenthal and L. Jacobson. *Pygmalion in the Classroom.* (NY: Holt, Rinehart and Winston, 1968).

30   G. Verma and P. Pumfrey. *Educational Attainments: Issues and Outcomes in Multicultural Education*. (London: Falmer Press, 1988).
31   G. J. S. Dei. J. Mazzuca, E. McIsaac, J. Zine. *Reconstructing 'Drop-Out': A Critical Ethnography of the Dynamics of Black Students' Disengagement from School*. (Toronto: University of Toronto Press, 1997).
32   S. Aronowitz and H. Giroux. *Education Under Seige: Conservative, Liberal and Radical Debate Over Schooling*. (Massachusetts: Bergin and Garvey, 1985).
33   Ibid.
34   G. J. S. Dei. J. Mazzuca, E. McIsaac, J. Zine. *Reconstructing 'Drop-Out': A Critical Ethnography of the Dynamics of Black Students' Disengagement from School*.
35   We employ data from the 1990 Statistics Canada survey in general and from the Ontario data sets specifically because they are broken down by race and ethnicity relative to both the general population and to minoritized groups.
36   D. Woo. 'The Socioeconomic Status of Asian American Women in the Labour Force'. *Sociological Perspectives*. Vol. 28(3), 1985.
37   E. N. Glenn. 'From Servitude to Service Work: Historical Continuities in the Racial Division of Paid Reproductive Labour'. *Signs: Journal of Women in Culture and Society*. Vol. 18(1), 1992.
38   S. Sherwin. *No Longer Patient: Feminist Ethics and Healthcare*. (NY: Temple University Press, 1992), p. 222.
39   Ibid., p. 226.
40   W. Dressler cited in Hunter College Women's Studies Collective. *Women's Reality, Women's Choices: An Introduction to Women's Studies*. (Oxford: Hunter College Women's Studies Collective, 1995).
41   A. Todd cited in S. Sherwin. *No Longer Patient: Feminist Ethics and Healthcare*. (NY: Temple University Press, 1992), p. 225.
42   I. R. G. Waldron. 'African Canadian Women Storming the Barricades! Challenging Psychiatric Imperialism Through Indigenous Conceptualizations of "Mental Illness" and Self-Healing'. Ph.D. Thesis. (Toronto: OISE/University of Toronto, 2002), p. 33.
43   S. Sherwin. *No Longer Patient: Feminist Ethics and Healthcare*, p. 235.
44   Ibid., p. 235.
45   Ibid.
46   Ibid.
47   See C. M. Renzetti and D. J. Curran. *Women, Men and Society*. (Toronto: Allyn and Bacon, 1999), p. 361.
48   See M. A. Paludi. *The Psychology of Women*. (New Jersey: Prentice Hall, 1998), p. 88–97; C. Travis, *The Mismeasure of Women*. (NY: Simon and Schuster, 1992).
49   Ibid., p. 371.
50   Ibid., p. 370–371.
51   See J. S. Jackson, T. N. Brown, D. R. Williams, M. Torres, S. L. Sellers and K. Brown. 'Racism and the Physical and Mental Health Status of African Americans: A 13 Year National Panel Study'. *Ethnicity and Disease*. Vol. 6,

1996, p. 132–147; E. A. Klonoff, H. Landrine and U. B. Ullman. 'Racial Discrimination and Psychiatric Symptoms Among Blacks'. *Cultural Diversity and Ethnic Minority Psychology*. Vol. 5, 1999, p. 329–339; R. Clark, N. B. Anderson, V. R. Clark and D. R. Williams. 'Racism as a Stressor for African Americans.' *American Psychologist*. Vol. 54, 1999, p. 805–816.

52   See K. Nader, N. Dubrow and B. H. Stamm (eds.). *Honoring Differences. Cultural Issues in the Treatment of Trauma and Loss.* (Philadelphia: Brunner/Mazel, 1989); and S. L Halligan and R. Yehuda. 'Risk Factors for PTSD'. *PTSD Research Quarterly*, Vol. 11(3), 2000, p. 17.

53   R. M. Scurfield. 'Positive and Negative Aspects of Exposure to Racism and Trauma: Research, Assessment and Treatment Implications'. *Clinical Quarterly.* Vol. 10(1), 2001.

54   C. Ungerleider. 'Police Minority Conflict in Democratic Societies'. *Currents.* Vol. 8(1), 1993, p. 3–5.

55   Ibid., p. 4–5; See also R. Neugebauer. 'First Nations Peoples and Law Enforcement: Community Perspectives on Police Response', In R. Neugebauer (ed.). *Criminal Injustice: Racism in the Criminal Justice System.* (Toronto: Canadian Scholar's Press Inc, 2000).

56   C. Ungerleider. *Police Minority Conflict in Democratic Societies.*

57   F. Henry, W. Mattis and C. Tator. 'Racism in the American and British Justice Systems'. *Currents.* Vol. 8(4), 1994.

58   F. Henry and C. Tator. *The Ideology of Racism—Democratic Racism*, p. 29.

59   K. K. Russell. *The Color of Crime: Racial Hoaxes, White Fear, Black Protectionism, Police Harassment and Other Macroaggressions.* (NY: New York University Press, 1998).

60   Ibid., p. 20–32.

61   Ibid., p. 4.

62   Ibid., p. 62.

63   E. Summers-Effler. 'The Micro Potential for Social Change: Emotion, Consciousness, and Social Movement Formation.' *Sociological Theory.* Vol. 20(1), 2002, p. 43.

CHAPTER SIX
The Banality of Racism: Living 'Within' the Traumatic

1   L. L. Karumanchery. *The Color of Trauma: New Perspectives on Racism, Politics and Resistance.*

2   Y. Danieli. 'Introduction: History and Conceptual Foundations'. In Y. Danieli (ed.). *International Handbook of Multigenerational Legacies of Trauma.* (NY: Plenum Press, 1998), p. 4.

3   L. L. Karumanchery. *The Color of Trauma: New Perspectives on Racism, Politics and Resistance.*

4   Ibid., p. 177.

5   J. L. Herman. *Trauma and Recovery,* p. 33.

6   Ibid., p. 33.

7   R. Delgado. *Words that Wound*, p. 164.

8   J. L. Herman. *Trauma and Recovery*, p. 34.
9   P. Freire. *Pedagogy of the Oppressed*, p. 55.
10   J. L. Herman. *Trauma and Recovery*, p. 35.
11   A. Kardiner and H. Spiegel. *War, Stress and Neurotic Illness*. (NY: Hoeber, 1947), p. 13.
12   L. L. Karumanchery. *The Color of Trauma: New Perspectives on Racism, Politics and Resistance*, p. 180.
13   T. Eagleton. *The Significance of Theory*. (Cambridge: Blackwell, 1990).
14   R. Delgado. *Words that Wound*, p. 160.
15   J. L. Herman. *Trauma and Recovery*, p. 36.
16   A. Shalev, S. Orr, T. Peri. et al. 'Impaired Habituation of the Autonomic Component of the Acoustic Startle Response in Post-Traumatic Stress Disorder'. A Paper presented at the American Psychiatric Association Annual Meeting. (New Orleans, LA, 1991), cited in J. L. Herman. *Trauma and Recovery*.
17   R. Delgado, *Words that Wound*, p. 161.
18   L. L. Karumanchery. *The Color of Trauma: New Perspectives on Racism, Politics and Resistance*, p. 189.
19   H. Bannerji. *Thinking Through: Essays on Feminism, Marxism and Anti-Racism*. (Toronto: Women's Press, 1995), p. 56.
20   J. L. Herman. *Trauma and Recovery*, p. 37.
21   Ibid., p. 37.
22   Ibid., p. 37–38.
23   L. L. Karumanchery. *The Color of Trauma: New Perspectives on Racism, Politics and Resistance*, p. 193.
24   J. L. Herman. *Trauma and Recovery*, p. 38.
25   P. Freire. *Pedagogy of the Oppressed*, p. 51.
26   L. L. Karumanchery. *The Color of Trauma: New Perspectives on Racism, Politics and Resistance*, p. 243.
27   J. L. Herman. *Trauma and Recovery*, p. 83.
28   L. L. Karumanchery. *The Color of Trauma: New Perspectives on Racism, Politics and Resistance*, p. 202.
29   L. Terr. 'What Happens to Early Memories of Trauma? A Study of Twenty Children Under Age Five at the Time of Documented Traumatic Events'. *Journal of the American Academy of Child and Adolescent Psychiatry*. Vol. 27, 1988, p. 96–104.
30   L. Terr. *Too Scared to Cry*. (NY: Harper-Collins, 1990), p. 238–239.
31   L. L. Karumanchery. *The Color of Trauma: New Perspectives on Racism, Politics and Resistance*, p. 203.
32   P. Russell. 'Trauma, Repetition and Affect'. (A paper presented at Psychiatry Grand Rounds, Cambridge Hospital, Cambridge, MA, 5 September, 1990).
33   J. L. Herman. *Trauma and Recovery*, p. 41–42.
34   L. L. Karumanchery. *The Color of Trauma: New Perspectives on Racism, Politics and Resistance*, p. 208.
35   See G. J. S. Dei. J. Mazzuca, E. McIsaac, J. Zine. *Reconstructing 'Drop-Out'*.

36   L. L. Karumanchery. *The Color of Trauma: New Perspectives on Racism, Politics and Resistance*, p. 213.

37   J. L. Herman. *Trauma and Recovery*, p. 42.

38   D. Chopra. The Path to Love: Spiritual Strategies for Healing. (NY: Harmony Books, 1997), p. 111.

39   See M. Horowitz. *Stress Response Syndromes*. (Northvale: Jason Aronson, 1986); R. Janoff-Bulman. 'The Aftermath of Victimization: Rebuilding Shattered Assumption'. In C. Figley (ed.). *Trauma and Its Wake*. (NY: Brunner/Mazel, 1985); and J. L. Herman. *Trauma and Recovery*.

40   L. L. Karumanchery. *The Color of Trauma: New Perspectives on Racism, Politics and Resistance*, p. 218.

41   Ibid., p. 221.

42   J. L. Herman. *Trauma and Recovery*, p. 51.

43   L. L. Karumanchery. *The Color of Trauma: New Perspectives on Racism, Politics and Resistance*, p. 246.

44   Ibid., p. 285.

45   See L. H. Bowker, M. Arbitel and J. R. McFerron. 'On the Relationship Between Wife-Beating and Child Abuse'. In K. Yllo and M. Bograd (eds.). *Feminist Perspectives on Wife Abuse*. (California: Sage, 1988), p. 158–174; L. Walker. *The Battered Woman*. (NY: Harper and Row, 1979), p. 76.

46   L. L. Karumanchery. *The Color of Trauma: New Perspectives on Racism, Politics and Resistance*, p. 249.

47   Ibid.

48   H. K. Bhabha. *The Location of Culture*, p. 78.

49   L. L. Karumanchery. *The Color of Trauma: New Perspectives on Racism, Politics and Resistance*, p. 228.

50   R. Delgado. *Words that Wound*, p. 161.

51   J. L. Herman. *Trauma and Recovery*, p. 74–75.

52   Ibid., p. 57.

53   Ibid., p. 76.

54   L. L. Karumanchery. *The Color of Trauma: New Perspectives on Racism, Politics and Resistance*, p. 235.

55   J. L. Herman. *Trauma and Recovery*, p. 77.

56   L. L. Karumanchery. *The Color of Trauma: New Perspectives on Racism, Politics and Resistance*, p. 238.

57   F. Fanon. *Toward the African Revolution*. (NY: Grove Press, Inc., 1967), p. 39.

CHAPTER SEVEN
Weaving the Tapestry: Anti-Racism Theory and Practice

1   H. K. Bhabha. 'Signs Taken for Wonders: Questions of Ambivalence and Authority Under a Tree Outside Delhi, May 1817'. In H. K. Bhabha. *The Location of Culture*.

2   G. Spivak cited in B. Parry. 'Current Theories of Colonial Discourse'. In B. Ashcroft, G. Griffiths and H. Tiffin (eds.). *The Post-Colonial Studies Reader*. (NY: Routledge, 1985), p. 43–44.

3   G. J. S. Dei. *The Denial of Difference: Reframing Anti-Racist Praxis*, p. 17–38.

4   F. Fanon cited in B. Parry. 'Current Theories of Colonial Discourse'. In B. Ashcroft, G. Griffiths and H. Tiffin (eds.). *The Post-Colonial Studies Reader*. (NY: Routledge, 1985), p. 43–44.

5   A. Butler. 'Review of Class Readings from SESE 1921Y: Principles of Anti-Racism Education.' Unpublished. (OISE/University of Toronto, 2000).

6   J. Zine. 'Negotiating Equity: The Dynamics of Minority Community Engagement in Constructing Inclusive Educational Policy'. A Paper read at the International Conference on 'Nationalism, Identity and Minority Rights: Sociological and Political Perspectives'. University of Bristol, September 16–19, 1999.

7   M. Brettschneider. 'Theorizing Diversity from a Jewish Perspective'. *Race, Gender and Class*. Vol. 6(4), 1999, p.17.

8   Ibid., p. 17.

9   Ibid., p. 20.

10   Ibid., p. 20–21.

11   Ibid., p. 16.

12   Ibid., p. 16.

13   See also A. Davis. *Women, Race and Class*; A. Lorde. *Sister Outsider*; S. Razack. *Looking White People in the Eye*; E. Dua and A. Robertson (eds.). *Scratching the Surface of Racism: Canadian Anti-Racist Feminist Thought*; A. Calliste and G. J. S. Dei. *Anti-Racist Feminism*.

14   J. Greenebaum. 'Placing Jewish Women into the Intersectionality of Race, Class and Gender'. *Race, Gender and Class*. Vol. 6(4), 1999, p. 42.

15   Ibid., p. 44.

16   See also P. J. Williams. 'Spirit-Murdering the Messenger: The Discourse of Finger-Pointing as the Law's Response to Racism'. In. A. K. Wing (ed.). *Critical Race Feminism: A Reader*. (NY: New York University Press, 1997), p. 229–238; A. K. Wing, 'Brief Reflections Toward a Multiplicative Theory and Praxis of Being'. In. A. K. Wing (ed.). *Critical Race Feminism: A Reader*. (NY: NY University Press, 1997), p. 44–50.

17   J. Greenebaum. 'Placing Jewish Women into the Intersectionality of Race, Class and Gender'. *Race, Gender and Class*. Vol. 6(4), 1999, p. 47.

18   J. Bourne. 'Homelands of the Mind: Jewish Feminism and Identity Politics'. *Race and Class*. Vol. 29, 1987, p. 1–24; J. Greenebaum. 'Placing Jewish Women into the Intersectionality of Race, Class and Gender'. *Race, Gender and Class*. Vol. 6(4), 1999.

19   T. Connolly. 'Representing Whiteness in the Black Imagination'. In L. Grossberg. et al. (eds.). *Cultural Studies*. (NY: Routledge, 2000), p. 338–346.

20   See G. Brandt. *The Realization of Anti-Racist Teaching*. (London: Falmer Press. 1989); and M. Lee. *Letters to Marcia: A Teacher's Guide to Anti-Racist Education*. (Toronto: Cross Cultural Communication Centre, 1998).

21   See C. Sleeter. 'How White Teachers Construct Race'. In C. McCarthy and W. Crichlow (eds.). *Race, Identity and Representation in Education*. (NY: Routledge, 1993), p. 157–171; and C. Sleeter. 'White Racism'. *Multicultural Education*. (Spring) 1994, p. 5–8.

22 G. J. S. Dei. 'Race and Equity in the Academy'. In K. Armitage (ed.). *Equity and How to Get It: Rescuing Graduate Studies.* (Toronto: Inanna Publications, 1999), p. 79–90.

23 P. Freire. *Pedagogy of the Oppressed.*

24 P. Butler. 'Reflections on Class Discussions'—SESE 1921Y: Principles of Anti-Racism Education'. Unpublished Paper. (OISE/University of Toronto, 2000), p. 4.

25 Ibid., p. 4.

26 M. Cheng. 'Anti-Racism Education'. Ph.D. Thesis. (Toronto: OISE/University of Toronto, 2000); M. Cheng and M. Yau. *The 1997 Every Secondary Student survey: Preliminary Findings.* (Toronto District School Board. Academic Accountability Office, Report No. 227, 1998).

27 I. Shah. 'Faculty Diversity at the University of Toronto'. Unpublished Paper. University of Toronto, 2000.

28 M. Cheng and M. Yau. *The 1997 Every Secondary Student survey: Preliminary Findings.*

29 See G. J. S. Dei. J. Mazzuca, E. McIsaac, J. Zine. *Reconstructing 'Drop-Out': A Critical Ethnography of the Dynamics of Black Students' Disengagement from School.*

30 M. Cheng. 'Anti-Racism Education'. Ph.D. Thesis. (Toronto: OISE/University of Toronto, 2000).

31 G. J. S. Dei. J. Mazzuca, E. McIsaac and J. Zine. *Reconstructing 'Drop-Out': A Critical Ethnography of the Dynamics of Black Students' Disengagement from School.*

32 G. J. S. Dei and L. L. Karumanchery. 'School Reforms in Ontario: The Marketization of Education and the Resulting Silence on Equity'. *The Alberta Journal of Educational Research.* Vol. 45(2), 1999, p. 111–131.

33 R. Hatcher. 'Social Justice and the Politics of School Effectiveness and Improvement'. *British Race, Ethnicity and Education.* Vol. 1(2), 1998, p. 274–285.

34 Ibid., p. 268.

35 L. L. Karumanchery. 'Educational Reform: Marketization and Anti-Racism as Competing Discourses'. *Trans/forms.* Vol. 5, 2000, p. 88–100.

36 S. Hall cited in G. Crozier. 'The Deracialisation of the Initial Teacher Training: Implications for Social Justice'. *Race, Ethnicity and Education.* Vol. 2(1), 1999, p. 79–91.

37 G. J. S. Dei and L. L. Karumanchery. 'School Reforms in Ontario: The Marketization of Education and the Resulting Silence on Equity.' p. 115.

38 B. D. Tatum. 'Talking About Race, Learning About Racism: The Application of Racial Identity Development Theory in the Classroom'. *Harvard Educational Review.* Vol. 62, 1992, p. 1–24.

39 R. Hatcher, *Social Justice and the Politics of School Effectiveness and Improvement.*

40 S. Razack. *Looking White People in the Eye: Gender, Race and Culture in Courtrooms and Classrooms*, p. 19.

41 G. J. S. Dei. *Anti-Racism Education: Theory and Practice.*

CHAPTER EIGHT
Cultivating Culture: Consciousness and Resistance

1   F. Fanon. *Toward the African Revolution*, p. 41.
2   J. L. Kincheloe and S. R. Steinberg. *Changing Multiculturalism*. (Philadelphia: Open University Press, 1997), p. 206.
3   G. J. S. Dei. 'The Role of Indigenous Knowledges in the Academy'. *International Journal of Inclusive Education*. Vol. 4(2), 2000, p. 111–132.
4   H. Thiophene. 'Post-Colonial Literatures and Counter-Discourse'. In B. Ashcroft, G. Griffiths and H. Thiophene (eds.). *The Post-Colonial Studies Reader*, p. 95–98.
5   See L. Abu-Lughod. 'The Romance of Resistance: Tracing Transformations of Power Through Bedouin Women'. *American Ethnologist*. Vol. 17(1), 1990, p. 41–55; D. S. Moore. 'Remapping Resistance: "Ground for Struggle" and the Politics of Place'. In S. Pile and M. Keith (eds.). *Geographies of Resistance*. (London: Routledge, 1997); B. Parry. 'Resistance Theory/Theorising Resistance, or Two Cheers for Nativism'. In F. Barker, P. Hulme and M. Iversen (eds.). *Colonial Discourse/Postcolonial Theory*. (Manchester: University Press, 1994), p. 172–196.
6   J. Muteshi. 'Women, Law and Engendering Resistance: A Pedagogical Project'. Ph.D. Thesis. (Toronto: OISE/University of Toronto, 1996).
7   F. Shroff. 'New Directions in Canadian Health Policy: Lessons of Holistic Medicine'. Ph. D Thesis. (Toronto: OISE/University of Toronto, 1996), p. 23.
8   I. D. Yalom. *The Theory and Practice of Group Psychotherapy*. (NY: Basic Books, 1985),
9   L. L. Karumanchery. *The Color of Trauma: New Perspectives on Racism, Politics and Resistance*, p. 263.
10 Ibid., p. 270.
11 Ibid.
12 J. L. Herman. *Trauma and Recovery*, p. 215.
13 L. L. Karumanchery. *The Color of Trauma: New Perspectives on Racism, Politics and Resistance*, p. 271.
14 Ibid., p. 276.
15 Ibid., p. 277.
16 See J. L. Herman. *Trauma and Recovery*; and Y. Danieli. *Introduction: History and Conceptual Foundations*.
17 See P. Freire. *Pedagogy of the Oppressed*.
18 L. L. Karumanchery. *The Color of Trauma: New Perspectives on Racism, Politics and Resistance*, p. 278.
19 E. Stark and A. Flitcraft. 'Personal Power and Institutional Victimization: Treating the Dual Trauma of Woman Battering'. In F. Ochberg (ed.). *Post Traumatic Therapy and Victims of Violence*. (NY: Brunner, 1988), p. 140.
20 J. L. Herman. *Trauma and Recovery*, p. 134–135.
21 P. Freire. *Pedagogy of the Oppressed*, p. 66.
22 L. L. Karumanchery. *The Color of Trauma: New Perspectives on Racism, Politics and Resistance*, p. 170.

23 Ibid., p. 254.
24 Ibid., p. 258.
25 H. Bhabha cited in B. Parry. *Resistance Theory/Theorising Resistance, or Two Cheers for Nativism*, p. 43.
26 Ibid.

CONCLUSION
Transcending Racism, Transcending Trauma

1   E. Said. *Out of Place: A Memoir*. (New York: Knopf, 1999).
2   F. Fanon cited in H. K. Bhabha. *The Location of Culture*, p. 40.
3   G. J. S. Dei and I. M. James. 'Becoming Black: African-Canadian Youth and the Politics of Negotiating Racial and Radicalized Identities'. *Race, Ethnicity and Education*. Vol. 1(1), 1988; A. K. M. Ibrahim. *'Hey, Wassup Homeboy?' Becoming Black: Race, Language, Culture and the Politics of Identity: African Students in a Franco-Ontarian High School.*
4   J. L. Herman. *Trauma and Recovery*, p. 32.
5   The American Psychiatric Association. *Diagnostic and Statistical Manual of Mental Disorders* (4th ed.). Text Revision. (Washington, DC: American Psychiatric Association, 2000).
6   R. M. Scurfield. 'Positive and Negative Aspects of Exposure to Racism and Trauma: Research, Assessment and Treatment Implications'. *Clinical Quarterly*. Vol. 10(1), 2001.
7   Ibid., p. 1.
8   R. Delgado. *Words that Wound*, p. 160.
9   See R. M. Scurfield. 'Exposure to Racism Trauma and Other Race-Related Experiences: A Guide to Issues, Assessment and Treatment'. Educational Credits. Online continuing education course (www.educational-credits.com, 2000); A. Y. Davis. 'Gender, Class and Multiculturalism: Rethinking "Race" Politics'. In A. F. Gordon and C. Newfield (eds.). *Mapping Multiculturalism*. Minneapolis: University of Minnesota Press, 1996), P. C. Loo, K. Singh, R. M. Scurfield and B. Kilauano. Race-Related Stress Among Asian American Veterans: A Model to Enhance Diagnosis and Treatment'. *Cultural Diversity and Mental Health*. Vol. 4, 1998, p. 75–90; and The American Psychiatric Association. *Diagnostic and Statistical Manual of Mental Disorders*.
10 See *The International Handbook of Multigenerational Legacies of Trauma*.
11 D. T. Wellman. *Portraits of White Racism*. (Cambridge: Cambridge University press, 1977).
12 L. L. Karumanchery. *The Color of Trauma: New Perspectives on Racism, Politics and Resistance*, p. 113.
13 Y. Danieli. *Introduction: History and Conceptual Foundations*, p. 4.
14 J. L. Herman. *Trauma and Recovery*, p. 1–33.
15 M. Foucault cited in H. Drefus and P. Rabinow. *Michel Foucault: Beyond Structuralism and Hermeneutics*. (Chicago: University of Chicago Press, 1982), p. 226.

16	J. H. Sechi. 'Being Japanese-American Doesn't Mean 'Made in Japan'. In D. Fisher (ed.). *The Third Woman: Minority Women Writers of the United States.* (Boston: Houghton Mifflin, 1980), p. 444.

17	L. L. Karumanchery. *The Color of Trauma: New Perspectives on Racism, Politics and Resistance,* p. 326.

18	H. K. Bhabha. *The Location of Culture,* p. 191.

19	Ibid., p. 191.

20	J. L. Herman. *Trauma and Recovery,* p. 211.

21	L. L. Karumanchery. *The Color of Trauma: New Perspectives on Racism, Politics and Resistance,* p. 328.

22	Y. Danieli. *Introduction: History and Conceptual Foundations,* p. 4.

23	L. L. Karumanchery. *The Color of Trauma: New Perspectives on Racism, Politics and Resistance,* p. 329.

24	J. L. Herman. *Trauma and Recovery,* p. 61.

25	See J. N. Capella and K. H. Jamieson. *Spiral of Cynicism: The Press and the Public Good.* (NY: Oxford University Press, 1997); R. Jacoby. *The End of Utopia.* (NY: Basic Books, 1999); Z. Bauman. *In Search of Politics.* (Stanford: Stanford University Press, 1999); and C. Boggs. *The End of Politics: Corporate Power and the Decline of the Public Sphere.* (NY: Guilford Press, 2000).

26	H. A. Giroux. *Impure Acts: The Practical Politics of Cultural Studies.* (NY: Routledge, 2000).

27	L. L. Karumanchery. *The Color of Trauma: New Perspectives on Racism, Politics and Resistance,* p. 331.

INDEX

Studies in the Postmodern Theory of Education

General Editors
Joe L. Kincheloe & Shirley R. Steinberg

Counterpoints publishes the most compelling and imaginative books being written in education today. Grounded on the theoretical advances in criticalism, feminism, and postmodernism in the last two decades of the twentieth century, Counterpoints engages the meaning of these innovations in various forms of educational expression. Committed to the proposition that theoretical literature should be accessible to a variety of audiences, the series insists that its authors avoid esoteric and jargonistic languages that transform educational scholarship into an elite discourse for the initiated. Scholarly work matters only to the degree it affects consciousness and practice at multiple sites. Counterpoints' editorial policy is based on these principles and the ability of scholars to break new ground, to open new conversations, to go where educators have never gone before.

For additional information about this series or for the submission of manuscripts, please contact:

Joe L. Kincheloe & Shirley R. Steinberg
c/o Peter Lang Publishing, Inc.
29 Broadway, 18th floor
New York, New York 10006

To order other books in this series, please contact our Customer Service Department:
(800) 770-LANG (within the U.S.)
(212) 647-7706 (outside the U.S.)
(212) 647-7707 FAX

Or browse online by series:
www.peterlang.com